The Catskill 67

"The mountains are like a museum where the exhibits change every month."
—*Ralph Ryndak*

"The Catskills are a different kind of pretty."
—*Fran Shumway*

The Catskill 67

A Hiker's Guide to the
Catskill 100 Highest Peaks under 3500'

by Alan Via

edited by Fred LeBrun

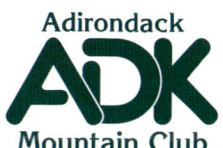

Adirondack Mountain Club, Inc.
Lake George, New York

Adirondack Mountain Club, Inc.
814 Goggins Road, Lake George, NY 12845-4117
www.adk.org

© 2012 by Adirondack Mountain Club, Inc.
All rights reserved. Published 2012.
First edition 2012
Printed in the United States of America

No part of this publication may be reproduced or trasmitted in any form or by any means without express written permission from the publisher. Requests for permission should be addressed in writing to the Publication Director of the Adirondack Mountain Club at pubs@adk.org or the address shown above.

20 19 18 17 16 15 14 13 12   1 2 3 4 5 6 7 8 9 10
ISBN-13: 978-1-931951-08-1 (softcover)

The Adirondack Mountain Club (ADK) is dedicated to the protection and responsible recreational use of the New York State Forest Preserve, parks, and other wild lands and waters. The Club, founded in 1922, is a member-directed organization committed to public service and stewardship. ADK employs a balanced approach to outdoor recreation, advocacy, environmental education, and natural resource conservation.

ADK encourages the involvement of all people in its mission and activities; its goal is to be a community that is comfortable, inviting, and accessible.

Cover photographs by Tony Versandi, Joanne Hihn, Bill Chriswell, Alan Via, and Moonray Schepart. Back-cover Rochester Hollow by Mike Cruz.
Text photographs by Bill Chriswell, Mike Cruz, Joanne Hihn, Cheryl Miller, Mark Schaefer, Moonray Schepart, Tony Versandi, and Alan Via.
Illustrations by Eileen Catasus-Chapman and Barbara Via.
Maps by Liz Cruz of Cruz Cartography.
Design by Ann Hough.

Library of Congress Cataloging-in-Publication Data

Via, Alan, 1948–
  The Catskill 67 : a hiker's guide to the Catskill 100 highest peaks under 3500' / by Alan Via ; edited by Fred LeBrun.
      p. cm.
  Includes bibliographical references and index.
  ISBN 978-1-931951-08-1 (softcover)
  1. Hiking--New York (State)--Catskill Mountains--Guidebooks. 2. Catskill Mountains (N.Y.)--Guidebooks. I. LeBrun, Fred, 1941– II. Title.
  GV199.42.N652C373 2012
  796.52209747'38--dc23
                                                    2011050130

Contents

Preface 7
Acknowledgments 11
Respect for the Mountains, Their Stewards, and Private Property 15
Catskill 100 Highest Peak List 19
Before You Begin 23
Map 1: Southwest Peaks 27
   Mill Brook Ridge 28
   Woodpecker Ridge 30
   Beaver Kill Range 31
   Willowemoc 34
   High Falls Ridge 35
   Mongaup Mt. 36
   Cradle Rock Ridge 38
   Barkaboom Mt. 40
   Sand Pond Mt. 42
   Hodge Pond Mt. 43
Map 2: South-Central Peaks 47
   Spruce Mt. 48
   East Wildcat 49
   Winnisook Lake Mt. 51
   Van Wyck Mt. 53
   Giant Ledge 55
   West Wildcat 58
   Denman Mt. 60
   Woodhull Mt. 62
   Red Hill 63
Map 3: Southeast Peaks 65
   Ashokan High Point 66
   Little Rocky 68
Map 4: East Peaks 71
   Olderbark Mt. 72
   Overlook Mt. 75
   Plattekill Mt. 76
   Silver Hollow Mt. 78
Map 5: Northeast Peaks 81
   Roundtop Mt. (Kaaterskill quad) 82
   Stoppel Point 84
   Onteora Mt. 86
   Burnt Knob 86
   East Jewett Range 88
   Acra Point 89
   West Stoppel Point 90

- Map 6: North Peaks 93
  - Huntersfield Mt. 94
  - St. Anne's Peak 96
  - Richmond Mt. 98
  - Pine Island Mt. 99
  - Cave Mt. 101
  - Packsaddle Mt. 103
  - West Cave Mt. 104
- Map 7: North-Central Peaks 107
  - Roundtop (Prattsville quad) 108
  - Belleayre Mt. 109
  - South Bearpen 111
  - Sleeping Lion 112
  - South Vly 115
  - Shultice Mt. 116
  - White Man Mt. 117
  - Red Kill Ridge 117
  - Rose Mt. 118
  - Irish Mt. 120
  - Montgomery Hollow 121
- Map 8: Northwest Peaks 123
  - North Plattekill Mt. 124
  - South Plattekill Mt. 127
  - Moresville Range NW Peak 129
  - Narrow Notch Mt. 130
  - Utsayantha Mt. 131
  - Cowan Mt. 133
  - Churchill Mt. 134
  - Round Top (Hobart quad) 134
  - Moresville Range SW Peak 136
  - Southeast Warren 137
  - Old Clump 138
  - East Gray Hill 140
  - Meeker Hollow Mt. 142
- Map 9: West Peaks 145
  - Dry Brook Ridge 146
  - Mt. Pisgah 147
  - Little Pisgah 149
  - Hubbell Hill 151
- Appendix 1: Bushwhacking Basics 153
- Appendix 2: A Subjective Look at the Peaks 158
- Appendix 3: Tandem Peaks 159
- Glossary 160
- References and Suggested Reading 171
- About the Author 175
- Adirondack Mountain Club 176
- Index 180

Preface

Why this book? Nearly all hiking guides owe a debt to the good works of those writers who have come before, and this one is no exception. It is also a truism that the 35 highest Catskills mountains, those over 3500 ft, captured the romantic imagination of young America as its first definition of wilderness nearly two hundred years ago. These are well-trod trails. In addition they are well documented and have been commented upon in detail in a variety of other guides and histories. So a natural question arises: Why do we need another Catskills hiking guide?

The answer is that this guide is different. It builds on the past by assuming you have, or can easily acquire, one of several existing guides to the 35 highest peaks in the Catskills, but it introduces a whole new set of mountains. The guide in your hand focuses exclusively on the 67 next highest peaks in the Catskills. Many of these are just a few feet shorter than the famed 35, and just as challenging and rewarding to hike as their slightly bigger sisters. These 67 offer a trove of hiking gems known to and appreciated so far by only a small minority of the hiking population. This guide is different because the peaks are different.

This guide also differs significantly by providing Global Positioning System (GPS) coordinates for more challenging trailhead locations and road intersections. It offers a perfect opportunity to combine your map and compass and GPS skills. (See the glossary for more about GPS.)

In these pages I share with you my experience hiking or bushwhacking these 67 Catskill peaks. For the many 'whacks, I try to identify the best lines of ascent and descent, and the pitfalls and joys you're apt to encounter along the way. Trailless hiking offers the twenty-first–century explorer the same exhilaration of discovery felt by those who first set foot on these mountains, because you are creating your own wilderness experience.

I want to emphasize, though, that this guide is not just about providing bushwhacking alternatives to established trails. Standard guides provide mileage and elevation, and tell something about the trails and a little about the peak. All good stuff. This book provides the same. You'll also read about the plant life, wildflowers and ferns, the birds and beasts that live here. The best view spots and exceptional photo opportunities will be identified, as well as what the woods are like, and difficulty ratings are given for both trailed and untrailed peaks.

My goal is to have you see the 67 mountains through my eyes and experience them before you step into the woods. You'll be able to tell easily which hikes are a good match for your interests and abilities. You'll also learn when it's a fine idea to bring along your kayak, canoe, fishing rod, or bicycle. All the necessary details

Chickadee. Barbara Via

are included for how to get to trailheads, including coordinates for the GPS minded. The nine topographic maps included in the book also indicate trailheads, fishing spots, good cycling routes, places for camping and paddling, and more. These regional maps overlap, making it easy for the hiker to navigate from one area to another.

A large-format folded map is located in a pocket inside the back cover of the book. The folded map illustrates the areas covered by the nine maps within the book, and it also provides the locations of the 100 Highest Catskill peaks.

An explanation is in order about references to the "Catskill 100 Highest." The Catskill 100 Highest list actually consists of 102 mountains. It begins with the list of 98 Catskill peaks 3000 ft or higher put together by Catskills legend Father Ray L. Donahue. Reverend Donahue's list first appeared in 1975 in *Guide to the Catskills* by Adams, Coco, Greenman, and Greenman (see the reference list for more details).

The guide states, "Elevations given for summits are based on latest known U.S. Coast and Geodetic Survey Maps. To be included in this list, peaks must rise at least 200 feet above the low point of the nearest adjacent high peak" (p. 9). Father Donahue was the first to include SW Hunter (Leavitt Peak) as a separate mountain; it was subsequently added to the peak list of the Catskill 3500 Club.

In 2006, Mark Schaefer published the "modern" Catskill 100 list, beginning with Reverend Donahue's list as the starting point. Mark checked the latest map editions and verified current elevations and peak locations of the 98 peaks, using the same 200 ft topographic prominence between peaks. Where no col or peak elevations were displayed on the latest maps, highest contours, not interpolations or estimates, were used. The order of the peaks is based on actual elevations shown on the most current United States Geological Survey (USGS) maps.

Mark's research agreed completely with Reverend Donahue's original 98 peak list, as well as the list of excluded peaks. To come up with an even 100 mountains, Mark scoured the USGS maps for 2 more qualifying summits. Hodge Pond Mt. at 2985 ft garnered number 99, and an eye-straining review of all the Catskill mountain map quadrangles came up with a three-way tie for number 100: East Gray Hill, Meeker Hollow, and Red Hill, each with a 2980 ft summit. Thus the list of the Catskill 100 Highest peaks was born. Yes, it's really 102 mountains, but the "100 Highest" does have a certain ring, and the name—for the most part—has stuck.

Why these mountains? The 67 peaks in this guide have been around since the last ice age, but it's curious how little known most of them remain to the general public. That's probably because many are outside of the Catskill Forest Preserve Blue Line. They're still in the Catskills, but because they're outside of the Forest Preserve boundaries, they're out of the sight and consciousness of most hikers. Further contributing to the anonymity of these peaks is that a number of them had their summits mislocated or misnamed by the USGS and, until recently, were frequently unnamed on most maps. So it's hard to blame folks for not paying attention to the majority of these mountains.

Like other mountain hiking lists I've completed, I began the Catskill 100 Highest without a firm plan to actually complete it. I believed that by climbing the 3500 ft summits in all seasons, months, and under differing weather conditions, I knew the Catskills. I'd been aware of a Catskill 3000 footer list for many years, but the publication of the Catskill 100 Highest Peaks list in 2006 rekindled my interest in taking on what grew into a surprisingly rewarding challenge.

Were there really mountains southwest and northwest of the Catskill 3500ers? New places and trails to discover, and many real bushwhacks without herd paths? Few hikers had ever visited most of these summits, so I said to myself, "Let's go look."

What I discovered and I hope you will, too, are wild and unknown areas of Sullivan, Delaware, Ulster, and Greene counties. What a pleasant shock for someone who'd previously spent so much time in the Catskills. I found gorgeous agricultural valleys and 3000 ft peaks scattered about, and some of the most beautiful trailhead drives anywhere in the greater Catskills. There were stunning backcountry roads, ancient family graveyards, abandoned stone fences, and overgrown fields at the feet of peaks that few hikers know. These too are very much the Catskills. Their slopes are draped with deciduous forests that are a hiker's delight. The valleys have small trout streams, and the peaks different and sometimes strange names, like Barkaboom, Cradle Rock Ridge, Pine Island, Old Clump, and Sleeping Lion.

What I discovered was a whole new hiking world to explore, standing tall in plain sight and ignored for too long. There is real wildness left in some of these lower 67 peaks, precisely because they have been largely ignored. I think you'll get as intoxicated as I did with exploring a new set of mountains and the country surrounding them. Whether you are an avid peakbagger, casual hiker, or armchair climber; whether you will climb some or just a few of these mountains, open the guide, get out a map, and begin a new adventure.

Devil's Path from the south. Eileen Catasus-Chapman

View from North Point, on the trail to Stoppel Point. Tony Versandi

Acknowledgments

This book would not have been possible without the support and encouragement of my wife, Barbara. She's the stalwart who has for decades ignored my frequent departures, early morning starts, late night returns, and missed dinners and engagements with patience and understanding. I cannot imagine another partner having the same cheerful acceptance of my shenanigans and decades-long hiking obsession.

My heartfelt but inadequate thanks and appreciation go to the following people who provided invaluable assistance along the way.

I am especially indebted to Professor Michael Kudish, who has been a constant and valuable resource. Mike read the early manuscript and provided ten pages of handwritten annotations on vegetation, geography, woods and bark roads, history, old settlements, ancient bogs, long gone rail beds, old-growth forests, factual and topographical errors, and my favorite, "Alan's anthropomorphisms." Dr. Kudish is Emeritus Professor of Forestry, Paul Smith's College. His PhD dissertation is *Vegetational History of the Catskill High Peaks*.

Editor Fred LeBrun was the patient teacher who guided me through the process of turning a manuscript into a book. Much of the enjoyment you may receive is in large part owing to his insights and keen observations. I've read and admired Fred's work for almost forty years and could not believe my good fortune when he agreed to edit the project. What a joy to begin a project as colleagues and end as friends.

Good hiking guides need great maps. Cartographer and Catskill native Liz Cruz of Cruz Cartography outdid herself. Using her own GIS database, Liz put together the big map in the back of the book and designed the topographic maps found throughout this book. She rescaled the maps, adjusted trails and other land features, placed and relocated map icons, relocated trails that USGS had misplaced, and smiled through the innumerable "Liz, do you think you might be able to" changes I sent her. I'm indebted beyond thanks for her talent, creativity, enthusiasm, attention to detail, skill, and ideas. Liz provided the second pair of eyes that critiqued the entire manuscript before it went to the copy editor.

Life sometimes smiles at you. I received a big grin when Lisa Crosby Metzger was asked to do the final copy edit on the manuscript. She pored over every word, fixed my "English as a second language" sentences throughout the book, caught inconsistencies, poor phrasing, and repetitions, and in general made the final book more effective. It was a pleasure to work with this talented professional.

My forever appreciation to Ann Hough, the wonderful designer whose vision turned the black and white manuscript into the book you are enjoying. I thank her for the cover layout, design, fonts, photo placements, and more. Ann patiently guided me to where she knew we had to go—and did it with a sharp eye for what looks good.

Mark Schaefer did the research on the "modern" Catskill 100 Highest list. He put together an online interactive peakfinder that listed mountain names, elevations, locations, and topographic map information. His tireless replies to inquiries assisted many hikers in locating a number of these formerly obscure Catskill 100 summits. Without Mark's attentive detail, most recent Catskill 100 completers would have never set out to climb the peaks in the first place. Mark's encyclopedic replies to questions on background, history, and trails were invaluable. I'm further indebted to him for his early review and comments on the manuscript.

Mike Cantwell reviewed and offered essential updates on the changing conditions and trails around Huntersfield and Richmond mountains shown on Map 6, the North Peaks. He is a genuine Catskill authority, a font of Catskill lore, natural history, flora, and fauna. Mike's website, The Catskill Mountaineer, www.catskillmountaineer.com, provides information on the entire Catskill mountain range and is a source of up-to-date material and news for hikers, travelers, and others.

In addition to his enjoyable company on many hikes, Moonray Schepart's GPS tracklogs provided invaluable input for the proper location of maintained trails on the peak maps. He was a patient sounding board on formatting the peak list and has been one of my go-to guys on technical matters of all sorts.

Thank you to retired DEC biologist Dick Henry for his generous sharing of information and perspective gained from his years of experience and for providing the essential information on black bear and fisher population and behavior contained in the glossary.

It's my fortune to be friends with Ralph Ryndak, Moonray Schepart, Mike Cantwell, Bill Chriswell, Jay Hui, Cindy Kuhn Yourdon, Tony Versandi, Laurie and Tom Rankin, Jim Bouton, Shawn Turner, George Dudar, Bill Schirmer, and Ron Cusmano. Each in her or his own way contributed information on routes, local and natural history, fauna, flora, and perspective. Thanks also to Maddy Hand for the good trail conversation and wonderful refreshments at her and Ralph's home after hikes.

A further thank you goes to George Dudar who created the Catskill 100 design and decal and to Tom and Laurie Rankin for turning George's design into a patch.

My Lab, Bookah, would like to thank Dick and Joanne Hihn for enduring her muddy paws, bad breath, and summit table manners. She commiserates with them for putting up with my bad jokes and puns on many a hike. I'm sure Boo feels I too am often barking up the wrong tree.

I hiked most of the trailless Adirondack 100 Highest with fellow bushwhackers Spencer Morrissey and Brian Yourdon. They provided another impetus to tackle the Catskill 100 and Spencer's guide to the Adirondack 100 Highest, *The*

Other 54, got me thinking about writing a guide to the Catskills. Brian showed me how to supplement my map and compass background with GPS skills and graciously endured my persistent GPS questions in the midst of Adirondack bugs, rain, snow, and blowdown. One of my life goals is to someday be able to float up a mountain like Brian does.

Neil Woodworth, Executive Director of the Adirondack Mountain Club (ADK), has been a close friend since our first hikes together to the Adirondack High Peaks almost forty years ago. Neil has provided guidance on the software and hardware ends of GPS technology and regularly provides sound advice when I get stumped with a new development in this rapidly evolving technology. His active and enthusiastic encouragement kept me going through manuscript doldrums. My gratitude to Neil extends beyond this book. His irreplaceable behind-the-scenes work with environmental and land acquisition issues is unrivaled. I would encourage readers who are not members of the Adirondack Mountain Club to join if for no other reason than to support ADK and Neil's work on conservation projects of all sorts. Everyone who loves the mountains owes Neil a debt of enduring gratitude.

A huge thanks goes to Bill Chriswell, Mark Schaefer, Tony Versandi, Moonray Schepart, Mike Cruz, and Joanne Hihn for their photographic contributions and to Eileen Catasus-Chapman and Barbara Via for their wonderful artwork.

Dr. Jennifer Bull, DVM, at the Delmar Animal Hospital, is Bookah's veterinarian and her excellent care and advice has kept Bookah strong, healthy, and in the woods all of her life.

And a final acknowledgment to my dog, Bookah, who has been at my side all the way. I watched her grow up in the woods and become one of the best bushwhackers of them all. Wherever I am in the woods, she is either right next to me or orbiting within sight. Her trust allowed me to become comfortable removing porcupine quills from dogs in the woods. Boo has her own 3500 Club certificate and is the first canine and second "female" to complete the Catskill 67—probably having climbed them all three or more times.

Mike Kudish dating an old cherry tree. Alan Via

'Whacking through a fern glade on Delaware County peak. *Joanne Hihn*

Respect for the Mountains,
Their Stewards, and Private Property

Some of these mountains are a patchwork of public and private properties. If your objective is to hike any of these less traveled and sometimes trailless peaks, asking for permission is not only part of the game but is required. Private property is noted in each chapter, with the predictable caveat that land changes hands, or becomes public property.

Please take the time to do your homework and research and review maps and other sources ahead of your hike. There is a wealth of information available. The Venture Out and New York–New Jersey Trail Conference maps show places you can hike by simply parking your car and putting on a pack. They show the location of public land, and I urge you to hike public property routes where possible.

Seeking permission from landowners can be time consuming. Approached with the right attitude, though, it's interesting, enjoyable, and a great way to meet the people who live on and support the land where you want to hike. The landowners pay the taxes, keep the fields clear, repair fences, remove blowdown, and maintain woods roads.

Of all the mountains where we have asked permission to hike on private land, only once were we turned away—when we unwittingly interrupted a Sunday afternoon football game on which the caretaker had a wager. We enjoyed a laugh about it the next day, when we heard about the rebuff from a friend who lives in the area. He knew the caretaker, who told him about "some of your nutty hiking friends." It still brings a smile to my face a few years later. As it turned out, we asked at another home on the other side of the mountain and found friendly and willing hosts.

Seeking Permission to Hike

When seeking permission to hike on private land, please take to heart the following suggestions, which may ease the process for you.

Drive around to scout your next hikes. Obtain owner information from posted signs or from town clerks, then take the time to meet the landowners and always try to put yourself in their place. How would you want to be approached? Look for a friendly face and ask if you can hike or return another time. My experience is that many people find our affliction amusing and are often fascinated that the hills behind their homes are of interest to anyone other than themselves or perhaps hunters.

Avoid asking the landowner for permission to hike via a telephone call or e-

mail. Calling a complete stranger to ask about using their property is difficult for the person on either end of a conversation. Do it in person. When you do seek permission, try to make it a small delegation that walks up to the porch. Knock, knock from seven strangers on the front porch in an isolated area would probably be unnerving for the homeowner.

Remember the old adage, "You catch more flies with honey than with vinegar"? Knocking on the landowner's door at 6:30 AM Sunday morning is generally not a great way to win friends or get an OK to hike. Nor is leaving a pasture gate open, dog poop in yards, or litter and coffee cups near where you parked. Don't block driveways or woods roads' entrances.

If you're given permission from a landowner, please keep it to yourself. By doing so you are protecting the landowner and spreading out the number of places people will approach to hike. Your discretion will help keep access open for the future. Common sense, common courtesy, a smile, and "thank you" go a long way.

We've brought home-baked desserts, bottled beverages, and gift cards as ways to say thank you to landowners. My wife, Barbara, mailed a watercolor thank you note she'd painted to show appreciation to a landowner who was proud of his property and anxious to show us around. He'd even offered to drive us part way up a trailless peak in his golf cart.

Many of these landowners are sportsmen. They pay taxes on the land and

Old sugarhouse on the slopes of one of the Catskill 67. Alan Via often like to hunt and fish on their property. Consider remaining on public trails during the turkey and deer seasons. Let the landowners enjoy a few weeks without hikers scaring their quarry.

This bears repeating: Respecting the landowner's privacy will be repaid in kind. Passing along to other hikers the names and locations where you have received permissions is one of the surest ways I know to alienate landowners. If someone allows you to hike, don't assume it is OK to give their name to others or post the contact information on the Internet. Jealously guard the privacy of your contacts and let those who are interested in hiking these mountains do their own homework and get to know the owners themselves.

Good Stewardship

Respect for the landowners goes hand in hand with respect for the mountains. The Catskill 67 are very different from the Catskill 3500 ft peaks in ways other than their elevations. Herd paths, blazes, markers, route cairns, canisters, or flagging are almost nonexistent on the trailless 67 (see "herd paths" and "cairns" in glossary). Use woods roads where possible to minimize signs of your passing and refrain from breaking branches that are in the way of your hiking or views.

Please let the hikers who come behind you enjoy the same sense of discovery and adventure that you experienced. When you mark a route with a blaze, flag, or cairn, it encourages herd paths, as those following assume "this is the way to go." Consider removing recently installed cairns and other markers placed by hikers who are, in essence, stealing the sense of discovery from those who follow.

The spring 1966 issue of *Peeks*, the Adirondack 46ers newsletter, had an editorial I think of often: "As you go on your trailless hikes, please destroy old cairns, markers, strings, etc. that were put up by hikers, thoughtless or incompetent. Such signs spoil the fun for true 46ers." This advice is as timely and fitting for the untrailed Catskill 67 peaks today as it was for the Adirondack summits almost fifty years ago.

The Catskill 67 is a unique group of mountains. Please do all you can to keep it that way.

Cairns are almost nonexistent on the trailless 67. Mike Cruz

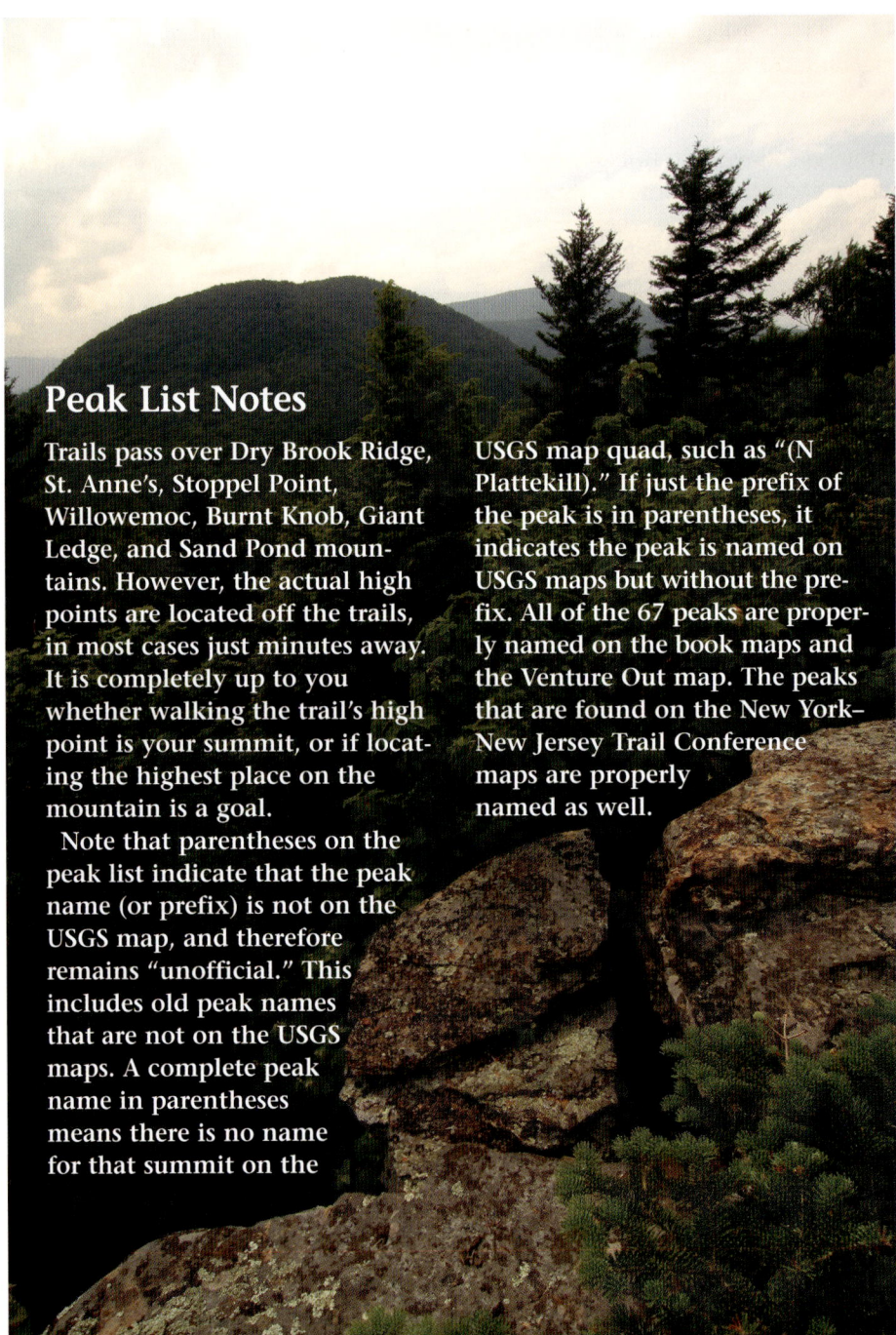

Peak List Notes

Trails pass over Dry Brook Ridge, St. Anne's, Stoppel Point, Willowemoc, Burnt Knob, Giant Ledge, and Sand Pond mountains. However, the actual high points are located off the trails, in most cases just minutes away. It is completely up to you whether walking the trail's high point is your summit, or if locating the highest place on the mountain is a goal.

Note that parentheses on the peak list indicate that the peak name (or prefix) is not on the USGS map, and therefore remains "unofficial." This includes old peak names that are not on the USGS maps. A complete peak name in parentheses means there is no name for that summit on the USGS map quad, such as "(N Plattekill)." If just the prefix of the peak is in parentheses, it indicates the peak is named on USGS maps but without the prefix. All of the 67 peaks are properly named on the book maps and the Venture Out map. The peaks that are found on the New York–New Jersey Trail Conference maps are properly named as well.

Burnt Knob from Acra Point. Tony Versandi

Catskill 100 Highest Peak List

Abbreviations: B = bushwhack, no canister
C = bushwhack, with canister
CHH = Catskill 100 Highest
CoHP = county high point
F = fire tower
R = rough road
S = ski area
T = trailed
U = unmaintained trail

For the genesis of this list, and an explanation of criteria, please see Preface.

CHH Rank	Catskill 67 Rank	Elev.	Code	CHH Peak Name	USGS Topo Map	Catskill 67 Map
1		4180	T	Slide Mt. (Ulster CoHP)	Peekamoose Mt.	
2		4040	F,T	Hunter Mt. (Greene CoHP)	Hunter	
3		3980	T	Black Dome	Freehold	
4		3940	T	Blackhead	Freehold	
5		3940	T	Thomas Cole Mt.	Hensonville	
6		3880	T	West Kill Mt.	Lexington	
7		3868	U	Graham Mt.	Seager	
8		3860	T	Cornell Mt.	Phoenicia	
9		3860	C	Doubletop Mt.	Seager	
10		3847	T	Table Mt.	Peekamoose Mt.	
11		3843	T	Peekamoose Mt.	Peekamoose Mt.	
12		3840	T	Plateau Mt.	Hunter	
13		3800	T	Sugarloaf Mt.	Hunter	
14		3780	T	Wittenberg Mt.	Phoenicia	
15		3740	C	(Leavitt Peak / SW Hunter)	Hunter	
16		3721	C	Lone Mt.	Peekamoose Mt.	
17		3720	F,T	Balsam Lake Mt.	Seager	
18		3720	T	Panther Mt.	Shandaken	
19		3700	C	Big Indian Mt.	Shandaken	
20		3694	C	Friday Mt.	West Shokan	
21		3680	C	Rusk Mt.	Lexington	
22		3655	U	(Kaaterskill) High Peak	Kaaterskill	

CHH Rank	Catskill 67 Rank	Elev.	Code	CHH Peak Name	USGS Topo Map	Catskill 67 Map
23		3640	T	Twin Mt.	Hunter	
24		3623	C	Balsam Cap	West Shokan	
25		3620	C	Fir Mt.	Shandaken	
26		3610	C	North Dome	Lexington	
27		3600	T	Balsam Mt.	Shandaken	
28		3600	U	Bearpen Mt.	Prattsville	
29		3600	U	Eagle Mt.	Seager	
30		3573	T	Indian Head Mt.	Woodstock	
31		3540	C	Mt. Sherrill	Lexington	
32		3529	C	Vly Mt.	West Kill	
33		3524	T	Windham High Peak	Hensonville	
34		3520	C	Halcott Mt.	West Kill	
35		3508	C	Rocky Mt.	West Shokan	
36	1	3480	T	Mill Brook Ridge	Arena	1
37	2	3460	T,B	Dry Brook Ridge	Seager	9
38	3	3460	B	Woodpecker Ridge	Seager	1
39	4	3440	B	Olderbark Mt.	Bearsville	4
40	5	3440	B	Roundtop Mt.	Kaaterskill	5
41	6	3440	U	Roundtop	Prattsville	7
42	7	3423	T	Huntersfield Mt. (Schoharie CoHP)	Ashland	6
43	8	3420	S	Belleayre Mt.	Fleischmanns	7
44	9	3420	T,B	(St. Anne's Peak / W West Kill)	Lexington	6
45	10	3420	T,B	Stoppel Point	Kaaterskill	5
46	11	3410	B	(S Bearpen)	West Kill	7
47	12	3408	B	(Sleeping Lion Mt./NE Halcott)	West Kill	7
48	13	3380	B	Spruce Mt.	Shandaken	2
49	14	3377	B	Beaver Kill Range	Claryville	1
50	15	3360	B	(S Vly)	West Kill	7
51	16	3345	S	Mt. Pisgah	Margaretville	9
52	17	3340	B	(E Wildcat)	Peekamoose Mt.	2
53	18	3340	B,S	(N Plattekill)	Hobart	8
54	19	3280	B	Shultice Mt.	Roxbury	7
55	20	3260	B	(S) Plattekill Mt.	Hobart	8
56	21	3260	B	(Winnisook Lake)	Shandaken	2
57	22	3240	B	(NW) Moresville Range	Roxbury	8
58	23	3224	T,B	(Willowemoc/Beaver Kill Ridge)	Willowemoc	1
59	24	3220	B	(Narrow Notch)	Roxbury	8
60	25	3220	B	Onteora Mt.	Hunter	5
61	26	3220	B	Richmond Mt.	Ashland	6
62	27	3214	F,R	Utsayantha Mt.	Stamford	8

CHH Rank	Catskill 67 Rank	Elev.	Code	CHH Peak Name	USGS Topo Map	Catskill 67 Map
63	28	3211	B	(High Falls Ridge)	Claryville	1
64	29	3206	B	Van Wyck Mt.	Peekamoose Mt.	2
65	30	3200	T,B	Giant Ledge	Shandaken	2
66	31	3180	T, B	Burnt Knob	Freehold	5
67	32	3177	B	Mongaup Mt.	Willowemoc	1
68	33	3160	B	Cradle Rock Ridge	Arena	1
69	34	3160	B	(W) Wildcat Mt.	Peekamoose Mt.	2
70	35	3140	B	East Jewett Range	Hunter	5
71	36	3140	F,T	Overlook Mt.	Woodstock	4
72	37	3140	B	(Pine Island Mt.)	Lexington	6
73	38	3140	B	White Man Mt./Hack Flats	Roxbury	7
74	39	3100	T	Acra Point	Freehold	5
75	40	3100	B	Barkaboom Mt.	Arena	1
76	41	3100	S,B	Cave Mt.	Hensonville	6
77	42	3100	B	Cowan Mt.	Hobart	8
78	43	3100	B	(Packsaddle Mt./Lexington Mt.)	Lexington	6
79	44	3100	B	Plattekill Mt.	Woodstock	4
80	45	3100	B	(Red Kill Ridge/Butternut Mt.)	Fleischmanns	7
81	46	3100	B	(W Stoppel Point)	Kaaterskill	5
82	47	3090	B	Rose Mt.	West Kill	7
83	48	3080	T	(Ashokan) High Point	West Shokan	3
84	49	3062	T,B	(Sand Pond / Beaver Kill Ridge)	Willowemoc	1
85	50	3060	B	Churchill Mt.	Stamford	8
86	51	3060	B	Irish Mt.	Roxbury	7
87	52	3060	B	Round Top	Hobart	8
88	53	3053	T,B	Denman Mt.	Claryville	2
89	54	3040	B	(Montgomery Hollow)	Roxbury	7
90	55	3040	B	(SW Moresville Range)	Roxbury	8
91	56	3040	S,B	(W) Cave	Ashland	6
92	57	3040	B	Woodhull Mt.	Peekamoose Mt.	2
93	58	3020	B	(Little Pisgah)	Margaretville	9
94	59	3020	B	(SE Warren)	Hobart	8
95	60	3015	B	Little Rocky	West Shokan	3
96	61	3000	B	(Hubbell Hill)	Margaretville	9
97	62	3000	B	Old Clump	Roxbury	8
98	63	3000	T	(Silver Hollow / Edgewood)	Bearsville	4
99	64	2985	B	(Hodge Pond)	Willowemoc	1
100	65	2980	B	(E Gray Hill)	Roxbury	8
101	66	2980	B	(Meeker Hollow)	Hobart	8
102	67	2980	F,T	Red Hill	Claryville	2

Plattekill Falls. Mark Schaefer

Before You Begin

Please consider a few things before you begin to hike. The GPS coordinates you find throughout the book are WGS 84. If your maps are based on USGS maps, their coordinates are set at the older NAD 27 standard. For GPS users, please be sure your GPS unit and your computer mapping software are set to the same datum, WGS 84.

Hunting season in the Catskills normally starts on October 1 for turkey and early archery. Big game season starts around the third week of November. The spring turkey hunting season is the month of May. Consider avoiding bushwhacks and some trails during the hunting season, and leave the hunters to pursue their sport for the few weeks their season is open.

There are a few places in the Catskills with timber rattlesnakes. The timbers are shy and endangered. In the unlikely event you are lucky enough to see one, it will undoubtedly be looking for the best way to disappear. Copperheads, while not common, can be found here and there, especially in Ulster County.

Many of the 67 peaks involve bushwhacking. Although there is a section in the appendix on bushwhacking, this book isn't a "how-to" manual. There is a basic assumption that if you leave roads and trails behind, you know how to safely return. Be sure you carry clothing appropriate for 'whacking and the weather, safety glasses, and adequate fluid, and that you know how to use a map and compass. I believe that if you don't know how to use a map and compass in concert with each other, and carry them, the only bushwhacking you should do is in the company of someone who does. A GPS is a fine and useful tool and saves time, but electronics can fail.

The New York State Department of Environmental Conservation (DEC) allows public access to vast

Navigating by compass on a Catskill 67 bushwhack. Joanne Hihn

tracts of public land in the Catskills. New York City, through its Department of Environmental Protection, allows public access to its water-supply lands with a DEP permit. (See DEC and DEP in glossary.)

Private property abounds in the mountains. If you encounter posted signs or yellow-blazed property lines, please be certain you skirt private property or have permission from the property owner in advance of your hike.

Ratings

For each of the 67 peaks included in this guide, you'll find ratings for view, interest, difficulty, and bushwhack. For view and interest, a "1" is a peak without great views that doesn't have a terrific overall interest. A "5" for both means the views and hike interest are excellent. A peak receiving a "1" for difficulty or bushwhack correlates with a relatively easy hike or easy bushwhack. A "5" should be approached with caution and commitment.

Note that these ratings are completely subjective, based on the author's experiences and the views of others familiar with the peaks. Temperature, humidity, precipitation, snow, and other factors will all affect your personal experience.

Top: DEP sign, Catskills
Above: View from Giant's Ledge. Mark Schaefer

Map Legend

△ **Pine Island Mt.**	Peak under 3500 feet in elevation
△ Thomas Cole Mt.	Peak over 3500 feet in elevation
● **Phoenicia**	City or Town
Weaver Hollow Road	Road Name
Ashokan High Point Trail	Trail Name
Pepacton Reservoir	Water Body Name
3000	Contour Label
——	100' Contour
——	500' Index Contour
—(214)—	State Road (NY214)
—[47]—	County Road (CR47)
——	Local Road
- - - - -	DEC Maintained Road
	DEC Maintained Trails
- - - - - (red)	Red Trail Markers
- - - - - (blue)	Blue Trail Markers
- - - - - (yellow)	Yellow Trail Markers
- - - - - (green)	Other Trails
—— (orange)	Catskill Scenic Trail
—·—·—	County Line
P	Trail Access Parking Area
★	Scenic View
✝	Cemetery
🗼	Fire Tower
	Recreation Opportunities
🎣	Fishing
🚴	Biking
🛶	Paddling
🏊	Swimming
⛷	Cross-country Skiing
⛺	Camping
⛩	Picnicking

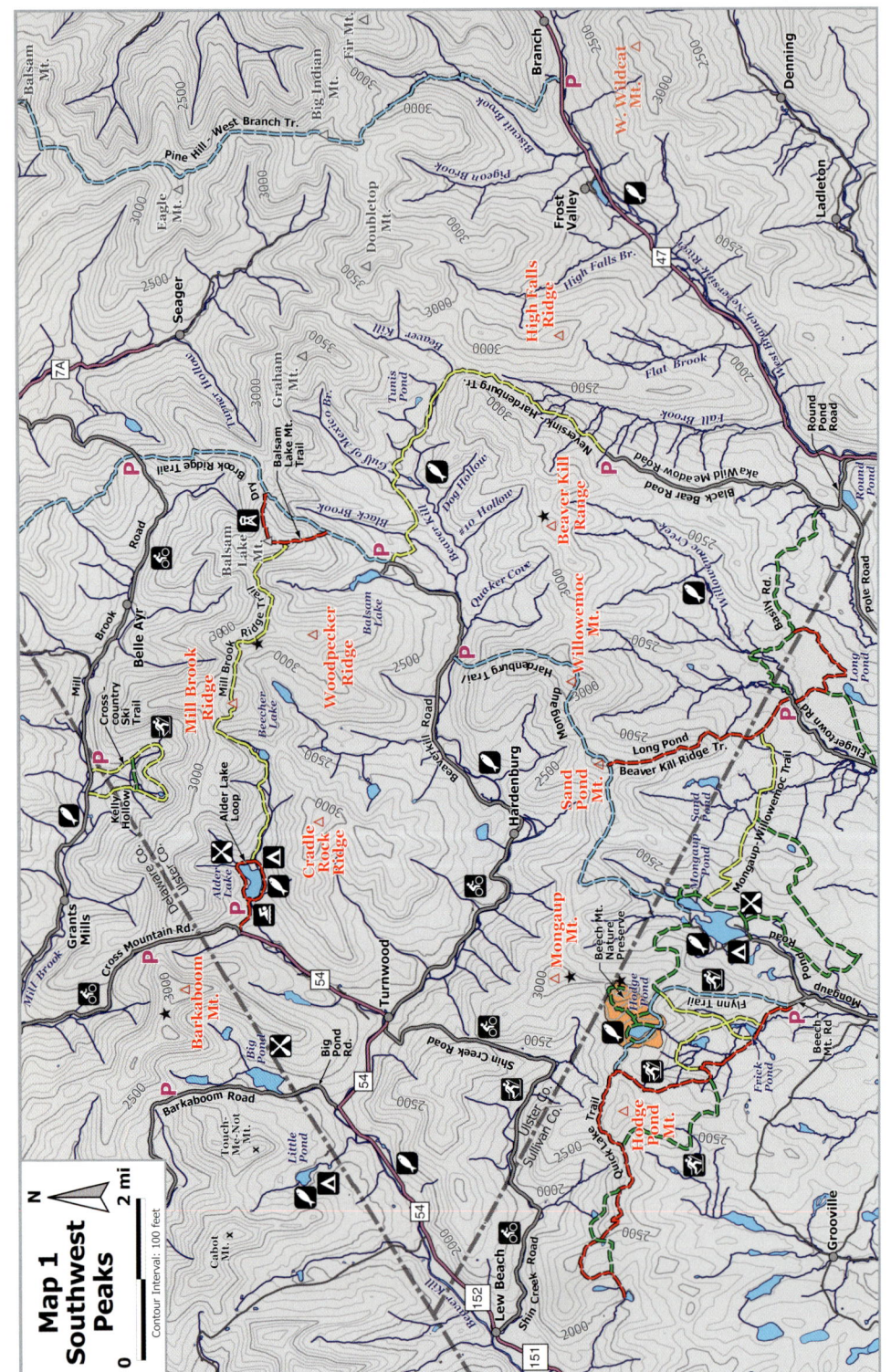

Southwest Peaks

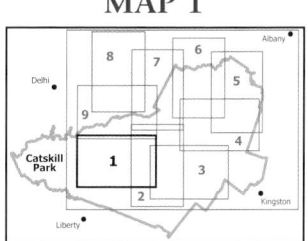

MAP 1

Mill Brook Ridge
Woodpecker Ridge
Beaver Kill Range
Willowemoc
  (Beaver Kill Ridge)
High Falls Ridge
Mongaup Mt.

Cradle Rock Ridge
Barkaboom Mt.
Sand Pond Mt.
  (Beaver Kill Ridge or
  Sand Pond Ridge)
Hodge Pond Mt.

What a great area for hiking! This region contains a fantastic mix of trailed and bushwhack peaks, small lakes and ponds, and trailhead drives that are scenic. Many of the summits have fern glades, and the bushwhacks are often through open, deciduous forests.

In general, the forests in this area are largely pricker-free (see more about "prickers" in the glossary). Although most of the summits are wooded, there are good views to enjoy along the way, particularly when the trees are bare. Many of the trailheads are fairly remote, but the directions to them are straightforward. Campgrounds and camping areas in the region include Little Pond, Willowemoc, and Mongaup Pond.

Fishermen can try their luck on public stretches of the nearby Neversink River and Beaver Kill and Willowemoc creeks, as well as at Alder Lake, Mill Brook, and Big Pond. Paddlers can enjoy beautiful Alder Lake, Mongaup Pond, and Big Pond.

The Beech Mountain Nature Preserve is a destination all by itself, or it can be combined with hikes to Mongaup or Hodge Pond mountains. Alder Lake is a great spot to cool off after a day in the woods.

Cyclists have miles of rolling hills as well as some very challenging ascents. Shin Creek, Beaverkill, and Black Bear roads are just a few excellent ones to choose from. Shin Creek Road between Lew Beach (N42° 00.297', W74° 47.106') and Turnwood (N42° 01.479', W74° 42.578') is a wilderness ride that will be a highlight of the season for off-road bicyclists. The seasonal Cross Mountain Rd. is a thigh burner up and over the Barkaboom–Mill Brook col (see "col" in glossary).

Squirrel corn at Barkaboom. Bill Chriswell

Mill Brook Ridge, 3480'   Arena Quad
Catskill 67 Rank: 1
View: 4, Interest: 4, Difficulty: 3, Bushwhack: 4

HIGHLIGHTS AND SUMMARY: This is a trailed peak with bushwhack options. Impressive shoulder-high fern glades and large birches cover the summit. The picturesque ridge trail offers a spectacular view spot between Woodpecker Ridge and Mill Brook's summit. Views are outstanding when the leaves are off the trees. Mill Brook Ridge is the highest of the sub-3500 ft peaks, and some believe that if the summit were remeasured with sophisticated modern equipment, Mill Brook might "grow" another map contour and join the Catskill 3500 footer list.

BEST TIME TO HIKE: Any season, but winter is preferred for bushwhacking.

The mountain is a five-summit peak with a trail passing over the summit and one of its other sub-peaks. The other three summits are trailless. Since trail hikes on the mountain are well covered in other guides we'll touch only briefly on those and concentrate on bushwhack routes.

You can climb Mill Brook Ridge on trail by first going over Balsam Lake Mt. The Mill Brook Ridge Trail begins about a quarter mile below the summit of Balsam Lake Mt. and heads downhill, switchbacking on a soft and lightly used footpath. It then ascends Mill Brook's first bump and descends into a col. Then it heads to the summit. (Although USGS maps show this first bump as part of Mill Brook Ridge, from a topographic standpoint it might better be considered a false summit of Woodpecker Ridge due to the 40 ft rise from Woodpecker Ridge but more than 320 ft rise from Mill Brook Ridge's col.)

Inestimable trail maintainer, Laurie Rankin, the first woman Catskill 100 completer, does a great job maintaining this lightly used footpath. Enjoy Laurie's handiwork and the screened views all along the way to the top of Mill Brook (N42° 03.156', W74° 38.000'). For the full-view visual treatment, hike the trail when the leaves are off the trees. There is an open ledge on the trail located a few minutes E of the col between Woodpecker Ridge and Mill Brook's summit. Standing at this view spot you can see Woodpecker Ridge, Beecher Lake, Alder Lake, and the summit of Mill Brook Ridge. The climb up to Mill Brook's wooded summit is gradual, and in midsummer there are acres of shoulder-high cinnamon ferns. While they're beautiful to look at, walking through them is like doing leg lifts at a gym. They hide rocks, holes, and blowdown, making for a very challenging off-trail walk in summer. Mill Brook Ridge is about 3 mi of hiking and 700 ft of ascent from Balsam Lake Mt.

Does the trail pass over the actual summit? There is a large rock right next to the trail on the N side. This appears to be the high point, but the tall ferns may give the impression that a higher spot could be off the southern side of the trail. Judge for yourself.

Another lightly used trail to Mill Brook Ridge comes from Alder Lake. This pleasant trail is lightly used but not difficult to follow for anyone who regularly hikes the Catskills. Regardless of direction, Mill Brook is a fine ridge hike. See the section on Cradle Rock Ridge for details to the trailhead and hike from Alder Lake.

Hiking from Alder Lake, the beaver meadow/swamp near the lean-to is a scenic visit in the spring or autumn. In spring, the views open up and you're likely to see ducks and geese nesting. On a quiet, windless day in early spring, every sound echoes off the mountain slopes, including the raspy voices of the spring peepers. There is first-growth forest (see glossary) in the area. Hiking from Alder Lake is 6+ mi round-trip with 1400 ft of ascent.

For the adventurous, Mill Brook can be bushwhacked from Kelly Hollow. The trailhead is on Mill Brook Rd., NW of the summit. The trailhead has a sign with the parking area set back 50 ft from the road (N42° 04.754', W74° 38.998'). Kelly Hollow has some snowmobile and cross-country ski trails, as well as a pond and lean-to.

The easternmost of the Kelly Hollow trails terminates somewhere around 2100 ft. From here, you can bushwhack S to Mill Brook's 3260 ft sub-peak or directly toward the summit. The Kelly Hollow trails can be done as a loop hike, and depending on the direction of travel, you might have time to explore what appears to be an old farmstead, with foundations and an old graveyard. There is a lot to see in this area, and it is rich with birdlife and wildflowers in the spring. High on the trail is an old Civilian Conservation Corps dam that beavers have turned into a pond with great views of the N side of the Mill Brook range.

Depending on weather, bushwhacks beyond Kelly Hollow tend to be damp in spring, and there are areas of tall undergrowth hiding blown-down branches and rocks. Many of the small trees along the northern flanks of Mill Brook appear to be in poor health, as you'll unwittingly discover if you grab them for a handrail (see "portable handrails" in glossary). This bushwhack is an interesting route up or down the mountain when the vegetation is gone and snow has covered the rocks and cemented them in place.

Another 'whack goes over Mill Brook's dogleg (see glossary) northern ridge. This is an attractive route on a map, but accept my word about its challenges. The ridge appears to be a gentle ramp connecting the summit to Mill Brook Rd., but it is guarded by steep drop-offs on both flanks. In summer the tall ferns on the upper half of the ridge hide mobile rocks and fallen branches. Tall weedy bushes force you to wade with arms held high. The top of this nice-looking ridge is strewn with downed branches, hidden from late spring on. You are left with

Woodpecker Ridge. Moonray Schepart

the option of struggling across on the ridge crest, or sidehilling to keep from diving into the steep drainages on either side. (See "sidehilling" and "drainage avoidance" in glossary). This route is much better in midwinter with firm snow. You'll gain or lose about 1800 ft of elevation for the 'whack up or down from Mill Brook Rd.

Despite the trail over Mill Brook Ridge, this entire area still has a wild feel. Take a step off the trail and you can sense the wilderness. Off-trail, the woods have almost no sign of human activity. The animals seem to agree, given the deer and bear sign. Don't be surprised if you encounter porcupines as you ramble.

Woodpecker Ridge, 3460   Seager Quad
Catskill 67 Rank: 3
View: 2, Interest: 3, Difficulty: 2, Bushwhack: 2–3

HIGHLIGHTS AND SUMMARY: Can you imagine a better name for a mountain? All routes are bushwhacks. The lightly traveled woods lend themselves to seeing more wildlife and fewer people. Deer, bear, coyotes, rabbits, and birds abound. There are completely open woods for 'whacking in springtime, fern glades in summer, and showy deciduous woods, particularly in autumn. The bushwhack from the Mill Brook Ridge Trail is short and straightforward, but other routes are longer and more interesting.

BEST TIME TO HIKE: It's a simple 'whack anytime, but late autumn to early spring is best for open views and easy travel.

The shortest and surest way to Woodpecker's trailless twin summits is a bushwhack from the Mill Brook Ridge Trail. This trail connects Alder Lake (N42° 02.980', W74° 40.835') to Balsam Lake Mt. (N42° 02.740', W74° 35.683'). The bushwhack from the trail consists of a half mile of route-finding, and the best spot for starting is from near the 3420 ft Mill Brook Ridge sub-summit, located directly N of Woodpecker. You can begin the bushwhack on either the N or E side of this bump, but having gone both ways, I'd suggest approaching Woodpecker from the northern side. It is shorter, easier, and more pleasant.

While this 'whack to Woodpecker is short, it is loaded with beech whips (see glossary) that affect your visibility and slow down progress. It will take longer than the distance suggests. There are also large areas of ferns in season. They are attractive and interesting, but hide the blown-down branches near your legs.

The summit of Woodpecker is completely wooded. Although you can glimpse screened views along the route when the leaves are gone, it's not a bushwhack for those interested in scenery when the leaves are on the trees. In the winter or spring you can easily navigate Woodpecker by sight, when the beech leaves and ferns are gone.

In early spring the first summit of Woodpecker almost resembles a meadow, and its twin summits are an easy 0.1 mi apart. Both have identical map contours, and the wooded terrain makes it difficult to determine whether the N or S is the true top. Decide for yourself. Once you've come this far, it'll be difficult to resist trying to discover which is taller.

A shorter hike but longer bushwhack to Woodpecker originates at the Balsam Lake Mt. trailhead (N42° 01.429', W74° 35.993') on Beaverkill Rd. From the trailhead you have two options. One is to start the hike to Balsam Lake Mt. and after a few minutes bushwhack W, skirting private property that surrounds the SE side of Balsam Lake. Or head directly W from the trailhead, avoiding private property around the lake. In either case, your objective is to get onto Woodpecker's southern ridge and follow the open woods to the summit. It's pretty easy 'whacking for the most part, with the occasional steeper section and some blowdown along the southern ridge. Either hike is approximately 2 mi round-trip and 1000 ft of ascent.

You can get on that same southern ridge of Woodpecker by parking at the trailhead for the northern trail to Willowemoc Mt. (N42° 00.740', W74° 37.367') on Beaverkill Rd. and follow Woodpecker's southern ridge. See page 34 in the Willowemoc section for details on the start of this route. This route is a little over 2 mi with 1300 ft of ascent.

Beaver Kill Range, 3377'   Claryville Quad
Catskill 67 Rank: 14
View: 5, Interest: 4, Difficulty: 3, Bushwhack: 3

HIGHLIGHTS AND SUMMARY: This is one of the wild and wonderful Catskill 100 summits, with spacious open woods and a wilderness feel once away from the trails on the N or S sides. It is a bushwhack from any direction. The spectacular and remote fern and birch glade just below the summit offers one of the most arresting viewing spots in the Catskills. The peak is adorned with wildflowers in the springtime and has gorgeous autumn finery. Birds and wildlife are quite apparent, particularly on the northern side of the peak.

Beaver Kill Range has five prominent summits and a number of smaller ones that run in a SW to NE direction. The highest is the second summit from the SW end; it is labeled 3377 ft on topographic maps.
BEST TIME TO HIKE: Early spring into autumn.

The most common route is from the S. To get to the parking area, take CR47, Slide Mountain Rd. Turn onto Round Pond Rd. (N41° 56.144', W74° 34.532') and make your first right after the pond. Bear right onto Wild Meadow Rd. (N41° 56.634', W74° 35.239'). Continue right at a sign for Basily Rd., where Wild Meadow Rd. becomes Black Bear Rd. You'll see a mix of woods, meadows, and camps as you drive this scenic road to its end. In non-winter months, park at the snowplow turnaround at the road's terminus, but don't leave your car there in the snowy season. You can also drive beyond the turnaround onto public land. The continuation of Black Bear Rd. is drivable with a car most of the time unless wet or snowy.

The road becomes a yellow-marked hiking trail, and the 'whack begins anywhere from the car to the nicely situated Fall Brook lean-to, located about 1.5 mi from the turnaround. Many hikers choose to jump into the bushwhack just beyond where they park their cars.

The deciduous forest is almost blowdown-free, with beeches predominating in the lower elevations. Inasmuch as you begin hiking at 2600 ft, the vertical gain to Beaver Kill Range is not great and the gradient is moderate all the way. The only barrier to easy travel is the abundance of face-high beech whips and saplings. They obscure your visibility, but it's their sharp tips you need to watch for. Only the lower branches of conifers manage to find a way around my glasses more frequently than beech whip tips!

Birch and cherry trees make their appearance at 2900 ft. Due to numerous small springs, there are some nettles near moist areas, but there are almost no blackberry prickers, which makes for a delightful bushwhack. Because this is a wild area, you'd expect to see deer and bear sign on the southern side of Beaver Kill Range. This is unfortunately not the case, and my guess is it's because of the proximity of camps and hunting clubs along the road. Although the beech habitat is ideal, there is no evident porcupine activity.

You can head for the top anywhere, but the most obvious way is via the mountain's wide and inviting SE ridge. After a few hundred feet of climbing, there is a series of small rock bands. These rock bands are easily negotiated.

There is an old and difficult-to-follow woods road that climbs the southern ridge. It's grown over and most visible when the beeches have dropped their leaves. A much more prominent woods road hugs the SE side of the drainage immediately E of Beaver Kill Range's 3340 ft sub-summit. To locate the beginning of the woods road, walk the trail less than a mile, passing a large, white hunting camp on the left. Continue another 100 yd on the trail and then head NW into the woods, staying to the E of private property. The woods road comes into sight in a couple of minutes on public property and continues all the way to within 0.3 mi of the ridgeline. Though this road is a handy and quick way to bypass much of the beech whips, it's unfortunate that illegal ATV use (see glossary) is prevalent here, in an otherwise wild area.

With the exception of the woods roads, human activity is nonexistent in the area. As you approach the summit from almost any direction you'll see ferns and beeches, with the occasional birch and cherry.

An excellent way to gain the last couple of hundred feet is to approach the summit via its NE ridge. Just a minute or two below the top is one of the most breathtaking fern glades in the Catskills. This open slope is a magical spot, smothered with tall ferns and dotted with widely spaced mature birches. If the glade weren't spectacular enough on its own, across the valley is Balsam Lake Mt. with its prominent fire tower. To its right, in order, are Schoolhouse Peak,

Graham Mt., and Doubletop Mt., all in profile. And on the left, Woodpecker Ridge, part of Mill Brook Ridge, and Cradle Rock Ridge. What a grand spot for pictures, lunch, or lingering.

Once on the summit the woods are open, with more ferns and large birch trees. To enjoy the views, try the hike in early spring or after autumn leaf fall. This route covers about 3+ mi round-trip and 800 ft of ascent.

Another route begins on the northern side of the mountain, from a parking area on Beaverkill Rd. (N42° 00.740', W74° 37.367'). See next page, in the Willowemoc Mt. section, for trailhead details. At its start, the trail crosses an interesting bridge over a scenic but private section of historic Beaver Kill Creek. The Beaver Kill is thought to be the most important fly-fishing stream and the American birthplace of the sport. Take care to stay on the trail as the stream and its banks are private property and patrolled.

After crossing the stream, climb 1000 ft, most of the way up Willowemoc Mt., another Catskill 100 peak. As you climb there are views through the trees towards Woodpecker Ridge, Cradle Rock Ridge, and Balsam Lake Mt. Arriving at the first (NE) summit of Willowemoc, bushwhack E toward Beaver Kill Range, losing 400 ft of elevation in the 0.4 mi to the first col. The woods are easy bushwhacking with a couple of easy ledges. The next 0.9 mi regains the 400 ft and picks up another 100 ft of climbing to the top of Beaver Kill Range's 3310 ft SW sub-summit. From here, it's an easy 0.5 mi along the ridge up to the highest point. This route is about 3.5 mi and 1600 ft of ascent from the trailhead.

A second route from the N has the identical starting point, but once across the bridge and past the private property, jump into the bushwhack by heading directly SE until picking up the main drainage in Quaker Cove. The stream drains Beaver Kill Range's NW flank. You can either ascend the NW ridge or follow the drainage up to the col. The ridge has a gentle contour in its bottom 300 ft, gets steeper in the middle, and eases up for the last 500 ft to the summit. This route is about 2.5 mi one-way, but is a bushwhack the entire distance.

For campers, the Fall Brook lean-to, located between Beaver Kill Range and High Falls Mt., is well maintained with nearby water available. It is a good place to lunch or stay over for easy access to both peaks.

Fern glade below summit of Beaver Kill Range. Joanne Hihn

Willowemoc, 3224'
Willowemoc Quad

(Beaver Kill Ridge)
Catskill 67 Rank: 23
View: 2, Interest: 2, Difficulty: 2, Bushwhack: 1

HIGHLIGHTS AND SUMMARY: The route to Willowemoc is 99 percent on trails, with a short and untrailled bushwhack to the high point. It's an excellent hike that anyone who appreciates open woods, birds and other wildlife, and an absence of crowds will enjoy. Look for porcupine, deer, and bear sign. The entire trail is through open deciduous forest. Willowemoc Mt. is called Beaver Kill Ridge on some maps, but its summit is unnamed on the USGS map quad.

BEST TIME TO HIKE: This is an easy hike any time of the year. It is especially easy as an autumn or winter ascent.

Start from Beaverkill Rd. (N42° 00.740', W74° 37.367'), a short distance W of the southern trailhead for Balsam Lake Mt. There is a small parking area, and a blue-marked trail leads downhill for 50 ft to a register. The trail then crosses a scenic swinging bridge over the historic Beaver Kill Creek, a holy place for fishermen and thought to be the stream where fly-fishing got its start in America. This section of the Beaver Kill Creek is heavily posted against trespassing and is patrolled by the caretaker. You can gaze down at the creek, take pictures, or enjoy its beauty from the bridge or any place on the trail, but do not trespass unless you want to visit the local justice of the peace.

Once across the Beaver Kill, the trail heads uphill, SW and then S through open deciduous forest. It's a moderate and steady climb for about 800 ft, with a few rocky sections. The trail then reaches the ridgetop and levels off.

When you think you're almost there, a check of your map or GPS will show that you have reached Willowemoc's shorter NE summit. From here it's less than a mile of easy hiking to the top. As you near the summit, the blue-marked trail starts to head downhill. Take a look around and consult your map, as the top is only a few bushwhacking minutes away. Although the summit is wooded, you'll be able to tell where the high point is. This route is a little over 4 mi round-trip and 1100 ft of easy ascent.

I have a soft spot for Willowemoc as friends Laurie and Tom Rankin completed their ascent of the Catskill 100 here in January 2008 and I enjoyed being part of the group. Laurie was the first woman to complete the Catskill 100.

You can double up Willowemoc by combining it with a second Catskill 100 summit, Sand Pond Mt., located 1.3 mi to the SW (see page 43 in the Sand Pond Mt. section).

Willowemoc can also be climbed from the DEC trailhead on Flugertown Rd. (N41° 56.945', W74° 38.125'). Hike N on a red-marked trail. The trail slowly picks up 300 ft of elevation in the first 1.5 mi until climbing up onto Sand Pond Mt.'s southern ridge. Bear right (E) at the trail junction near Sand Pond's summit, then descend 300 ft into the Sand Pond–Willowemoc col. It's an easy 400 ft climb to near Willowemoc's summit before the short bushwhack described in the previous route.

Eager and adventurous bushwhackers can get up and onto the range of small peaks E or W of Willowemoc, bushwhacking from Beaver Kill Range to its E, or from Mongaup Mt., much farther to the W. Both are trailless Catskill 100 peaks. The woods all around Willowemoc are deciduous and easy bushwhacking. Unfortunately, the summit is wooded, but you can see screened views of Graham and Balsam Lake mountains, Woodpecker Ridge, Mill Brook Ridge, and Cradle Rock Ridge.

High Falls Ridge, 3211'   Claryville Quad
Catskill 67 Rank: 28
View: 3, Interest: 3, Difficulty: 3, Bushwhack: 3

HIGHLIGHTS AND SUMMARY: Seclusion is the theme on this bushwhack peak. You'll feel the solitude once you begin, with only the birds and other wildlife to keep you company. The forest is all hardwoods, predominately beech, and though the summit is wooded, there are views from along the edge of the western summit ridge, in the last 0.25 mi to the summit. Enjoy the acres of ferns in warm weather and the beautiful colors in autumn.
BEST TIME TO HIKE: This is a nice hike any time, but spring and autumn are unexcelled.

High Falls Ridge was given its name because of its proximity to High Falls. The most common hiking route is from the S. See page 31 in the Beaver Kill Range section for location of shared trailhead and parking details. During winter months, don't block the snowplow turnaround at the end of Black Bear Rd.

The unpaved road/trail becomes rougher the farther N you hike from the parking area. About 0.25 mi from the parking area is a large, white house on the left. The trail skirts the lawn, and just beyond the road splits; keep straight ahead as the turn doesn't head toward the mountain.

At about 1.5 mi the trail reaches Fall Brook lean-to, a great location if you're interested in an overnight. It's secluded, in good condition, and often stocked with firewood. An added bonus is the many interesting entries in the logbook.

You can begin your bushwhack within 0.25 mi before or after the lean-to; however, the farther S you start your 'whack, the more elevation you'll need to regain from the descent into the High Falls Brook drainage. Although the woods on the western side of High Falls Ridge are deciduous, the trees have grown close together until near 2900 ft to 3000 ft, when the woods begin to open up. On the hike you may cross an old woods road but it won't lead toward the summit.

Climbing higher, you'll find leafy views of Beaver Kill Range, which improve in late autumn. The summit has acres of ferns surrounding the wooded high point. Expect a round-trip of about 5 mi and between 900 ft and 1200 ft of ascent, depending on where you cross High Falls Brook.

Another route for High Falls Ridge starts on its NW side. Follow Beaverkill Rd. from Turnwood (N42° 01.479', W74° 42.578') through Hardenburg (N42° 00.094', W74° 39.590') to a DEC parking area at its end (N42° 01.429', W74° 35.993'). This is also the trailhead for Balsam Lake Mt. and the Neversink-Hardenburgh Trail. Follow the Neversink-Hardenburgh Trail for about 3.2 mi, passing Tunis Pond, until reaching the col between the northern ridges of Beaver Kill Range and High Falls Ridge. The woods are deciduous.

Begin the bushwhack by descending slightly and crossing a stream before beginning the climb toward High Falls Ridge. Aim for its 3200 ft northern sub-summit, the 3211 ft summit, or the col in between. The woods are not difficult to bushwhack, but midway up there are small rock bands and, in places, beech whips mixed with maple and birch saplings. This route is under 9 mi round-trip and approximately 1400 ft of ascent.

Hikers can combine High Falls Ridge with Beaver Kill Range. If climbing Beaver Kill Range first, you can return to the trail, or hike NE along Beaver Kill's ridge, selecting where to descend to climb High Falls Ridge.

Regardless of route, you will have a sense of being alone on this bushwhack once you leave the access trail. The woods are pleasant, there is a minimum of blowdown, and there is lots and lots of animal and bird activity. In springtime, the woods are speckled with wildflowers and the absence of ferns opens the woods considerably. Seeing High Falls in autumn is a gift you deserve.

Mongaup Mt., 3177'

Willowemoc Quad

Catskill 67 Rank: 32
View: 4, Interest: 5, Difficulty: 3, Bushwhack: 3

HIGHLIGHTS AND SUMMARY: Depending on the route chosen, Mongaup can be a complete bushwhack, or you can get to within a half mile of the summit by trail. Shin Creek Rd. and its surroundings are wild and filled with birds and other wildlife. All routes are spectacular in spring and autumn. Beech Mountain Nature Preserve is a destination worth visiting by itself. There is an open view spot along Beech Mountain Rd. and another along Mongaup's unusual southern ridge.

BEST TIME TO HIKE: Although you can hike the peak any time of year, spring and autumn are best. Shin Creek Rd. is likely to remain unplowed in winter.

The most common way to climb Mongaup Mt. is from the S. Drive N from Debruce onto Mongaup Pond Rd. (N41° 54.766', W74° 43.493') and make a left onto Beech Mountain Rd. Continue to the Frick Pond parking area (N41° 57.047', W74° 42.425').

Begin on the blue-marked Flynn Trail (described on some maps as the continuation of Beech Mountain Rd.). The markers lead into the woods around a private home near the trailhead. The Flynn Trail is a woods road; from springtime onward it's a grassy lane that gradually leads uphill along what is essentially the Mongaup–Beech Mt. ridge. As the trail passes a benchmark at 2714 ft, the Flynn Trail curves NW and then W, reaching a junction at a flat area. As Yogi Berra once said, "When you reach a fork in the road, take it." In this case, keep right (N), leaving  the blue-marked Flynn Trail, following the 2700 ft contour along the SW and then N side of Beech Mt. Near its high spot, there is an excellent view point where you can see Hodge Pond Mt. and Hodge Pond.

In the Beech-Mongaup Mt. col you can take a quick side trip up Beech Mt., Sullivan County's high point. Although it's the county high point, Beech Mt. misses being considered one of the Catskill 100 Highest because the drop from the summit to the Mongaup-Beech col is under 200 ft. If you decide not to hike to Beech Mt., leave the woods road and begin your bushwhack towards Mongaup's southern ridge. From the col to the summit, it is 0.75 mi and 200 ft of ascent along Mongaup's razor-thin southern ridge.

As you step into the woods, animal paths funnel along the ridge and it narrows to mere feet in places. To the W the topography descends steeply but to the E it is a sharp and immediate drop-off. In springtime, the forest floor is filled with trout lilies, trillium, spring beauties, and other wildflowers, and porcupines have stripped the bark on many of the beech trees. As you hike towards the summit, you pass through a section of first-growth forest while enjoying two or three excellent view spots looking toward Sand Pond, Willowemoc, Graham, Beech, and Doubletop mountains, with others in the distance.

The ridge widens as it nears the summit cone of Mongaup, and the woods are easy to hike. Only a few brambles remind you that you are not on a trail. The abundance of bear scat, bird sounds, and lots of other wildlife is likely because the Beech Mountain Nature Preserve is immediately S. The hike is about 8 mi round-trip and a little under 1000 ft in ascent.

An interesting and lightly used approach for Mongaup is from photogenic Shin Creek Rd. One end is at Turnwood (N42° 01.479', W74° 42.578') and the other at Lew Beach (N42° 00.297', W74° 47.106'). This seasonally maintained road is picturesque and lightly traveled. Its isolation and beauty make for a scenic drive, or mountain bike ride, worthy of the travel all by itself. The Turnwood half of the road is rougher, but drivable with regular car in its entirety if you are careful. Count yourself fortunate to see a bear, fox, coyote, or a deer with fawns,

Fiddleheads, Mongaup Mt. Joanne Hihn

and know that it is unlikely you'll run into another hiker heading for the peak.

Shin Creek Rd. is bordered by private property for more than half its length. From Turnwood, look for DEC signs at 2450 ft (near N42° 00.062', W74° 43.065' or N42° 00.514', W74° 42.877') and look for places to pull over to begin your bushwhack. The public land parcels are just W of Mongaup Mt.'s NNW ridge.

A dead E 'whack keeps you on public property. Head steeply uphill for 300 ft of boulder-strewn climbing until you get onto Mongaup's NNW ridge. The next 0.5 mi is on an easy gradient, and you pass over a small bump before the rise to Mongaup's wooded summit.

While the 700 ft of ascent and 4 mi round-trip isn't taxing to experienced bushwhackers, terrain and weather can affect your perception of its difficulty. In the early spring or during autumn, this route is a snap, when the ferns, nettles, and undergrowth are missing and it's easy to pick a clear route. With summer bugs, heat, humidity, nettles, and other prickers, this route hikes longer than it appears on a map. The few Catskill ledges along the way are small and easily climbed, and high up there is a woods road that passes through a grassy field with excellent views. Regardless of the season, this is a nice vantage point to take a break and enjoy the vista.

Another route from Shin Creek Rd. starts with the bushwhack originating 200 yd W of the road's hairpin turn. Head SSW into the woods for 0.15 mi, skirting private land. As you cross the border between Ulster and Sullivan counties, head SE. Eventually you will intercept a small trail/woods road leading into the Beech Mountain Nature Preserve. The Open Space Institute acquired 5000 acres of land around Beech, Hodge Pond, and Mongaup mountains from the Onteora Scout Reservation in the 1980s. The preserve is home to a diversity of animals, birds, plants, and amphibians.

Inside the preserve, there are a series of trails and woods roads; look for the woods road described in the first route above (that begins on the Flynn Trail). The routes from Shin Creek Rd. are under 3 mi round-trip and under 1000 ft of ascent.

Cradle Rock Ridge, 3160' — Arena Quad
Catskill 67 Rank: 33
View: 3, Interest: 3, Difficulty: 2–3, Bushwhack: 3

HIGHLIGHTS AND SUMMARY: This mountain has one of my favorite names and all of its scenic routes are bushwhacks. The hikes are camera-ready, with wildflowers in the spring and ferns in the summer; it's easy bushwhacking when the woods are leafless, and handsome in autumn. There is also pretty Alder Lake nestled at the mountain's feet. The peak and its surroundings are among the best the Catskills have to offer. Because of summer fern growth, hiking poles are really helpful. I've seen more bear scat in some places on the slopes of Cradle Rock Ridge than in any other place in the Catskills.

BEST TIME TO HIKE: When the leaves and vegetation are missing.

The most direct route begins at the spacious Alder Lake trailhead (N42° 02.992', W74° 40.933'), which is reached off of Cross Mountain Rd. from either Mill Brook Rd. (N42° 05.669', W74° 42.767') or CR54 (N42° 01.476', W74° 42.543'). From either direction, it's a long uphill drive on a seasonal dirt road that gets steeper and narrower, and is rocky in spots. I've driven it a number of times in a sedan, but bring a high-clearance vehicle when road conditions are questionable. Cross Mountain Rd. is not maintained in winter.

The short spur road to Alder Lake can be rough at times. It ends at a large DEC parking area. The elevation here is about 2250 ft. A very old masonry fence leads you down a path towards the site of the former Coykendall Mansion. Samuel Coykendall was a canal and rail magnate who built the dam and mansion just before the turn of the century. The property was sold to a sportsmen's club after World War II, and then to a scout council before becoming DEC property in 1980. The state razed the mansion in 2008, causing a controversy, as it was spectacular in its day and sited on an impressive lawn overlooking Alder Lake.

From the lawn you're looking across at one of Mill Brook Ridge's summits, and as you hike the trail along Alder Lake's northern shore, Cradle Rock Ridge's northwestern ridge comes into view. Alder Lake has a population of brook trout and a family of otters, and the entire area abounds with deer and bear. The trail hugs the shoreline on the northern side of Alder Lake, with nice campsites tucked slightly uphill in the hardwoods. As the trail comes around the lake's southern side, it's hillier, farther away from the water, and less scenic.

There are a variety of routes up and down Cradle Rock Ridge from the lake. A preferred one follows Alder Lake's northern shore until it intersects with the Mill Brook Ridge Trail. Take this trail for about 0.5 mi along Cradle Rock's northern flank until the trail gets very near the stream, at an altitude of 2300 ft to 2400 ft. Hop across the stream and head S into the woods. Begin climbing the ridge that terminates below the Cradle Rock summit plateau, staying out of the drainages E and W of the ridge. The woods are easy hiking on the lower slopes of the mountain, but in summer they are covered in a sea of tall cinnamon ferns as you climb higher. The forest is predominately beech, with some maples and birch. While beautiful, the ferns cover blowdown, and there are face-high beech whips and maple saplings in places.

As you climb the northern side of the mountain, the woods transform. The trees grow more closely together and the fern glades appear more frequently and are denser. At 2900 ft to 3000 ft the entire summit ridge is crowned by tall, dense ferns, making it a challenge to see your feet. Large birch and cherry trees are scattered all over this beautiful summit.

Any views during the leaf season are screened, but from autumn on you'll be treated to great views of the Mill Brook Range, Woodpecker Ridge, and Mongaup and Barkaboom mountains. Although the summit is not large, it is wooded enough and the contours gentle enough that you'll spend a few minutes looking for the highest spot. This route is 1.75 mi and 1050 ft ascent from the parking area to the summit.

You can also begin your bushwhack farther along the Mill Brook Ridge Trail toward the lean-to. There is a large meadow just below the lean-to that in wet weather may be flooded, presenting a possible obstacle for a bushwhacker. In fall or early spring the meadow is one of the most glorious places in the Catskills. In early spring, especially, you experience a stunning valley at high elevation located in a first-growth forest. The valley is filled with the sounds of nesting birds, frogs, and other selections from nature's wonderful springtime soundtrack.

You can also climb Cradle Rock from Alder Lake's southern side, going up the ridge just E of the drainage mentioned in the above route. The lower 300 ft to 400 ft of the 'whack is through remarkably open woods. The price for this easy bushwhacking lurks above in the form of substantial patches of stinging nettles, in addition to the ubiquitous heavy fern growth. Approaching the western edge of the NW summit, the cinnamon ferns are shoulder high in spots, hiding loose rocks and fallen tree branches.

Another way up or down Cradle Rock is via Alder Lake's S side trail and up the drainage that enters its SW shore. This is a direct route to the edge of the mountain's NW ridge and an excellent choice if you pick a good line. In summer, you'll find the same nettles and ferns as on other ways up this side of the mountain.

Other routes combine the mountain with a second peak, bushwhacking SSW from Mill Brook Ridge, dropping to the Mill Brook–Cradle Rock col and then up to the summit. Or you can hike from a parking area on Beaverkill Rd. (N42° 00.625', W74° 39.048') and bushwhack NNW to Cradle Rock's southern summit and continue NNE to the top. This is about 5 mi round-trip and a bit over 1200 ft of ascent.

On all of these routes expect to be slowed down considerably in the summer. They are ferny and scenic, but they transform into great routes after the hard frosts kill the green meanies and before they grow back in springtime.

Barkaboom Mt., 3100' *Arena Quad*
Catskill 67 Rank: 40
View: 3, Interest: 5, Difficulty: 2, Bushwhack: 3

HIGHLIGHTS AND SUMMARY: Barkaboom has a lot to offer the hiker/explorer. It is a bushwhack hike rewarded by fern glades, hardwood giants, deer, bear, birds, and a wonderful seep (see the glossary). Springtime wildflowers, including trillium, spring beauties, and Dutchman's-breeches, will brighten your path, as will the melodies of songbirds. According to the *History and Genealogy of Delaware County,* the mountain received its hard-to-improve-upon name from early Native Americans; the name means "birch." The views from the NNE ridge and col are enjoyable, especially when the leaves have departed. We came across a pair of tiny fawns hiding in the ferns on our last outing.

BEST TIME TO HIKE: Spring and summer are the best times to hike. The area is popular with hunters in autumn and Cross Mountain Rd. is not fully maintained in winter, making access questionable.

This small peak is located S of Pepacton Reservoir. The USGS unfortunately misplaced the actual summit on its maps, locating the "x" on Barkaboom's western sub-summit. This mistake puts an uninformed hiker 1.3 mi W of the true top, with an intervening middle summit to climb along the way to the true summit.

The most straightforward route is from the height of land on Cross Mountain Rd. in the col between Mill Brook Ridge and Barkaboom Mt. There is a small parking area on the western side of the col with space for two or three vehicles (N42° 04.068', W74° 41.365'). With the start at a height of 2600 ft, the 500 ft climb makes Barkaboom one of the shorter Catskill 100 hikes.

Head W from the parking area on a woods road. After passing through a marshy area, get onto Barkaboom's NE ridge. You quickly gain 400 ft in the first 0.5 mi, and then another 100 ft in the remaining 0.5 mi to the wooded summit. Along the way there is an abundance of plant life, including a few patches of nettles. The hike up the ridge is through a pretty deciduous forest with acres of ferns and a few easy ledges in the first half mile. At around 2800 ft look for a gorgeous seep. This source of running water allows an amazing variety of ferns, plants, and shrubs to concentrate here. Sit quietly. The seep is a great spot for birds and many four-footed residents who live in the area. If your luck holds, you might spot a Goldie's fern near the seep, a species not common in the Catskills.

While there are some good view spots when the leaves are off the trees, a summer 'whack on the ridge won't produce a view of many peaks except the close-by Mill Brook Ridge. Cross Mountain Rd. to the summit and back is 2 mi and 500 ft of ascent.

A longer but more interesting and rewarding way to experience everything Barkaboom has to offer is a through-hike. Leave one vehicle at the parking area on Cross Mountain Rd., described above, and then drive around the mountain to Barkaboom Rd. Near the height of land on Barkaboom Rd. there is a grassy DEC parking area (N42° 03.924', W74° 43.719') located at approximately 2350 ft. The narrow sliver of DEC land behind it provides access to the entire western and northern sides of the mountain.

Begin 'whacking NE through completely open hardwoods and acres of hay-scented ferns in the first half mile of your hike. Stay on the DEC land corridor until you attain the SSW ridge of Barkaboom's western summit. The woods are open all the way and the trees are a mixture of beech,

Fawn on Barkaboom Mt. Alan Via

maple, and oak, with some large black cherry. As you climb towards the western summit there are screened views of Touch-Me-Not Mt. and lots of deer sign. The last couple of hundred feet to the western summit is through remarkably open woods with black cherry trees in a sea of ferns. It would be difficult to find a more scenic woodland setting.

The western summit actually has two tops, one of which is slightly more distinct. Only one summit shows on topographic maps, as the twin summits don't break the 20 ft contour interval between them. The walk to and over Barkaboom's middle summit is similar, with ferns, black cherry, maple, and beech trees everywhere. As in the woods near the western summit, some of these trees are giants. There are more blackberry bushes on this section of the hike—great for bears, but not so much fun for hikers.

The screened views of the Huckleberry Range, Dry Brook Ridge, and Cabot and Touch-Me-Not mountains are better with the leaves off the trees, but the immediate surroundings are so beautiful you won't feel cheated in the height of summer. After the leaves have gone there are some extraordinary views from the col between the middle and actual summit. The terrain is a slow and gentle rise on the way to the eastern and highest summit of the peak, with the highest point near the center of the summit plateau. It's a little over 3.25 mi and 1075 ft of ascent between the two roads.

Sand Pond Mt., 3062'
Willowemoc Quad
(Beaver Kill Ridge or Sand Pond Ridge)
Catskill 67 Rank: 49
View: 2, Interest: 2, Difficulty: 3, Bushwhack: 1

HIGHLIGHTS AND SUMMARY: Sand Pond Mt. is reached by a trail that passes close to the summit. It's also known as Sand Pond Ridge by local sportsmen. The hike is a good one for those who don't need fabulous views or a dramatic summit, but appreciate the open, deciduous forest, numerous wildflowers, the trill of summer birds, and the quiet of a mountain most folks pass by. Look for porcupine, deer, and bear sign. The bushwhack to the summit is short and easy, so long as you understand land navigation and how to find your way off-trail.

BEST TIME TO HIKE: It is an easy hike any time of the year, and especially easy as an autumn or winter ascent.

Hobblebush on Barkaboom Mt. Bill Chriswell

Like the trail on neighboring Willowemoc Mt., the trail on Sand Pond Mt. approaches but does not go over the summit. The most direct route begins at the trailhead near the end of Flugertown Rd. (N41° 56.945', W74° 38.125') and follows the Long Pond–Beaver Kill Ridge Trail that passes E of Sand Pond and up onto Sand Pond Mt.'s southern ridge. The trail quickly gains about 450 ft in the first 1.5 mi, goes over a 2752 ft sub-summit, and then drops briefly into a shallow 60 ft col before climbing 400 ft up the main summit's narrowing ridge, nearing, but not going over, the summit. When the trees have shed their leaves, there are views of Sand Pond, Mongaup Mt., Cradle Rock Ridge, Woodpecker Ridge, Mill Brook Ridge, and Willowemoc Mt. The hike from your car to the summit is just over 3 mi and 1100 ft of ascent.

There is a second route from the N that first climbs Willowemoc Mt. from Beaverkill Rd (N42° 00.740', W74° 37.367'). It begins a short distance W of the southern trailhead for Balsam Lake Mt. (See page 34 in the section on Willowemoc Mt. for details on shared parking and first part of the hike.) Once on the top of Willowemoc Mt., hike 1.3 mi W then SW by following the blue-marked trail down 500 ft to the Willowemoc–Sand Pond Mt. col, and back up the easy and gradual 300 ft climb towards Sand Pond Mt. The woods between the two peaks are mostly birch with some maple and beech.

As on Willowemoc, the summit of Sand Pond Mt. is slightly off the trail, with the summit ridge a series of very small bumps. A good case could be made that either of the two competing high points is the actual wooded summit. To be sure, visit them both as they are thirty seconds apart. There are spotty views during the leaf season, but the best scenery is during cold-weather months. The round-trip over both peaks is just over 6 mi and 1800 ft of ascent.

For ambitious bushwhackers looking for a longer day, it's possible to link peaks and ridges by coming E from Mongaup's 3177 ft summit and whacking SE for 3 mi over three bumps of 2863 ft, 2989 ft, and then 2928 ft. This is a 900 ft gain in elevation. The same can be done from Beaver Kill Range and over Willowemoc Mt.

Hodge Pond Mt., 2985'

Willowemoc Quad

Catskill 67 Rank: 64
View: 2, Interest: 4, Difficulty: 2, Bushwhack: 2

HIGHLIGHTS AND SUMMARY: Hodge Pond is a great "little mountain" hike that can be either all bushwhack or a partial one, and it is easily combined with a climb of nearby Mongaup Mt. The beech, maple, and birch trees covering the peak allow for easy off-trail hiking, with wildflowers and spring birdsong early in the season, and fern glades from midsummer on. The mountain is a joy for birdwatchers and fans of wildflowers, and spectacular when wearing its autumn drapery. The lack of views from the wooded summit is more than compensated for by the profusion of trout lilies, spring beauties, trillium and ferns, and the open woods. Hodge Pond Mt. is not

much from a height standpoint, but any of the routes from Shin Creek Rd. or Frick Pond offer as nice a hike or bushwhack as you will find anywhere in the Catskill 100.
BEST TIME TO HIKE: This is a good peak to hike any time of year, but Shin Creek Rd. is only seasonally maintained.

Take your pick of three routes to climb. The first is via the Quick Lake Trail from the S with a short 'whack to the summit. A second is a bushwhack on DEP land from Shin Creek Rd., and the third is Hodge Pond Mt.'s northern ridge.

The Quick Lake Trail is reached by driving N from Debruce onto Mongaup Pond Rd. (N41° 54.766', W74° 43.493') and then taking a left onto Beech Mountain Rd. Continue to the Frick Pond parking area (N41° 57.047', W74° 42.425'). Begin your hike on the red Quick Lake Trail at the NW end of the parking area. The trail to Frick Pond can be a little soggy, but well worth it when admiring the view at Frick Pond.

Stay left (NW) on the red trail as it starts to climb at the pond outlet. The trail is a grassy woods road for most of its length beyond Frick Pond. Along the way, you'll intersect a few side trails and at 2300 ft you'll come to Iron Wheel Junction, a collection of old metal wheels. The red trail heads left at the junction and then takes a sharp right near 2400 ft. Look around at 2700 ft where the trail starts to level off, turns, and then starts heading downhill. Your route is uphill to your left (NW), into the open deciduous forest. It's a mere 0.3 mi and 300 ft of ascent to Hodge Pond Mt.'s summit. This is the shortest route to the top, but you can also follow the red Quick Lake Trail around the peak's E or N sides and bushwhack to the top from anywhere. The entire route is 6 mi round-trip with 900 ft of climbing.

The routes from Shin Creek Rd. begin from one of the most beautiful and isolated roads in the lower peaks. The NE end of the road begins at Turnwood (N42° 01.479', W74° 42.578') and the other at Lew Beach (N42° 00.297', W74° 47.106'). To begin the first bushwhack, park on DEP property where the peak's NE ridge intersects Shin Creek Rd., NW of where the road makes a sharp bend (N41° 59.646', W74° 43.305'). This route is half in Sullivan County and half in Ulster County. Scramble down a steep embankment, hop over "skinny" Shin Creek, and scramble back up its southern bank to begin your 'whack.

Before summer vegetation shows up, the deciduous forest will be completely open. Of any of the routes in this book, this may be the closest to a bushwhacking stroll that you'll find. The forest consists of nicely spaced beeches with almost no blowdown. An added treat is the almost complete absence of prickers or nettles. For the first half mile of your 'whack you will find it difficult to decide what to look at first. In springtime carpets of trout lilies decorate the toes of the beech trees. Or with leaves off the trees you will be amazed at how far you can see. A little later in the season, enjoy the numerous fern glades.

Aim for Hodge Pond Mt.'s NNW ridge and at around 2700 ft it shouldn't surprise you to find the woods even more open. The beech trees become larger and maples and ash become more plentiful. Up on the ridge a profusion of trillium compete with trout lilies and spring beauties in the wildflower beauty contest. At around 2700 ft to 2800 ft you cross the red-marked Quick Lake Trail that circles the mountain, likely the first sign of human activity you'll notice along the route. As you reach the wooded top of Hodge Pond Mt., locating the high point might require some looking around, but there is a 2 ft boulder that might serve the purpose.

A final route from Shin Creek Rd. is Hodge Pond Mt.'s NNE ridge. It is a little steeper, has a tad more understory and loose rocks, and the footing is a little lumpy (see glossary) in spots. While it's a little less scenic and the woods are a bit tighter, it's still a wonderful route and the most direct to and from your car parked on Shin Creek Rd.

A couple of small cautions about the Shin Creek routes are in order. In times of high water, a dry crossing of the creek can be a problem. In addition there is a thicket on the S side of Shin Creek Rd. near the sharp bend. While it may appear to be an open and inviting way to begin or end your bushwhack, don't be seduced by its charms. If you choose this shortcut it will be 0.2 mi of what Bogart and Bacall enjoyed in *The African Queen*. It is swampy, squishy, and thick, and not a great way to begin or end a hike. However, if you are not in a hurry and like to discover things on your own, incorporate it in the round-trip of just under 3 mi.

Hodge Pond Mt. Bill Chriswell

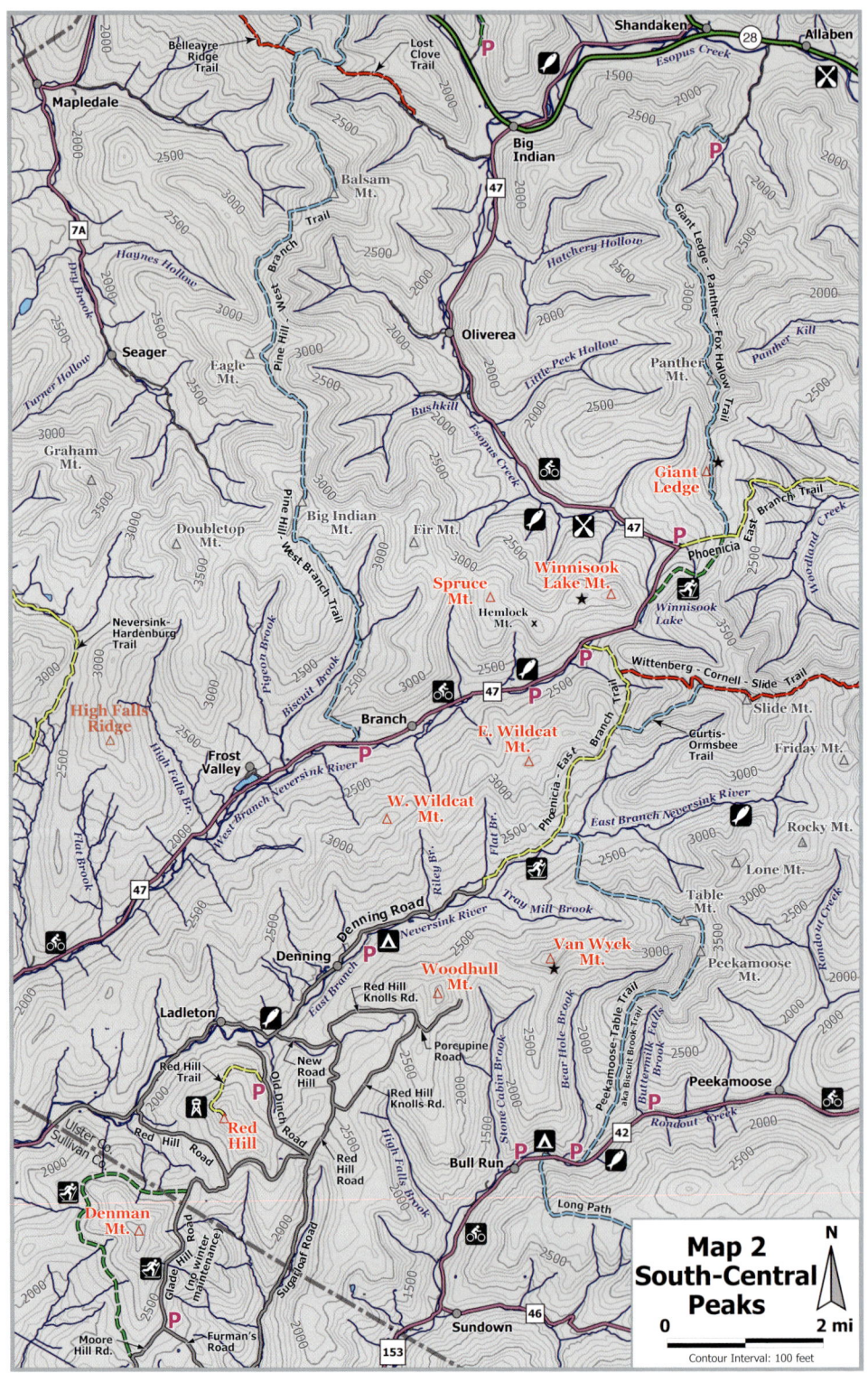

South-Central Peaks

MAP 2

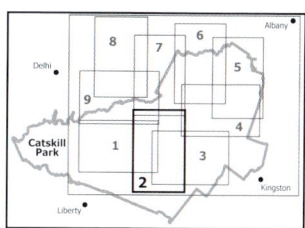

Spruce Mt.
East Wildcat
Winnisook Lake Mt.
Van Wyck Mt.
Giant Ledge

West Wildcat
Denman Mt.
Woodhull Mt.
Red Hill

The south-central peaks region is situated along the southern border of the Catskill 100 peaks, between Giant Ledge and Denman Mt. Eight of the peaks are bushwhacks, and a couple of these are very short. Some are of medium difficulty, and a few are more challenging. Although there are two good county roads that cross the region (CR47 and CR42), it's a long drive around mountain ranges to access Denman and Red Hill.

The woodlands in the northern two-thirds of the region are mostly deciduous, and ice storms have dropped blowdown above 2700 ft on some of the trailless peaks. Pricker bushes are not much of an issue on most of these mountains, but in places there are rocky slopes to contend with. The Wildcats might contain some of the best true wilderness in the Catskills, and the views from Giant Ledge, Van Wyck, and Red Hill make packing a camera a necessity. Hike Denman in June to enjoy sights and smells of mountain laurel.

On a hot summer day, a posthike swim in Rondout Creek or the Neversink River is incredibly refreshing. Fishermen can wet their lines in the Neversink River, in the Esopus, Rondout and Willowemoc creeks, or in one of dozens of small streams. Several parts of the Esopus Creek are suitable for canoeing and kayaking. Bicyclists have almost every country and town road waiting at their pedals.

Autumn reflections on Rondout Creek. Mark Schaefer

Spruce Mt., 3380'

Shandaken Quad

Catskill 67 Rank: 13
View: 2–3, Interest: 3, Difficulty: 3, Bushwhack: 3

HIGHLIGHTS AND SUMMARY: Hikers will enjoy a menu of short and long bushwhack routes to this trailless summit. The connecting ridge between Fir and Spruce is excellent and the col is one of the special places in the Catskills. Wildflowers, birds, and wildlife are plentiful on this lightly hiked peak. The beeches show a lot of porcupine activity and the Catskill bruins enjoy the area. Spruce Mt. can be one of the easier Catskill 100 bushwhacks or it can be linked with neighboring mountains for a more challenging or longer hike. The forest is almost completely deciduous and above 2800 ft there is blowdown from recent Catskill ice storms.

Be observant when reaching what seems like the high point. Depending on the direction you've come from, the highest point just might be another five minutes farther.

BEST TIME TO HIKE: Spruce Mt. is a good peak to hike anytime, but prime during either autumn foliage season or when the routes are covered by wildflowers. Winter provides the best views.

Spruce is probably most often climbed by those who first climb Fir Mt. and travel the connecting ridge between the peaks. Hikers usually start at the Pine Hills–West Branch trailhead (N41° 59.473', W74° 29.082') on CR47, then 'whack Fir's SW ridge. (Note that the Pine Hills–West Branch Trail is also referred to as the Biscuit Brook Trail, and CR47 is also called Slide Mountain Rd.) The route from Fir follows its gentle SE ridge to a narrow and attractive col. During warmer weather months, the small, open fern glade in the col might remind you of the Caudal on Thomas Cole Mt. From the Fir-Spruce col it is an easy 300 ft climb through open hardwoods to Spruce's wooded summit. Beech trees are predominant and wildlife sign is prevalent all over the ridge.

A variant of this route is to follow the same Pine Hills–West Branch Trail and bushwhack the ridge that begins directly E of the lean-to area. The climbing is steep at the bottom and leads to Fir's southern ridge. You can follow the top of this ridge towards Fir, or contour SE toward the Spruce-Fir col and climb by the route suggested above. Either route is around 7.5 mi and 2000 ft of climbing from Biscuit Brook to Fir, Spruce, and then back down directly to CR47.

A third and shorter route to Spruce Mt. starts at the Slide Mt. parking area on CR47 (N42° 00.543', W74° 25.673'). Cross the road from the parking area and pick a good line up to the Hemlock-Winnisook Mt. col. Aim for the center of the col as you near the ridge as there is steep terrain directly under each summit. Once in the col it's a short hiccup over Hemlock and 300 ft of easy ascent to

Porcupine. Barbara Via

Spruce's wooded summit. Keep going when you think you've reached the wooded summit, as the dense beech leaves might hide a higher area beyond. You can then either retrace your steps or descend via Spruce's SW ridge back to CR47.

Avoid a direct climb of Hemlock from the Slide Mt. parking area; there are some steep cliff bands on its southern and southeastern sides. Ice storms have terrorized the woods above 2700 ft on the Winnisook-Hemlock-Spruce ridgeline. Expect to run into broken branches above this elevation. These and the lumpy terrain will slow your progress in this otherwise beautiful deciduous forest. It's about 3.75 mi round-trip to Spruce and back with 1200 ft of ascent.

There is another nice way to climb Spruce, and it's one of my favorites. Look for the small point of public land that meets CR47 at the base of Spruce's SSW ridge (N42° 00.027', W74° 27.319'). In the summer you can either park a car on the side of the road here or walk from the Slide Mt. trailhead.

The beginning of the route starts at approximately 2200 ft and climbs through a beautifully open deciduous forest up Spruce's SSW ridge. The first 500 ft of ascent is gradual, the next 400 ft is steeper, and the final 300 ft is an easy ridge walk with chirping birds and signs of deer, bear, and porcupines. Trees screen the views from Spruce's wooded summit, but the scenery improves after the leaves fall. This route is 3 mi round-trip with 1200 ft of climbing.

East Wildcat, 3340'
Peekamoose Mt. Quad
Catskill 67 Rank: 17
View: 2, Interest: 4, Difficulty: 3, Bushwhack: 3

HIGHLIGHTS AND SUMMARY: The USGS map refers to this peak as Wildcat Mt. Catskill 100 hikers call it East Wildcat to differentiate it from the slightly shorter kitten to the W. All routes are interesting bushwhacks and you're guaranteed solitude in this truly wild range. There is a small, high-elevation hemlock forest that is a wonderful contrast to the deciduous woods surrounding it on all sides. The hike is a naturalist's delight, with wildflowers and bird and animal signs everywhere. Enjoy one of the nicest bushwhacks in the Catskills, with a profusion of interesting routes, fun ledges, and an all-day sense that you are lucky to be hiking where you are. Although East Wildcat lies between two large roads, the Neversink guards its northern side and the Frost Valley YMCA is a barrier to much of its southern side.

BEST TIME TO HIKE: A great hike any time of year, but best from autumn when the leaves are on display, through winter when the snow is untracked, right up to wildflower season. Take care with the Neversink stream crossing in times of high water.

The most direct route begins at the Slide Mt. parking area on CR47 (N42° 00.543', W74° 25.673'). Follow the yellow trail, which leads toward Slide Mt. Bear right at the first trail junction and again when reaching the junction with the Curtis-

Ormsbee Trail (N74° 00.220', W74° 25.108'). You continue on the yellow trail, which is both the Long Path and the Phoenicia–East Branch Trail. Your bushwhack up East Wildcat's NE ridge can commence at any time, up and over some easily climbed Catskill ledges on the way to the first of a pair of preliminary subsummits.

The forest in the Wildcat Range is almost all deciduous—beech, maple, birch, and cherry, with some blowdown from the spring 2007 ice storms. In places there are head-high saplings and beech whips that slow down progress. As you hike W, continue over the first and second small bumps, heading toward the third, which is the wooded summit. It's about 2.75 mi and a little under 1000 ft of ascent from the parking area to the top.

If you would like to do some exploring, the two high-elevation bogs (see glossary) on East Wildcat won't be a disappointment.

Another excellent route to East Wildcat begins at the trailhead on Denning Rd. (N41° 57.993', W74° 27.142'). Most hikers use this as the starting point to climb Lone and Rocky. The trailhead is at a little over 2100 ft and the route follows the yellow trail a little over a mile until it passes the intersection with the blue-marked Peekamoose–Table Mt. Trail. Just before reaching the intersection, the trail crosses onto public property. Although you might decide to bushwhack directly N towards East Wildcat at this point, if you continue on the yellow-marked trail you will pick up 400 ft of elevation and get 1 mi closer to the Wildcat ridgetop. At approximately 2750 ft, the gradient flattens out. Anywhere from here on is a good spot to jump into the bushwhack. Following the yellow trail much farther, however, will lead you away from the summit.

As in the previous route to East Wildcat, the woods you'll encounter are deciduous, with beech trees predominating and many small beech whips from 3 ft to 6 ft in height in between the more mature trees. The smaller saplings tend to block your navigation views from time to time. The mature beeches appear unhealthy, perhaps infected with beech fungus. From all appearances the large beech trees are in transition. Is the profusion of small trees nature's way of adjusting to the imminent loss of the older ones?

As you 'whack towards the ridge there is a steep rock band at about 2800 ft circling much of the SE portion of your route. At first glance, the foliage screens the view, giving the impression the cliffs will be more challenging than they are. With just a little scouting, experienced Catskill bushwhackers should have little difficulty. At this elevation the trees take on a broader arboreal mix, with the appearance of large birch, maple, and cherry trees, some of them twelve to twenty inches in diameter.

There is another band of cliffs at 3050 ft that is taller and at first appearance seems to extend for quite a distance. With some patience, finding a route up should be no problem as you walk along the base scouting for a way. In midsummer there is a beautiful fern glade all around the base of these cliffs. They provide another sight to distract you while you search for the way up through the rock band. The series of cliffs continues just beyond 3200 ft.

By now you may have discovered that the local animals know the best way through cliffs. A broken limb or other injury can condemn a deer or coyote to death. An animal path leading toward a break in a cliff is usually a pretty good sign that the "locals" know the easiest way through. My Lab, Bookah, quickly finds her way through steep sections of rocks. The two-legged hikers who accompany her learn that she's found the way when they see her peering down from a cliff top.

In the last couple hundred feet to the summit there are some very old cherry trees. Unfortunately, ice storms have inflicted the same fate on them as on other trees in the area. This route is 5 mi round-trip and 1400 ft of climbing.

A quick scan of a topographic map shows three nice ridges that rise SE from CR47 toward the peak. Crossing the Neversink River requires care, but if you decide to follow one of these ridges expect open woods and a few steep sections midway to the summit. These routes are all between 2.5–3.25 mi round-trip and about 1200 ft of climbing.

You can also climb East Wildcat from West Wildcat across the ridgeline. See page 59 in the West Wildcat section for routes across the ridgeline.

The Wildcat Range between the East and West peaks conveys a sense of true wilderness. There are few wild areas in the Catskills that are comparable. A trail has been proposed that would lead from the eastern end of Wildcat Range up and over East Wildcat, along the ridge, and then back down near West Wildcat. It would be a sacrilege to cut a trail through one of the Catskill high-elevation hemlock stands and the first-growth forest that comprises much of the ridgeline.

With the exception of an illegal trail that someone has tried to blaze, there are no tracks, blazes, paths, or litter of any sort. Please report any illegal flagging and cutting to DEC forest rangers.

There are occasional open areas for views, but the peace and quiet, serenity, woods, flora, and fauna are the reasons to be here. The wooded summit of East Wildcat won't provide much of a look at the surrounding mountains.

Winnisook Lake Mt., 3260'   Shandaken Quad
Catskill 67 Rank: 21
View: 3, Interest: 5, Difficulty: 2, Bushwhack: 2

HIGHLIGHTS AND SUMMARY: Winnisook Lake Mt. is the second summit NE of Hemlock Mt. It is unnamed on the USGS map quads and is a bushwhack from any direction. Winni can be climbed in a half-day, or made into a much longer outing by pairing it with another Catskill 100 summit, Spruce Mt. The top of Winnisook Lake Mt.'s western sub-summit has an interesting arrangement of boulders that are surrounded by a fern glade in warm weather months. You should definitely visit this sub-summit on your way to or from the main peak. The up-high views are nice when the leaves are off the trees, and porcupines and deer are abundant. There is blowdown and sections of the peak are very rocky. When the ground is bare, parts of the hike can be lumpy.

BEST TIME TO HIKE: Although the peak is a nice climb any time of year, Winnisook is a particularly attractive snowshoe when the blown-down branches and rocks are covered.

Winnisook Lake Mt. derives its name from the small lake across CR47 (aka Slide Mountain Rd). It is an excellent mountain with a lot to offer in a half-day hike by its shortest route from CR47. Begin at the Slide Mt. parking area (N42° 00.543', W74° 25.673') and begin walking the road NE for a few minutes. There is DEC property along the northern side of the road. When you see the first Winnisook Lake Club property sign, head into the woods, keeping W of the private property sign and blazes.

As you climb, the terrain steepens. You can avoid the cliffs underneath Winnisook's southern face by striking the ridgeline midway between the top and its 3200 ft western sub-summit. An ice storm threw damaged branches on the forest floor above 2700 ft. The ridgetop is very rocky, as is much of the terrain on the way up the mountain, yet the summit ridge is thinly wooded and easy to traverse. Views are best when the trees are leafless. You can see Slide, Panther, Fir, and the Wildcats on the way up and on along the ridge.

The real payoff for any hike to Winnisook, however, is a visit to its 3200 ft western sub-summit, located about 0.3 mi W of the true top. The western summit is gorgeous and unusual. and it puts the actual summit to shame. Here you'll find an unusual arrangement of large boulders that reminds some hikers of a small Stonehenge. How Mother Nature dropped and arranged these in one small area is an interesting question. The boulders must be the work of the last ice age!

On the west summt of Winnisook Lake Mt. Moonray Schepart

It's interesting that the lower summit of West Wildcat, just a few miles away, has the same sort of rock formation on a smaller scale.

In the summertime, Winnisook's sub-peak is a gorgeous fern glade, with large boulders and birches poking up through the ferns. It's at its most spectacular, though, in spring and autumn when the ferns are gone and you can really see this unusual 100-yd-long area. The round-trip to Winnisook and its western summit is under 2.5 mi and a tad under 1000 ft of climbing.

Another obvious route to Winnisook is a hike from anywhere along the Fir-Spruce-Hemlock-Winnisook ridge. From W to E, Fir is a Catskill 3500 peak, Spruce a Catskill 100 summit, and Hemlock, a nice peak immediately W of Winnisook Lake and not on any of the common peakbaggers' lists (see glossary). The woods are deciduous, but ice storm damage and the boulders and rocks scattered along the ridgeline make the bushwhack a little more effort than the map mileage might indicate. Figure on about 3.25 mi of bushwhacking and 700 ft of ascent from the summit of Fir to Winnisook.

There is another way to climb the peak. Park at the hairpin turn on CR47 (Panther Mt. trailhead, N42° 01.587', W74° 24.213') and walk NW (downhill) until you encounter DEC signs. While the ascent on this route begins at a moderate grade, it steepens considerably in the last 500 ft. This route is rocky, cliffy, and has more feet of ascent than the previous route.

Van Wyck Mt., 3206' Peekamoose Mt. Quad
Catskill 67 Rank: 29
View: 5, Interest: 5, Difficulty: 4, Bushwhack: 3–4

HIGHLIGHTS AND SUMMARY: Van Wyck is a bushwhack. The route from Woodhull features a cliff amphitheater, cold spring water, ferny woods, beautiful forest, the old bear holes, and a lack of prickers. There is almost too much to absorb in one hike. The many beech trees have a fan base in the large porcupine population, so pooches beware. You will often see bear sign on hikes. There is a spectacular open ledge just below the summit.
BEST TIME TO HIKE: This is a good hike at any time of year. It is especially fine in wildflower or foliage season.

Van Wyck is a favorite hike and has just about everything a great bushwhack should. It can be climbed by a number of attractive routes. One of the finest is along the beautiful dogleg ridge from Woodhull Mt. (See the Woodhull Mt. section later in this chapter, to choose your route up Woodhull.) The 'whack from Woodhull drops about 400 ft through a series of small shelves on the way down to the Woodhull–Van Wyck col. After gaining the Van Wyck ridge, hike SE, then E up the increasingly narrow northwestern, then western, upper ridge of Van Wyck. 'Whack the route to discover why it's special.

Nearing 2950 ft, there is a rock amphitheater where locals say Native Ameri-

cans held ceremonies. The amphitheater bisects the ridge but can be ascended on either side. For those camping or hiking in hot weather, an excellent spring providing cold, clear water pours from a pipe driven into the rock in a small, rectangular alcove at the base of this rock formation. The history of this is unknown.

At 3100 ft on the ridge there are stone stairs that look like they were placed a very long time ago. One can only guess their actual age and history. The woods along the ridge are deciduous, with beech, maple, and birch spaced just the right distance apart for easy passage. The ridge is wonderfully free of blowdown and prickers, and it's loaded with wildflowers in spring and areas of gorgeous ferns in summer. In some places you can walk with both arms outstretched and not bump a tree.

Nearing the summit you can look around through the large cherry and birch trees at the surrounding mountain scenery. Fifty feet below the top on the mountain's S side is an open ledge with a view few Catskill hikers get to enjoy. It's a fantastic spot to take a break, eat lunch, and take out the camera. The route is under 2.5 mi and 1000 ft of ascent from Porcupine Rd. over Woodhull to Van Wyck.

Another variation of this route begins at the cable barrier marking the beginning of DEC land at the end of Porcupine Rd. under the southeastern flank of Woodhull. The road gets more primitive the closer you get to the Woodhull–Van Wyck col. It's a short bushwhack up to the col. Once there, follow the route described above to Van Wyck. The variation is the same mileage but only 600 ft of ascent.

Van Wyck can also be climbed by its southern ridge. The route begins on CR42, Peekamoose Rd. (N41° 54.974', W74° 26.078'), and ascends its entire length through mostly beech forest. The beginning of the ridge can be found

Van Wyck Mt. Tony Versandi

between Bear Hole and Stone Cabin brooks, near any of the camping areas by Bull Run on CR42. The ridge gets very steep the last 400 ft to the summit. There is a good woods road that stays above the W side of Bear Hole Brook. One branch of the woods road heads towards Van Wyck's southern ridge, and the other heads farther up the Bear Hole Brook drainage.

If staying on the southern ridge, be on the lookout for the wreckage of two plane crashes. One is a private plane that crashed into the ridge in 1977 at around 2625 ft. The other is the remains of a military jet trainer from the 1960s.

Look around near 2750 ft on the ridge and you might get lucky and see two large bear holes, for which the stream is named. Many years ago, local people dug pits to trap bears. Although the sides of the large pits have since fallen in, you'll marvel at the amount of dirt that must have been excavated to construct these bear traps, and what a task it must have been. The round-trip from Peekamoose Rd. is 7.5 mi and 2000 ft of ascent.

Hikers can also bushwhack from Table Mt., losing 400 ft and gaining 1000 ft in the 1.75 mi between the summits.

Regardless of the route you select, the summit of Van Wyck is a delight. It's filled with ferns and wildflowers in season, and shaded by a grove of cherry and birch trees. If all of this is not enough, the view from just below the summit is breathtaking. To locate it, head E toward the sharp drop-off and then walk S until you come to an open ledge surrounded by grass and shade trees. Get out your cold drink and lunch, and enjoy the impressive views of Peekamoose and Table mountains.

Giant Ledge, 3200' Shandaken Quad
Catskill 67 Rank: 30
View: 5, Interest: 4, Difficulty: 3, Bushwhack: 1

HIGHLIGHTS AND SUMMARY: At 3200 ft, Giant Ledge is usually thought of as a bump on the way to Panther Mt. There is a trail over the summit ridge, but peakbaggers will want to take five minutes to bushwhack to the true summit. For everyone else, who cares? The views from the summit cliffs are excellent, as are the views looking up at the cliffs from a route along the peak's eastern side. Read on to learn of additional routes that may surprise you.
BEST TIME TO HIKE: Any time of year.

Trails to Giant Ledge come from three directions and all bypass the true summit, located a five-minute 'whack W of the trail. The first trail begins at the hairpin curve on CR47 (N42° 01.587', W74° 24.213'). Follow the yellow Phoenicia–East Branch Trail up 700 ft to the base of the Giant Ledge summit ridge. Hike left at the trail intersection and follow the blue markers to the top. The first part of the trail is steep in places and can be icy in winter. The round-trip from your car is 3.4 mi and 1050 ft of ascent.

Many hikers may not realize there is a DEC right-of-way along an old woods road that can be picked up near Winnisook Lake Club property. Though only members may park here, you can be dropped off or walk to the right-of-way. The unpaved road is scenic and mostly flat, and is a very pleasant walk. Starting at the club, it generally heads NE and intersects the yellow trail mentioned above.

You may also reach the woods road with a short bushwhack from CR47 right before the end of the DEC property line (N42° 01.174', W74° 24.554') at about 2500 ft. Continue driving uphill beyond the Giant Ledge hairpin-turn parking

Giant Ledge and Slide Mt. from Panther Mt. Tony Versandi

area mentioned above, and pull off the road. There is room to safely park off the road in warm weather months. Hike E uphill five minutes and intersect the woods road coming from the Winnisook Lake Club. It's about 4.5 mi round-trip and 800 ft of climbing from here to Giant Ledge.

For a longer day, begin hiking in Woodland Valley (see Map 3) and follow the yellow trail to where these other routes all intersect at the southern end of the Giant Ledge summit ridge. It's a 5 mi round-trip with 1850 ft of climbing.

Here's how to make a great hike even more interesting. From where the trails intersect at the base of Giant Ledge's southern ridge, hike N on the blue-marked trail about 0.4 mi, to just before the last 300 ft climb to the top. The trail is level here. Walk into the woods on your right (E) and skirt Giant Ledge's summit ridge on its eastern (right) side. In summer, this 1 mi bushwhack can be a little damp in places if you stray too far E. In winter it is a delightful hike through open woods. With the leaves off the trees you can see Panther and have unusual views looking right up at the summit cliffs of Giant Ledge. Huge boulders have fallen off the cliffs over the centuries, and with snow on the ground the smaller rocks and boulders are covered, minimizing the up-and-down hiking of other seasons.

Rock falls from the cliffs have created some large caves and other places to poke around and explore. The closer you are to the base of the cliffs, the more interesting the travel. Go too far E and you'll be sidehilling and in some wet areas. Like Goldilocks and the three bears, the middle course just outside of the rock fall zone and before the slope drops to the E is "just right." Take a look at a map; the flat area between map contours is the preferred route.

After you've gone a mile admiring the cliffs and superb echoes, contour W to the Giant Ledge–Panther col, intersecting the trail connecting the two peaks. Head left (S) and you will be on the top in no time. On the summit ridge, there are great views down and over the cliffs you were admiring from below. Watch your step here in the winter as the ice buildup can provide you a much closer look at the top of the cliff face than you had planned for, and keep an eye on your children and dogs.

Peakbagger readers—you know who you are already, so let's get you onto the real summit. Once on the summit trail high point, walk W into the woods away from the cliffs and views. In a couple of minutes you will hike up onto a small ridge that parallels the trail. Follow this little rocky ridge to its obvious high place. Congratulate yourself on a short little bushwhack that almost everyone else walks past.

West Wildcat, 3160'
Peekamoose Mt. Quad
Catskill 67 Rank: 34
View: 3, Interest: 5, Difficulty: 3, Bushwhack: 4

HIGHLIGHTS AND SUMMARY: As with its taller eastern sister, there are many ways to hike this gorgeous peak, all of them bushwhacks. For information on additional access points and trailheads, please refer to the section on East Wildcat, page 49. There are lots of reasons to hike West Wildcat, not the least being the wildlife, birds, deer, spring wildflowers, bears, and porcupines. The "Black Forest" located near the summit is worth the hike all by itself.

Most of the Wildcat ridgeline is first-growth forest. See the interesting rocks and fern glade about 0.2 mi E of the summit and try to locate the grove of white pine patriarchs lower on the mountain. The summer ferns are beautiful, but they cover up rocks and branches at their feet. Be cautious crossing the West Branch of the Neversink from the N during high-water conditions. BEST TIME TO HIKE: The best time to hike West Wildcat—one of my favorite mountains—is early spring, when it looks as if wildflowers have been flung all over the mountain.

The shortest, most direct, and favorite route starts at a DEC parking area on CR47 (aka Slide Mountain Rd.). Park almost directly N of the summit, about 1 mi NE of where Biscuit Brook crosses CR47. Walk into the woods from the back of the parking area, and scramble down the hill to the banks of the beautiful West Branch of the Neversink River. It's DEC land across the river and all the way to the summit. The Neversink is about 30 ft across and you can wet wade—bring water shoes—or use my garbage bag technique (see glossary) to cross.

Choose your day carefully and avoid periods of high water or a forecast of heavy rain while you're on the hike. Heavy precipitation will provide the bushwhacker with the opportunity to combine two sports: hiking and body surfing with your pack down the Neversink.

The woods on the S side of the 'Sink are completely open deciduous forest. Beech is the dominant species all the way to the summit, though there are also a variety of maples, large birch, and cherries. West Wildcat's summit lies just over 1 mi and 1100 ft of climbing in front of you. The average grade from this direction is very moderate. On the way up, check out some attractive rocks and easy-to-navigate ledges.

At around 2800 ft the beautiful woods open up even more, and small beech trees are scattered across acres and acres of spring trout lilies. In places you can walk with your arms out and barely bump a branch. The summit has some large birches and summer ferns.

After you're done exploring or having lunch, the enjoyment continues. Head down the NE ridge, dropping about 150 ft, and pass through a fern glade with scattered large boulders, much like the rocks on the two summits of Winnisook Lake Mt.

If you'd like to combine this peak with another, first climb East Wildcat (see section on East Wildcat, page 49) and select a pleasing route across the range. Leaving the summit of East Wildcat, head W by dropping through open woods about 300 ft and 0.5 mi to the next col. You'll notice that while the woods are otherwise not difficult to negotiate, there are enough broken treetops on the ground and the occasional ledge or cliff band to keep you focused. In summer this col is inviting and ferny. Combined with heavier foliage and limited visibility, though, it's sometimes difficult to see far ahead.

You can then choose the steep 200 ft climb W out of the col and back up onto the ridgeline. Another 0.75 mi of up and down deposits you in another col on the ridgeline's western side. I believe that by skirting this bump on its southern flank and staying on the contour, hikers can avoid some of the ledges and the elevation ups and downs. With careful planning and by watching your map contours, elevation, and bearing, you will lose about 125 ft of elevation as you head W and run right into the next col without having to regain elevation.

And what a surprise awaits you. After being in leafy birch, beech, and ferns all day, when you turn the nose of the ridge you've bypassed, you'll walk straight into a dark, cool hemlock forest that Catskill hiker Jim Bouton refers to as the "Black Forest." On a warm, sunny day, walking into the Black Forest is like standing in front of an open refrigerator. This three- to five-acre hemlock forest is first-growth. While there are a few limbs on its floor, the hemlocks are far enough apart that you can stroll through it before skirting the last tiny bump on the ridge and ascending the last 250 ft and 0.65 mi up West Wildcat's NE ridge. With the exception of the far southwestern end, the entire Wildcat Range ridgetop is first-growth forest.

From the Black Forest to the summit of West Wildcat the woods are much more open, and this last part of the ridge has delightful open areas of ferns and birches. There is a view spot on the Denning side of the summit ridge that is scenic when the leaves are off the trees.

From late spring until late autumn, it's difficult to find good views from West Wildcat, but there are a few open areas that provide glimpses of Woodhull, Van Wyck, Table, Lone, and other mountains in the distance. When the leaves are gone, though, a hike along the ridge allows easy navigation with views materializing here and there. Coming from the summit of East Wildcat, it is just over 2.25 mi between the peaks.

The southern side of the Wildcat Range has large tracts owned by Frost Valley YMCA. With a membership or by staying above the Frost Valley property line, you can be awed by some groves of ancient white pines. It is worth the time to locate them. Those who live in the area might consider joining the YMCA's Natural Resource Membership program, which allows hiking, hunting, and fishing anywhere on the property. Another option is to purchase a hiking-only membership. A background check is required if you want to be on the property when campers are there.

Denman Mt., 3053'
Claryville Quad
Catskill 67 Rank: 53
View: 3, Interest: 5, Difficulty: 2, Bushwhack: 2

HIGHLIGHTS AND SUMMARY: Denman can be an easy hike along a snowmobile trail, a bushwhack, or a combination. The mountain is a treat when the mountain laurels are blooming, and Denman's southern ridge in wildflower season or autumn foliage time is a fine hike. The views are mostly of the lesser peaks, but Denman is its own star. Birders, or any hikers who appre-

Crossing the Neversink River, using "garbage bag technique," West Wildcat.
Moonray Schepart

ciate nature, will enjoy the native creatures who call the mountain home.
BEST TIME TO HIKE: Although Denman can be climbed any time of year, autumn and springtime might be the best.

Denman Mt. is located NNW of the Rondout Reservoir and 2 mi SE of Claryville (N41° 55.103', W74° 34.331'). It is the most southern Catskill 100 peak. The low summit elevation and high trailhead make this a relatively short hike, and one easily combined with neighboring Red Hill.

Denman can be bushwhacked or climbed by a snowmobile trail that runs along its southern ridge. Let's begin with the bushwhack route. It starts at a large DEC parking area located at the intersection of Moore Hill Rd. and Glade Hill Rd. (N41° 52.872', W74° 32.336'). The road is unplowed beyond this point, but during warm weather months you can drive a little farther N. With the highway confusion not unknown to the backcountry Catskills, Moore Hill Rd. becomes Glade Hill Rd. as it runs along the E side of the peak.

From the DEC parking area, walk N along the road on the E side of Denman. Good bushwhackers know to use what the mountain offers you. Walking N on Glade Hill Rd. gets you 300 ft closer to the summit. When the road levels off and starts down, head left (W) uphill towards the summit through extremely open and easy-to-hike deciduous woods. Depending on where you leave the road, the actual bushwhack to Denman's southern ridge is between 0.25 and 0.4 mi.

Once on the ridgeline, take the excellent snowmobile trail that runs along its length and follow it right to the wooded summit. The summit plateau is large, and to be certain to reach the top walk N until the summit plateau starts to drop. The round-trip is a shade over 3 mi and 900 ft of climbing.

Once on the summit, you can either reverse your route to return to the parking area or make a loop of the hike by taking the snowmobile trail down Denman's southern ridge. A loop combining the bushwhack and snowmobile trail is almost 4 mi round-trip. Hikers with only a modest level of map and compass experience will have no trouble with the bushwhack portion of the loop, and little more than knowing how to read a topographic map is necessary for hiking the snowmobile trail to the top.

To follow the snowmobile trail up Denman, start at the same DEC parking area near the intersection of Moore Hill and Glade Hill roads. The trail runs N along Denman's southern ridge. The lower part of the trail passes through dense areas of mountain laurel, sometimes thick enough to obscure the trail. As you climb, bear right at a fork in the trail to remain on the ridgetop.

The trail weaves in and out of mixed hardwoods, conifers, acres of ferns, and large areas of overgrown meadows. These give the impression that the southern side of the mountain must have once been farmland. As you get to within about 0.75 mi of the summit, the woods transition to a forest of mixed hardwoods and conifers, providing screened views of the surrounding mountains and Rondout Reservoir.

Keep your eyes open as you hike. The variety of cover and flora attracts birdlife and provides food and cover attractive to deer and bear. In the springtime, mountain laurels light up the southern ridge, providing a second act to the profusion of wildflowers that bloom ahead of it. Hiking the snowmobile trail to the summit and back is almost 4 mi.

Woodhull Mt., 3040'   Peekamoose Mt. Quad
Catskill 67 Rank: 57
View: 3, Interest: 4, Difficulty: 2, Bushwhack: 2

HIGHLIGHTS AND SUMMARY: Woodhull is a short bushwhack hike, but it's a long drive to the trailhead. You can get up and down it quickly if your aim is a quick peak or if you want to climb nearby Red Hill on the same day. Combine the mountain with Van Wyck Mt. and you'll have a full day. There is deer, bear, and porcupine sign all over the peak. The woods are a joy, the bushwhacking is excellent, and the views are good from autumn through early spring. Woodhull is a birder's delight in springtime. As a courtesy to area landowners, please stay away during the big game and turkey hunting seasons. The last short distance to the summit is private property, so obtain permission if getting to the highest point is your objective.

BEST TIME TO HIKE: Any time of year is good, but autumn and early spring might be the most favorable.

The first challenge for Woodhull is locating the starting point. Take CR42, Peekamoose Rd., out of West Shokan past Sundown to the intersection with Sugarloaf Rd. (N41° 51.836', W74° 39.392'). (Note that CR42 becomes CR153 out of Sundown.) Drive N on Sugarloaf Rd., passing a number of roads on the left. Keeping right, Sugarloaf Rd. becomes Red Hill Knolls Rd. It eventually intersects Porcupine Rd. at the top of a long uphill (N41° 56.455', W74° 28.173'). Walk past seasonal homes and camps to a metal cable marking public property at the end of Porcupine Rd.

Porcupine Rd. becomes rougher as it continues N beyond the cable. You can either follow the DEC property line here NW to Woodhull's NE ridge, or stay with the road and choose another place to break off toward Woodhull's summit or its NNE ridge. The 'whack is under 1.5 mi and about 500 ft of climbing to the summit.

The summit is mostly beech, birch, and cherry trees, with large areas of summertime ferns. The absence of blowdown and pricker bushes makes for a delightful hike. The open woods along the top are marked by three small summit bumps. Unlike almost all of the Catskill 100 summits, two have small cairns on them. In my opinion, the third, unmarked summit is the highest by a few feet. Deciding for yourself is part of the fun. Although the top is wooded, there are screened views in many directions. The views in autumn or winter are even better as the deciduous trees turn colors or shed their leaves.

Porcupine Rd. parallels the eastern side of the summit. As you walk the road to the DEC property line, a friendly inquiry with one of the camp owners might lead to a short but steep 450 ft climb to the summit. An ascent from here is quick, but the steep slope is challenging due to loose rock in places.

If you approach Woodhull from its NNE ridge, expect open hardwoods and gentle grades. From this direction, you miss the steep ascent on Woodhull's eastern side. The woods on Woodhull Mt. are open and inviting, as large areas of the mountain were cut and cleared in the past.

For a route connecting Woodhull Mt. to Van Wyck Mt., see page 53 in the section on Van Wyck Mt.

Red Hill, 2980' Claryville Quad
Catskill 67 Rank: 67
View: 5, Interest: 4, Difficulty: 2

HIGHLIGHTS AND SUMMARY: Red Hill is a terrific short trail hike, which leaves time for other activities, including bagging another peak, birding, photography, or just loafing on the summit. It's a fire tower peak and one of the Adirondack Mountain Club's Fire Tower Challenge mountains. Red Hill is the southernmost on that list of towers, and has the dual distinction of being the lowest and last peak on the Catskill 100 highest list.

In spite of the remote trailhead, the wildlife, birds, and views make the drive to this peak worthwhile. It is located in the Sundown Wild Forest, SSW of Denning. The tower was last staffed by an observer in the early 1990s.
BEST TIME TO HIKE: Any time of year is good, but spring wildflower season or autumn foliage time might be the most satisfying.

The route up Red Hill used to be the tower access road that wound its way up the peak's SE ridge, but a change in ownership resulted in the road being closed. After the road was closed, a hiking trail was cut from a new trailhead (N41° 55.769', W74° 30.397') on Dinch Rd. The well-graded trail gains just under 900 ft of climbing in a little under 1.5 mi through a deciduous forest to the summit tower.

It is unfortunate that the service road is now closed to hikers, as along the switchbacks on the SE ridge of the mountain there are lovely open areas overlooking the tops of trees and fields. Though we can hope DEC might someday negotiate an easement for this side of the mountain, hikers should be content with the extraordinary views from the summit and its tower. On a clear day you can see some of the DEP reservoirs as well as Catskill summits. Woodhull, Peekamoose, the Wildcats, and many more of the higher peaks in the southern Catskills are visible.

Illustration by Barbara Via

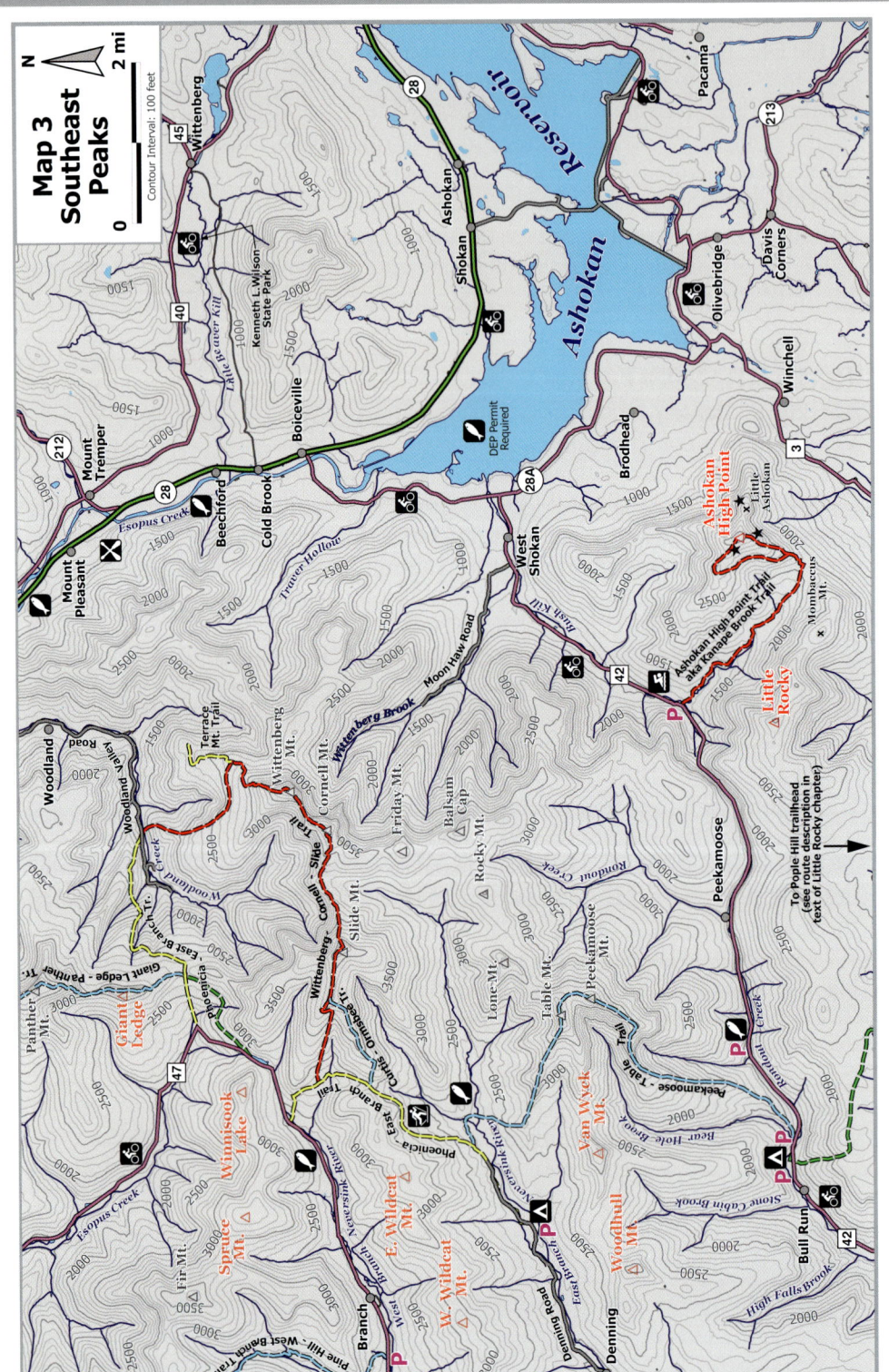

Southeast Peaks

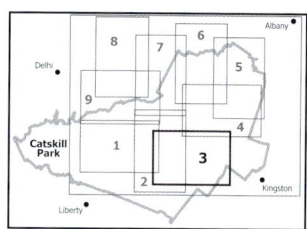

Ashokan High Point
  (High Point or Shokan High Point)
Little Rocky (Gulf Mt.)

While the southeastern region is loaded with mountains, it's home to only two of the Catskill 67. Ashokan is trailed, but offers some bushwhacking options. Little Rocky is a 'whack all the way. Both are easily accessible from CR42.

Ashokan High Point is one of the most interesting peaks in the Catskills, and one of the classic Catskills view points is located just below its summit. This is an excellent place to pick blueberries and take photographs. Its SW neighbor, Little Rocky, has some of the steepest climbing, tallest ledges, and biggest boulders you'll see in the mountains. Quiet bushwhackers on Little Rocky often encounter deer and grouse, and, on occasion, a bear.

On a hot day, bring along a bathing suit. There are swimming holes near the trailheads along the Bush Kill, Kanape, and Rondout creeks. Fishermen will find the Rondout and Esopus creeks, the nearby small streams, and the Ashokan Reservoir (DEP permit required) good destinations when in the area. Paddlers can get their boats wet on the nearby Esopus Creek.

Cyclists enjoy the roads circling the reservoir, including a bicycle-only path. Mountain bikers can sample the 15 mi Wallkill Valley Rail Trail (just outside the boundaries of Map 3) or the trails at the Kenneth Wilson State Park in Mt. Tremper or at Onteora Lake just west of Kingston.

Ashokan Reservoir. Barbara Via

Ashokan High Point, 3080'

West Shokan Quad

(High Point or Shokan High Point)
Catskill 67 Rank: 48
View: 5, Interest: 4, Difficulty: 3

HIGHLIGHTS AND SUMMARY: Regardless of which name you use, this is a top ten hike on the Catskill 100 list. The small oaks, ferns, spring wildflowers, blueberries, and the spectacular open meadow just beyond the summit are all highlights of this hike during different seasons. The unusual lineup of peaks seen from the summit meadow is extraordinary, as are the views of Ashokan Reservoir. It is a lovely trail hike.

BEST TIME TO HIKE: Spring wildflowers, June mountain laurel blooms, summer blueberries, and autumn foliage are all good reasons to visit the mountain. Did I leave out a season? Oops, this is a great winter snowshoe.

The trail begins across the road from the Kanape Brook (pronounced "Ka-Nape" by locals) trailhead (N41° 56.106', W74° 19.721') on CR42, Peekamoose Rd. The trail goes over a bridge and onto a rocky woods road that climbs steadily until it reaches the saddle between High Point and Mombaccus Mt. The hike to the saddle gains about 1000 ft in a little over 2.5 mi. The ascent is hardly noticeable owing to the gradual gradient and interesting surroundings. The hike to the col follows Kanape Brook or tributaries and is lined with mountain laurel and ferns, with a hardwoods forest backdrop. For overnighters, there are places to camp along the trail, and the brook provides a ready supply of water.

Above the High Point–Mombaccus col there is an alternate trail (N41° 55.103', W74° 18.401') to the summit. (If you follow the trail over the summit rather than doubling back, you will loop around and come out here. See the map and description on next page.) From here, the woods road/trail enters a grassy clearing and makes a sharp left up the ridge towards High Point. The ascent is gradual at first, then steeper. On the way to the summit there are ferns, laurels, and acres of blueberry bushes. The woods go through a very obvious transformation the higher you hike. Near the saddle, small oaks predominate, but as you climb they get much smaller, almost stunted. During your climb, take an occasional look over your shoulder at Mombaccus Mt. across the valley.

The grade eases as you enter an opening in the forest below the summit, with a great vantage point looking toward the surrounding mountains. You can also see Smiley's Tower in Mohonk and the Minnewaska Forest. Just below the summit there is a faint herd path descending E down the ridge. Besides leading to a small tent spot, it heads slightly S of E downhill 400 ft to a small bump on the ridge. This is Little Ashokan (N41° 55.408', W74° 16.850'). Besides looking back up at High Point, it offers wonderful views of the Ashokan Reservoir from its open top.

From the summit of High Point, the trail heads off the top and, in a minute, comes to a meadow that formed as a result of a years-ago fire. Besides being a great location to pick blueberries, its year-round charm is the fabulous view of Slide, Wittenberg, Cornell, Friday, Balsam Cap, Lone, and Rocky. You can't see these peaks from the summit ledge. Look around to find a small herd path that leads back into the woods behind you. Follow it for a very short distance and a view opens up towards the entire Ashokan Reservoir.

Returning to the trail, you can descend the way you came up. Or, to enjoy additional views and see more of the mountain, hike the loop mentioned earlier. To make the loop, follow the trail downhill through the meadow until the trail reenters the woods, with dense mountain laurel and stunted oaks on both sides. As you continue to follow the trail downhill, look left for the remains of an old plane crash about 30 ft off the trail. It may be difficult to see when the leaves are on the trees and laurels, as much of the debris has been removed from the site.

Continue along over two subsidiary bumps that are referred to by locals as Hoop Pole Mt. The name came from the era when wooden barrels were a daily part of life, and metal hoops were expensive or nonexistent. Locals would drive mules and oxen up the mountain and collect bundles of thin saplings that would be shaved and made into barrel hoops.

Local lore says that people used to set fires high up on the mountain to clear the forest for wild blueberry bushes. This is easy to believe if you're hiking the trail during the midsummer berry season. Before long the loop trail rejoins the trail you hiked on the way up. The entire hike is just under 7.5 mi and about 2050 ft of climbing if including the loop over Hoop Pole Mt.

A variation of the loop hike is to bushwhack Ashokan High Point's NW

Ashokan Reservoir with Ashokan High Point in the background. Mark Schaefer

ridge beyond Hoop Pole Mt. You will descend through areas of laurel, birch, blueberries, and ferns. There is a wonderful view spot on the crest of the ridge. If you stay NW and then W, the ridge should deposit you right on the Kanape Brook Trail a short distance from the trailhead. You can use this variant to either climb or descend the mountain. My friend Bill Chriswell and his dog, Shiloh, surprised a bear and her cub on the bushwhack described above.

Little Rocky, 3015'   West Shokan Quad
(Gulf Mt.)
Catskill 67 Rank: 60
View: 2, Interest: 5, Difficulty: 5, Bushwhack: 5

HIGHLIGHTS AND SUMMARY: The spectacular cliffs and rock formations make this a challenging peak for Catskill bushwhackers. It is not for casual bushwhackers or those uncomfortable on steep and unforgiving terrain. The steep terrain of this mountain suggests that there would be all sorts of great views, but there aren't. When the leaves are off the trees, some of Little Rocky's screened views open up nicely. Choose the Mombaccus Mt. route for the most forgiving way to the summit. There are a lot of birds and other wildlife on Little Rocky and you don't need to hunt around for the summit—the top has a small bump with a large rock cairn. It's a good spot for lunch. Please respect the private property on its northern and western sides.

BEST TIME TO HIKE: The best time to hike is when the nettles and leaves are gone, but be careful of steep routes during snow or icy seasons.

What Little Rocky lacks in height is more than made up for by its variety of routes and "interesting" flanks. Here is a Catskill 100 peak whose terrain will make Adirondack hikers feel right at home.

The "standard" bushwhack for Little Rocky begins at the Kanape Brook trailhead (N41° 56.106', W74° 19.721') on CR42, Peekamoose Rd., the same parking area you'd use for climbing Ashokan High Point (see previous section).

Begin hiking the Kanape Brook Trail and follow it to the saddle between Ashokan High Point (AHP) and Mombaccus Mt. Where the trail to AHP turns left (NNE), head SW into the bushwhack up Mombaccus's NNE ridge. The angle of ascent is moderate at first, but it gets steeper midway up as you pass some cliff bands. There is a small opening near the top of Mombaccus and from here it's a little less than 1.5 mi over to Little Rocky, a favorite walk for those who enjoy this peak.

The woodland between the two mountains is a mix of hardwoods, with some hemlock groves and lots of mountain laurel. Laurel is not common on the Catskill 100 mountains, and timing your hike to coincide with the white springtime blooms might be a good idea. Along the ridge, a quiet hiker might get lucky and see some of the numerous deer, bears, coyotes, or porcupines that call the mountain home. Springtime is a walk through an aviary. On the way to Little Rocky's summit there are rocky outcrops, a large open area, and a rock cairn on the peak's slightly shorter SE summit.

The summit of Little Rocky is wooded and it too has a large cairn marking the top. It's a good place to eat your lunch on the mostly viewless peak. By reversing the route back to the trailhead, you will walk about 9 mi and climb 2600 ft.

A second route starts at the same trailhead. Walk about 1 mi along the Kanape Brook Trail, then cross the brook on the E side of a large drainage. Pick up the short and very steep ridge that climbs over 1600 ft in 1.1 mi to Little Rocky's SE summit. As you begin your 'whack the woods are open. After a very brief warm-up, the route quickly gains elevation. The goal of remaining on the eastern side of the drainage is to hit the ridgetop a little E of Little Rocky's SE summit, avoiding a small wedge of private property. It's then a modest walk NW across the ridge to the actual summit. This route covers a little more than 2.5 mi from the trailhead with 2100 ft of climbing. While shorter than the Mombaccus route, be advised that there is very steep terrain on this route, and it should be used only by experienced bushwhackers.

A third route starts on the SW side of the mountain if you can drive to the Pople Hill parking area at the end of the deteriorated Trail's End Rd. (N41° 53.045', W74° 21.633') outside of Riggsville. Follow the trail N for about 0.5 mi and then bushwhack Big Rosy Bone Knob (2223 ft). Continue N and then NE to Little Rocky from this very intriguingly named peak. This route is doable, but complicated. If you want to try it, you'll need to do some map homework and plan a route.

The entire W and NW side of Little Rocky is private property. If you can obtain permission from landowners, there are wonderful but steep routes up the mountain's NE, W, and N ridges. One gains 1900 ft in 1.2 mi of hiking, with house-sized boulders that have calved off the cliffs above. Hikers on any of those ridges are tested with finding and following the cracks, ramps, and chutes up, through, and over the battlements of the peak.

The mountain has a lot to see: mountain laurel, a large deer population, areas of ferns and nettles in summer, and oak, beech, and hemlock woods. The mountain is also crisscrossed with old woods roads, some of which assist, and others that lead nowhere.

Blueberry Bald on Little Rocky. Bill Chriswell

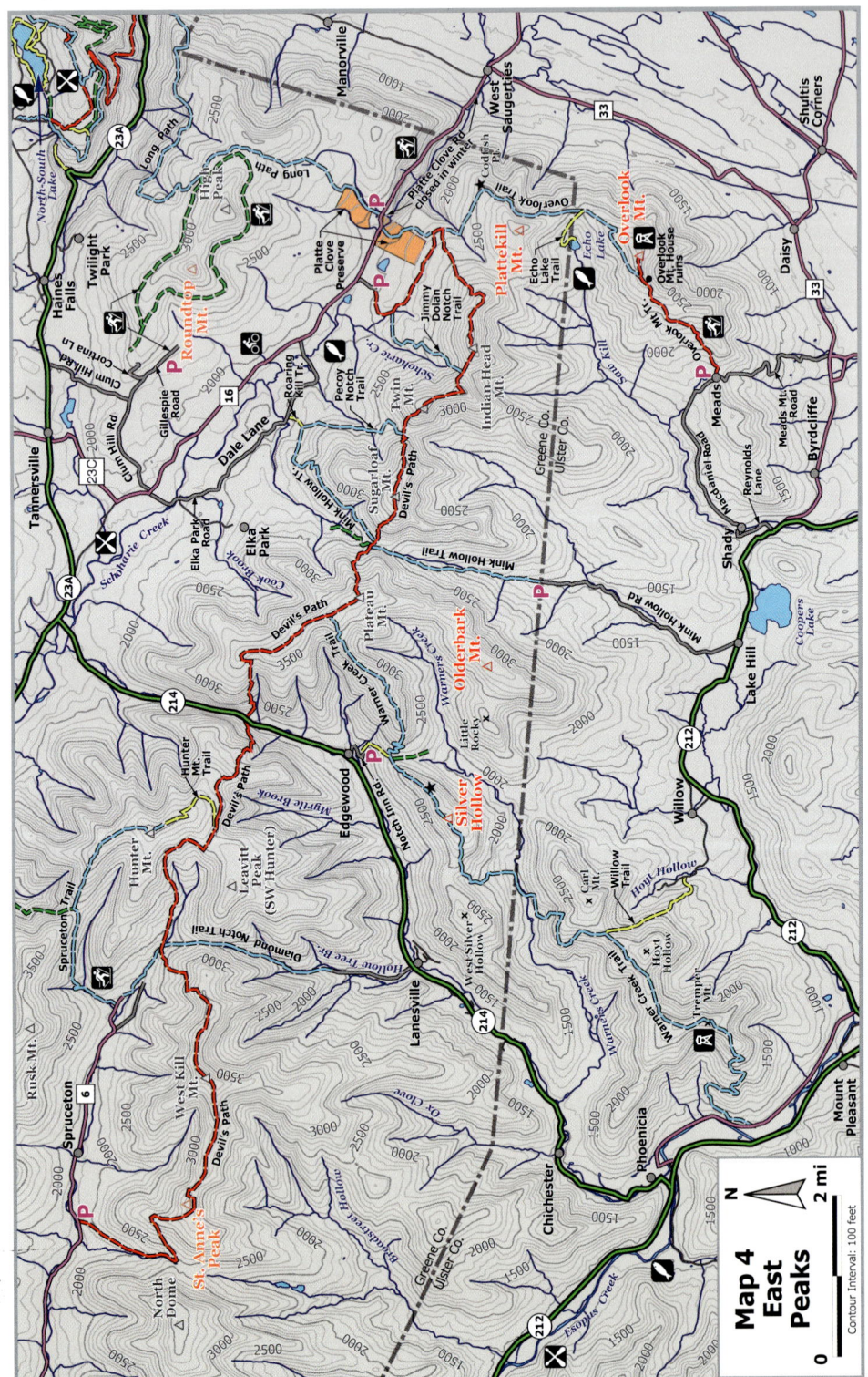

East Peaks

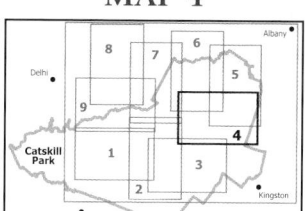

MAP 4

Olderbark Mt. (Oelberg)
Overlook Mt.
Plattekill Mt. (Kaaterskill)
Silver Hollow Mt. (Edgewood Mt.)

The eastern peaks region may have only four of the Catskill 67, but they are an interesting variety. Olderbark and Plattekill are bushwhacks, Overlook and Silver Hollow have trails. One is among the most challenging of the Catskill 100, another has a fire tower and superlative views overlooking the Hudson River Valley. One peak has a pair of old quarries, Codfish Point lookout, and some of the easiest bushwhacking woods anywhere.

The region has excellent highway access to the trailheads, and tucked into the eastern edge of the map is the spectacular Platte Clove Rd., one of the top drives to a trailhead anywhere in the state. The views from the summits or along the hikes are superb for three of the four peaks. Very steep terrain guards Olderbark's summit, and the top has an Adirondacks feel. Walk quietly and don't be surprised at the birds and other wildlife on all but the very busy Overlook Mt.

Fishing is allowed in the Ashokan Reservoir with a DEP permit. There are also North-South Lake and Colgate Lake, the Schoharie and Esopus creeks, and miles of smaller streams for anglers. For the more ambitious fisherman, Echo Lake between Plattekill and Overlook mountains provides hike-in fishing without a lot of competition.

Paddlers will enjoy North-South Lake, Colgate Lake, and the Schoharie and Esopus creeks. Bicyclists with strong legs and lung capacity will enjoy a memorable workout climbing Platte Clove Rd. from West Saugerties. Almost every local county road can be pedaled and mountain bikes are welcome at the Kenneth Wilson State Park in Mount Tremper, at Onteora Lake west of Kingston, or on Hunter Mt.

Ashokan High Point and Little Rocky from Overlook Mt. Mark Schaefer

Olderbark Mt., 3440'
Bearsville Quad
(Oelberg)
Catskill 67 Rank: 4
View: 2, Interest: 3, Difficulty: 5, Bushwhack: 5

HIGHLIGHTS AND SUMMARY: All routes are bushwhacks, on steep, exciting terrain. The woods just below the summit plateau abruptly transition from deciduous to conifers, and you'll feel like you've hiked from the Catskills to the Adirondacks. Olderbark has it all. Hike quietly and enjoy the bird and animal life. There are great places to camp on the eastern side of the mountain. You'll see wildflowers in early spring but nettles later on in the many drainages on Olderbark. A long-time local says the peak was named for the old bark roads (see glossary) that crisscross its flanks. The Adams *Gazetteer* offers that the name "Oelberg" likely came from the oil that was pressed from butternut trees found on its slopes. Another suggestion is that the name derives from the biblical "mountain of olives."

Looking at Olderbark from Mink Hollow, it's hard to believe the mountain is not one of the 3500 ft summits. It misses the cutoff by a mere 60' or less and its ridges seem to rise and soar when seen from the S.

BEST TIME TO HIKE: Anytime, although snow and ice would make the steep cliffs very challenging in winter.

The usual route starts from the parking area at the end of Mink Hollow Rd. (N42° 04.062', W74° 11.202'), located off of NY212 in Lake Hill, near Cooper Lake. There are many good places to begin your bushwhack between 0.3 and 0.6 mi along the Mink Hollow Trail. The trail crosses a stream, so when water levels are high keep to the western side of the brook until you start the bushwhack.

The woods are open on Olderbark's eastern flank, with beeches and young maples. The slope is gradual up to 2400 ft, and appreciably steeper above. At this elevation, the maples are larger and birch trees begin to appear. Stinging nettles, everyone's favorite ground cover, are prevalent in wet areas beginning at around 2500 ft. Can I be the only one who has taken a stumble, face first, into a hungry patch of nettles? To avoid the nettles, try to stay away from drainages. Avoid the woods road you might cross in the lower part of the mountain as well. It heads in the wrong direction. There are several good places to camp in the area.

The "interesting" part of the bushwhack begins around 2600 ft when the climbing gets steeper and you encounter the first cliffs. As with most Catskill rock bands, patience rewards with the inevitable way through, but the steep terrain is not for the fainthearted. Look for animal paths as wildlife know the safe and efficient routes through or around cliffs. My Lab, Bookah, is adept at finding routes through steep terrain. Using her nose, she disappears and then reappears at the top, looking down with a "how come it's taking you so long" expression.

On the mountain you might decide to head straight for the summit of Olderbark. A closer look at a topographic map shows very steep climbing right up

to the summit plateau. A better alternative might be to aim at the col at the northern end of Olderbark's summit plateau. You need to cross 500 ft of very steep terrain before you reach it, but it is doable for very experienced bushwhackers. Expect loose rocks and portable handrails (see glossary), and it is steep enough in spots that hikers need to be cognizant of where their companions are. On the eastern side of the mountain, the steepest terrain is between 2800 ft and 3000 ft.

The sub-peak immediately N of Olderbark has deciduous trees on its crown, mostly black cherry, and is peculiar since it doesn't have the conifers found on Olderbark's summit ridge. Take a breather and enjoy the screened views.

Olderbark's summit is long and flat, and the deciduous forest abruptly changes. At 3100 ft the first conifers appear, and from 3200 ft it's mostly conifers all the way to the summit. The conifers are thick in places with occasional blowdown. Wearing glasses for safety is a good idea on any bushwhack. This is not a place to get an eye poke or corneal abrasion.

Where's the summit? The conifers and occasional deciduous trees don't allow much visibility, so the only way to be sure is to hike across the entire top. About 0.15 mi from the southern end feels like the highest point, but you'll have to decide for yourself. When the leaves are off the trees, there are some views at the edges of the summit ridge.

This side of Olderbark has a secluded feel and, other than the occasional old woods road, there are few signs of current human activity. The steep terrain and remoteness of the summit all contribute to a wilderness feel complete with signs of deer, bear, porcupine, woodpeckers, and other wildlife. Routes from this direction are between 5 and 6 mi round-trip and about 2100 ft of ascent.

Another route to Olderbark is from its larger, northern neighbor, Plateau Mt.

Mink Hollow, on the way up Olderbark Mt. Bill Chriswell

Hiking from the summit of Plateau Mt. along its SSE ridge, you'll pass through conifer forest for the first few hundred feet of descent. Things opens up as you lose elevation toward the Olderbark col. It's a short climb from the col to the small bump on Olderbark's summit ridge mentioned previously. If you want to combine Olderbark and Plateau, I suggest climbing Olderbark first as it's easier to stay on the narrow connecting ridge while going uphill rather than down through the conifers. In this way your hike also ends on marked trails at the end of the day. It is just under 3 mi and 800 ft of ascent from Olderbark to Plateau Mt.

There is another way to summit Olderbark. From NY214 near Edgewood (N42° 08.470', W74° 12.747'), look for Notch Inn Rd. for access to the trailhead to Silver Hollow. You can either park along Notch Inn Rd. near NY214 and walk a short distance up the road to the beginning of the trail, or hope there is room in the small parking area up Notch Inn Rd. near the Silver Hollow trailhead. There is DEC land on the left (E) side of Notch Inn Rd. but private property on the right (W) side. If the small Silver Hollow trailhead parking area is filled, please don't block the driveway to the adjacent home. Leave your car closer to NY214.

The trail follows an old road toward Silver Hollow Notch. Nearing the height of land, you'll come to a trail intersection. One way, the trail leads towards Catskill 100 Silver Hollow Mt. and the other towards Plateau Mt. Pass this junction and stay on the unpaved road through Silver Hollow Notch and down the other side. Descend about 0.2 mi and after losing about 150 ft of elevation, leave the road and bushwhack ESE, passing above private property.

Once across Warner's Creek (can be impassable in times of high water), it's about 900 ft of moderate climbing to the Little Rocky–Olderbark col. From here, you can 'whack another 400 ft to the Olderbark summit plateau, or 200 ft to Little Rocky. Note that the Little Rocky on this side of Olderbark does not have enough elevation change to qualify as a "real" peak, and is not the Little Rocky on the Catskill 100 Highest list. Yet there are some spectacular views from just beyond its summit. From "little" Little Rocky, bushwhack SE to the Little Rocky–Olderbark col, and pick your way up Olderbark's moderately contoured NE side. Follow the summit ridge to the summit.

Although you'll have to regain the elevation climbing back up to Silver Hollow Notch on the way out, this alternative route on Olderbark's NW flank is much more gradual and gentle than a route over the castle walls guarding the eastern side. This route is around 7 mi round-trip and a bit over 2000 ft of ascent.

A southern approach to Olderbark presents a complete contrast to the first route. The climb is mostly gradual as it passes through DEP to DEC land and over some old woods roads. You'll encounter some steep sections before reaching some open, grassy areas and then the conifer zone near the summit. Along the way, enjoy views of Indian Head, Plattekill, Overlook, and Twin mountains, as well as Cooper Lake, a Kingston water supply.

There are significant areas of private property on the southern and SSE side of Olderbark, and permission is required from landowners.

Overlook Mt., 3140'

Woodstock Quad

Catskill 67 Rank: 36
View: 5, Interest: 5, Difficulty: 2

HIGHLIGHTS AND SUMMARY: There are superlative views from the tower and eastern overlook. The hike from the Meads Mountain Rd. trailhead is short and often crowded. In springtime look for blooming mountain laurel and wildflowers alongside the trail. The constant human traffic keeps the wildlife at bay during the daytime, but watch your step in warm weather; the chance to see a shy timber rattler along the upper reaches is a bonus for some hikers. Avoid shortcutting the last 0.1 mi to the summit for the sake of the mountain.

BEST TIME TO HIKE: The best time of year to hike Overlook is any of the twelve months of the year. Go early in the morning to avoid hiker traffic.

Overlook is a Catskill 100 gem, with trails from two directions. The shortest and quickest is from high on Meads Mountain Rd. N of Woodstock. Look for a large parking lot at the height of land (N42° 04.264', W74° 07.351'). This lot fills up on nice days. Many locals use the mountain for their early morning hike, run, mountain bike, or dog walk, and people-watching can often be part of the hiking experience.

Just beyond the barrier at Meads is the access road for the tower and an old hotel. It is now closed to vehicles except for cell tower service vehicles and ranger access. The road climbs steadily and gains about 1375 ft ascent in a little under 2 mi.

Near the top of the road are the ruins of the Overlook Mountain House. The hotel was located on the site where two previous versions, both destroyed by fire, had stood. The rebuilt hotel was constructed of masonry and was never completed. Unused and deteriorated, it suffered a series of fires over the decades. It is now an interesting spot to take a break and some photos.

Opposite the ruins is a modern cell and broadcasting tower. Just beyond, the trail forks and hikers bear right toward the summit. The trail passes under the summit plateau and takes you past the old fire observer's cabin and, just beyond, the tower. On weekends in warm weather, tower volunteers open the tower and cabin, which also serves as a small natural history museum. At the summit, you can enjoy the view, eat lunch at picnic tables, or climb the restored tower.

Behind the cabin is a well-worn path that heads 0.1 mi E to the overlook for which the mountain

Timber rattlesnake. Cheryl Miller

was named. From this open rock ledge you can see Connecticut, many miles of the Hudson River Valley, the Ashokan Reservoir, and farther S, the Mohonk Preserve.

Overlook Mt. is home to timber rattlesnakes and visitors to the mountain shouldn't be surprised to encounter these retiring creatures on sunny rocks or ledges, under or behind logs, or in rocky crevices. These rare and beautiful animals can make their appearance anywhere on the mountain. From spring to mid-autumn, keep your dog leashed and children out of the woods and away from rocky places or spots where a timber might be hiding.

Climbing Overlook from the Meads Mountain Rd. trailhead in this direction is a round-trip of 4.25 mi with 1380 ft of climbing. In nice weather, you will seldom have privacy on this hike. But that is more than made up for by the old hotel ruins, cabin, tower, and spectacular views.

Overlook Mt. can also be climbed from a trailhead on Platte Clove Rd. (N42° 08.001', W74° 05.152'), the beginning of which is described in the next section, Plattekill Mt. This excellent and scenic route passes next to (or over) Plattekill Mt., drops into the Plattekill-Overlook col, and ascends Overlook's NE ridge. It joins the trail near the site of the old hotel. This hike is 11 mi round-trip and gains 1650 ft of elevation. The hike can be considerably shortened by leaving a car at the Meads trailhead.

Plattekill Mt., 3100'   Woodstock Quad
(Kaaterskill)
Catskill 67 Rank: 44
View: 4, Interest: 5, Difficulty: 3, Bushwhack: 2

HIGHLIGHTS AND SUMMARY: This is another of my favorite Catskill hikes. It's one of the three Plattekills on the Catskill 100 list and it offers almost too much to see and do on one hike. Old bluestone quarries, the Codfish Point view spot, an interpretive trail, open woods, plus birds and wildlife all point to a full day. The spectacular drive or bike ride up Platte Clove Rd. to the trailhead sets the stage for a great day, and the peak is close to the Catskill Center's property, which is likely why birds and small creatures are abundant along this hike. The hike is on trails for most of the way, then follows an old woods road before a 300 ft bushwhack to the summit. The bushwhack is short and forgiving, making this a good mountain for a beginner to practice map, compass, and GPS skills.
BEST TIME TO HIKE: Though it's a terrific hike in any season, I would especially recommend it in autumn or springtime.

The most direct route—and maybe the best—begins on Platte Clove Rd. (CR16) at the Catskill Center for Conservation and Development (Platte Clove Preserve) trailhead. The drive from West Saugerties along the seasonal Platte Clove Rd. is spectacular. It's one of the best rides to or from a trailhead anywhere in the Northeast. In under 3 mi, Platte Clove Rd. climbs almost 1500 ft, hugging a mountainside on one shoulder and with a deep drop-off into the clove (see glossary) on the other. It switches back and forth and is scenic even with leaves on the trees.

From the small roadside parking area (N42° 08.001', W74° 05.152'), the trail drops down into the woods, crosses a striking hand-hewn King Post replica bridge, and then gently winds its way uphill. Along the trail, numbered stations explain what you see at different locations. The trail is well maintained and passes two junctions on your right. The first one goes to the Prediger Rd. trailhead and the second one leads to Indian Head Mt. Keep left, continuing on the blue-marked trail to Overlook Mt., your route.

The trail soon reaches the Devil's Kitchen lean-to, a good place for a quick break or gear adjustment. Just beyond, the trail passes over a small bridge, climbing more steadily until it reaches a short spur trail on the left (E) to Codfish Point. The junction is marked with a bluestone cairn. Taking the spur trail, in less than a minute you arrive at a magnificent vista looking at 60 mi of the Hudson River Valley and beyond. In the springtime, enjoy the sights and subtly fragrant pinksters found here.

Back on the trail, look around for a faint path on the opposite side; it's the beginning of an old quarry road. Although you can begin your 'whack at any time, my recommendation is to follow the quarry road uphill. At 0.2 mi you will reach an old bluestone quarry, with some stone "lawn chairs" and one "throne." You can sit and ponder the history of the quarry and the effort it took to bring stone down the mountain and back to the road.

Continue on the woods road a little farther uphill to a second quarry. You can see the Catskill Bruderhof, Roundtop, and Kaaterskill High Peak on the opposite side of the valley. This is an excellent place to begin your bushwhack up Plattekill, an easy 0.25 mi and about 300 ft of climbing up its NE ridge. The 'whack to the summit takes you through open woods that are free of blowdown and filled with wildflowers and the songs of birds in the spring.

At 2950 ft, ease your way over to the SE side of the ridge to take in more views of the Hudson River Valley. Nearing the summit there is a thin band of conifers to push through, with the two large summit boulders right on the other side.

Platte Clove Road. Mike Cruz

Wander another two or three minutes S of the summit and the woods return to open, parklike hardwoods and easy walking. You can see Overlook Mt. from a small grove of stunted birches. Drop down the ridge about 150 ft and Echo Lake and Overlook are visible from another open area.

You can return to the summit rocks for lunch and retrace your route, but if time allows consider a traverse of Plattekill. Descend 600 ft SSE down Plattekill's southern ridge—easy bushwhacking to where it intersects with the Echo Lake Trail in the Plattekill-Overlook col. Extend your day by hiking down to Echo Lake; climbing 600 ft to Overlook Mt.; or, if you make a left (N), by hiking along Plattekill's eastern shoulder to where you left the trail near Codfish Point.

If you follow the first up and back route, this hike is about 5 mi round-trip and approximately 1400 ft of ascent.

Hikers can also climb Plattekill from the Meads Mountain Rd. trailhead (N42° 04.264', W74° 07.351') on the other side of Overlook Mt. (see page 75 in the section on Overlook) and join one of the routes above.

Silver Hollow Mt., 3000'
Bearsville Quad
(Edgewood Mt.)
Catskill 67 Rank: 63
View: 4. Interest: 3, Difficulty: 2

HIGHLIGHTS AND SUMMARY: Silver Hollow Mt. is a short and rewarding trail hike with excellent views near the summit. The trail, from where it leaves Notch Inn Rd. until the summit, can be a little overgrown from late spring through summer, but it is easy to follow and the open woods along the summit ridge make up for it. Because the mountain is so lightly hiked, there are birds and other wildlife, and spring presents a bounty of wildflowers.
BEST TIME TO HIKE: The best time to hike is any time of year, but the largest rewards come when the leaves are off the trees or when fall foliage is at its peak. Silver Hollow would also be interesting for experienced cross-country skiers.

Silver Hollow Mt. is one of the shorter and easier of the Catskill 100 peaks. To locate the trailhead, drive on NY214 and near Edgewood (N42° 08.470', W74°

Stone chair at Codfish Point. Mark Schaefer

12.747'), look for Notch Inn Rd. This is a good but narrow unpaved road. In summer conditions there is little difficulty driving it all the way up to a parking area on the left side that has room for one or two cars. Please don't block the driveway of a home opposite the parking area. If the parking area is filled, there are numerous places to park near the highway on the E side of Notch Inn Rd.; this entire side is on DEC property.

Begin your hike on the trail just beyond the parking area. The trail gains a little over 500 ft to just before Silver Hollow Notch. The trail leaves the road and enters the woods on your right (N42° 07.942', W74° 12.814'), climbing more steeply up Silver Hollow's long, narrow NE ridge. From autumn through early spring, this is a beautiful hike: open hardwood forest with ash, maple, and beech's showy fall foliage, excellent snowshoeing, or a wash of wildflowers in early spring.

Look for a nice view point right at the top of your climb, on the NE part of the summit ridge about 10 minutes before the actual summit. Visible to the SSW is Carl Mt., to the SE Little Rocky (not the Catskill 100 one), to the NE part of Plateau Mt., and to the E a unique perspective of the entire summit ridge of Olderbark Mt., peeking over Little Rocky. There are also other open areas along the summit ridge as you hike along the top of Silver Hollow's steep and cliffy SE side.

Silver Hollow Mt. has three summits and the general consensus is that the second one is the true top. Hike the short distance to the third and final summit and decide for yourself.

A traverse of the top allows you to spend a few more minutes on this fine short hike. It's a mountain with a few surprises, and one where you'll likely have the wooded summit to yourself. Although there is not much to see from the actual summit, the views along the way, especially when the leaves are off the trees, are showy. Since the mountain was trailless until a few years ago, it's an excellent place for peace and solitude, and for observing birds, other wildlife, and flowers. From near NY214, it's just under 2 mi and 1150 ft of climbing to Silver Hollow's summit.

For the ambitious bushwhacker, Silver Hollow can also be combined with a series of Catskill 200 Highest summits that include West Silver Hollow, Carl, Hoyt Hollow, and Tremper mountains, throwing in a crossing of Warner's Creek along the way.

Silver Hollow Mt. Tony Versandi

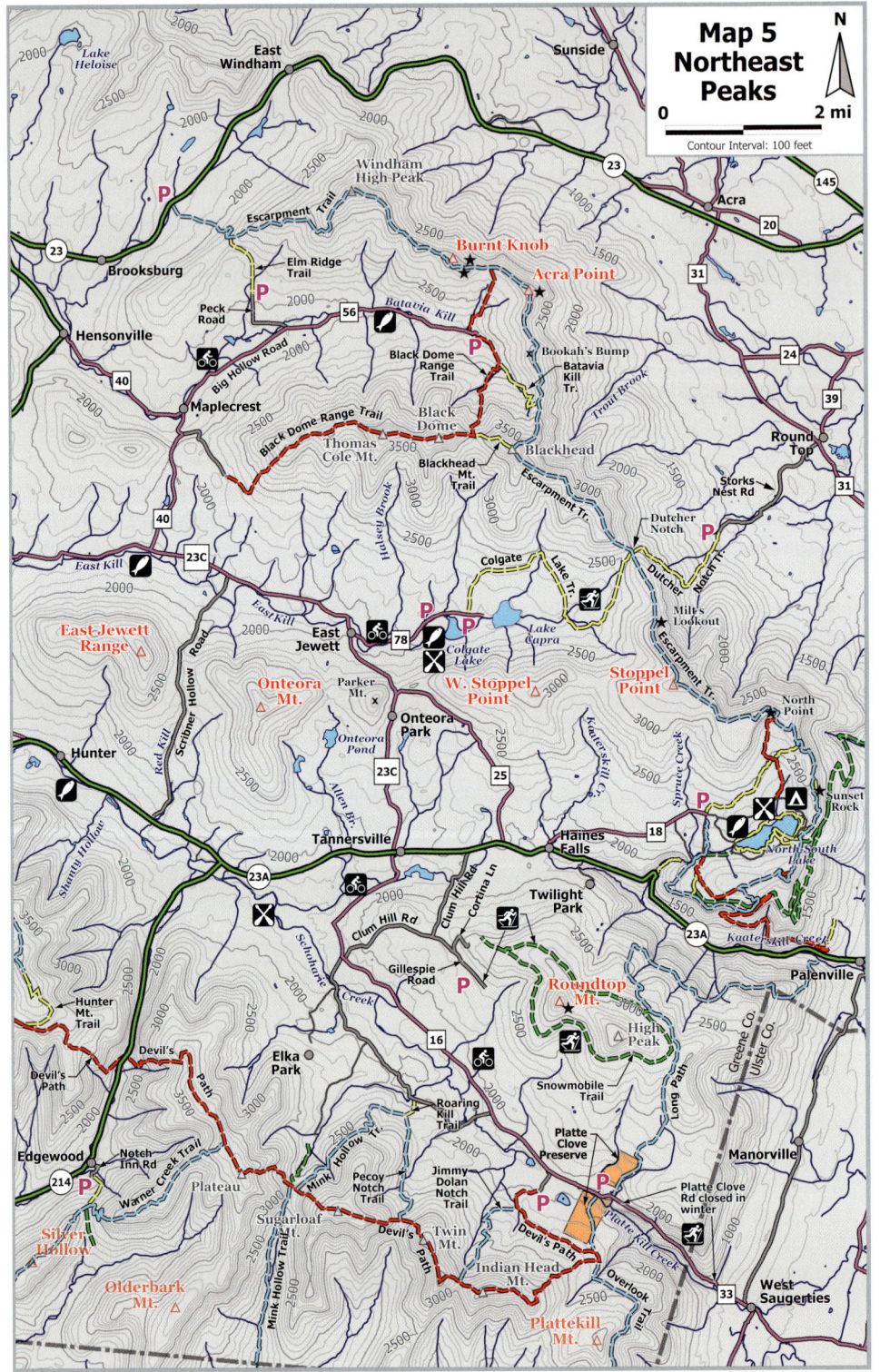

Northeast Peaks

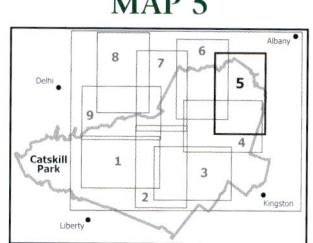

MAP 5

Roundtop Mt.
 (Kaaterskill Quad)
Stoppel Point
Onteora Mt. (East Kill Mt.)

Burnt Knob
East Jewett Range
Acra Point
West Stoppel Point

The seven mountains in the northeast region are varied. There are bushwhacks, semi-bushwhacks, and trail hikes. Some are on private property, so permission to hike must be obtained. Good highways surround the peaks providing for easy drives to the trailheads. The forests are mostly deciduous, but conifers often appear on the upper reaches of the mountains. Acra Point, Stoppel Point, and Roundtop have some of the best views of the group. Ice storm damage has left blowdown in different places but it isn't a large difficulty for bushwhackers. The hike along Acra Point's ridge is a wonder in spring wildflower season.

Cyclists with strong legs can tackle the 1400 ft ascent up the spectacular Platte Clove Rd. (CR16) or enjoy the rolling and sometimes steep hills throughout the region. Big Hollow Rd. is a great ride so long as bikers watch the hiker traffic coming and going.

The Schoharie, East Kill, and Batavia Kill creeks are prime fishing streams. Colgate Lake and North-South Lake offer still-water angling and also provide good paddling, as does the Schoharie Creek. For those looking to take a dip after a hike, any of these locales will do nicely.

View of Blackhead Range from Stoppel Point. Mark Schaefer

Roundtop Mt., 3440'
Kaaterskill Quad
Catskill 67 Rank: 5
View: 4, Interest: 4, Difficulty: 3, Bushwhack: 3

HIGHLIGHTS AND SUMMARY: This is one of three Roundtops on the Catskill 100 list. All of the routes are bushwhacks featuring beautiful woods with lots of ferns and birches. Bushwhacking conditions are excellent, with little need to don armor for blowdown or pricker bushes. The ledge near the summit is a great place to get out the camera or have lunch. The first route is a classic. Whether combined with neighboring Kaaterskill High Peak or not, it is likely to become one of your favorites.

BEST TIME TO HIKE: Any time of the year, although Roundtop is gorgeous in autumn. Hikers may have to walk Gillespie Rd. in winter.

DEP has acquired land near the peak and it forms the basis of a great route. This 337-acre parcel is located at the end of Gillespie Rd. (N42° 10.549', W74° 07.154'), which branches from Clum Hill Rd. S of Tannersville. Between this land and the Kaaterskill Wild Forest land that was already in place, hikers can easily access Roundtop Mt. from anyplace on the snowmobile trail that encircles both Roundtop and Kaaterskill High Peak. You can also climb Roundtop from the Kaaterskill High Peak trailheads on Platte Clove Rd. (N42° 08.191', W74° 05.653'), NY23A, or directly from Kaaterskill High Peak.

Gillespie Rd. is unpaved and it gets rougher the closer you get to the parking area at its eastern end. This is usually an easy drive in a 4WD or high-clearance vehicle from late spring to mid-autumn, unless Gillespie Rd. is snowy or really wet. It is also passable in a sedan if you drive slowly and park if the road looks out-of-condition. Get out of your car to take a look lest your undercarriage find washouts, exposed rocks, or muffler-devouring obstacles. At the eastern end of Gillespie Rd. there is a parking area at a small, remote turnaround. There is room for a few vehicles.

Catskill explorer and historian Mark Schaefer says the Gillespie Rd. access used to be called the Friends Nature Trail, and this mostly level, formerly privately owned parcel connected with Huckleberry Point. Beyond the current parking area the trail crossed a number of private land parcels and was marked by the locals with painted soup can lids. The Friends Nature Trail crossed the upper end of Josh Rd. on property that was owned by the police camp and now the Catskill Bruderhof. The extension of Gillespie crossed old roads and paths until it eventually ran into the beginning of the trail to Huckleberry Point, located on the eastern side of Kaaterskill High Peak.

From the Gillespie Rd. parking area, walk straight uphill through a grassy area that is visible from your car. This quickly turns into a slowly ascending woods road. As the road turns left you have two options. You can begin your bushwhack here, or stay on the road to pick up a little more elevation. In either case, at 2800 ft you will run into the snowmobile trail that encircles Roundtop Mt. and Kaaterskill High Peak.

You can cross the snowmobile trail and continue onto Roundtop's NW ridge. If you choose this option, you'll bushwhack uphill by first going NE, then SE, and eventually S following Roundtop's northern ridge as it doglegs around to the summit. You can also follow the snowmobile trail, pick up a half mile towards Roundtop, and then strike directly for the summit.

Illegal and irresponsible ATV usage has turned the snowmobile trail into a wet, muddy mess with deep puddles, wallows, and boot-sucking mud. Hikers and ATVs have started to widen the snowmobile trail by avoiding the quagmire, adding to the mess. Although DEC rangers are trying to patrol the area, it's been beyond their resources to keep the illegal users away. If you use this option, rock-hop the morass and remain with the snowmobile trail for 0.25 mi. Doing so, take note of the steep ridge that parallels the trail on the left. As the ridge gets its closest to the snowmobile trail, leave the trail and head for the summit.

Whether you choose to avoid the snowmobile trail or utilize it, the woods on the entire W and S of Roundtop Mt. are almost all deciduous and very easy going. The ice storms appear to have largely bypassed the mountain. As your bushwhack nears the summit, the woods are a delightful mix of birch and fern glades, with easily climbed or bypassed rock bands. There are some beautiful views in and out of the trees as you near the completely wooded summit.

Unlike most of the trailless Catskill 100 peaks, Roundtop has a large rock cairn marking the obvious top. When the leaves are on the trees the views are mostly of the here-and-there variety; go from late autumn until early spring for the best ones. Otherwise, look for the beautiful, grassy view point a couple of minutes from the summit. You won't be disappointed by the great views of the surrounding mountains. During the winter a few of the cliff bands are a bit more challenging, but the continual views through openings in the trees make the extra effort worth it.

Roundtop Mt. can be climbed by leaving the snowmobile trail at various points from the N, NW, or its nice southern ridge. Better yet, sample them all. Traveling from Gillespie Rd. it is about 1150 ft of ascent and 3 mi round-trip to the summit of Roundtop Mt. and back.

A bushwhack from Kaaterskill High Peak is another option, and features open woods the entire way. If the leaves are off the trees and visibility is good, you can see your route the entire way down Kaaterskill High Peak's NW ridge and then right up Roundtop's SE ridge.

Kaaterskill's NW slope is a bushwhacker's delight, with easily traveled open woods for 95 percent of the way. Other than a few conifer patches, it's mostly birches and ferns. The down slope is so gradual that you'll find yourself in the col quickly and with little effort. From the col the first vertical 100 ft toward Roundtop is a gentle rise. It then steepens. There is a very steep 100 ft section around 3300 ft, which eases off as you near Roundtop's summit. This is nothing an experienced Catskill 'whacker hasn't encountered before. It can be avoided by traversing N under Roundtop's steep terrain to more moderate terrain from the N.

You can reverse this route and hike from Roundtop to Kaaterskill High Peak with a NE bearing off the summit. After dropping 150 ft, contour to the SE and pick up the ridge down to the col.

If you first climb Kaaterskill High Peak and on to Roundtop from the trailhead on Platte Clove Rd., it is about 5.5 mi and 1900 ft ascent by the time you reach a second car at Gillespie Rd.

Stoppel Point, 3420'
Kaaterskill Quad
Catskill 67 Rank: 10
View: 5, Interest: 5, Difficulty: 3, Bushwhack: 1

HIGHLIGHTS AND SUMMARY: This is a trail hike almost to the summit then a short walk to the highest point. The view spots and points of interest almost wear you out—North and South lakes (or North-South Lake, as they're also known), Artists Rock, Badman Cave, Sunset Rock, Lookout Rock, North Point views, and more. Hikes from North-South Lake Campground can often be crowded. Other routes are less used but no less enjoyable. For solitude and the chance to observe birds and other wildlife, select less traveled routes or hike before the summer camping season.

BEST TIME TO HIKE: Early spring through autumn is the best time to hike.

Owing to its popularity, Stoppel Point's many trails are described in other hiking guides. I'll summarize some routes but spare mile-by-mile descriptions.

The more popular and crowded approaches to Stoppel Point originate from or near the North-South Lake State Campground. The Schutt Rd. parking area (N42° 12.039', W74° 03.505') is located a two-minute walk W of the gatehouse. Parking here saves you a campground entry fee. There are three options to reach Stoppel Point from the lakes.

You can take the yellow Rock Shelter Trail just before the campground gatehouse or walk the northern campground road a mile and pick up the red Mary's Glen Trail. A third trail begins at a parking area on the eastern end of North Lake just beyond the beach. The first two routes converge N of the lake at around 2300 ft. The third is the blue-marked Escarpment Trail that follows the Long Path.

While longer, the Escarpment Trail is one of the most picturesque trails in the Catskills. It passes the scenic Artists Rock and then intersects higher up with a short spur trail to the beautiful Sunset and Lookout Rock overlooks. Continuing higher, the trail passes Newman's Ledge and Badman Cave before heading back into the woods and climbing to North Point.

Whichever trail you've taken, you'll want to linger on the open rock at North Point, where the red-marked trail intersects the Escarpment Trail. Take in the great views of North and South lakes in the distance. This is the classic Catskill postcard view of the lakes seen in books, magazines, and on calendars. If you can tear your eyes away from views, step into the woods in the opposite direction to get a different perspective on the Blackhead Range and Acra Point. After putting your camera away head back to the trail for the remaining hike to Stoppel Point. You'll reach a clearing in the woods that most consider the summit, but

continue with a short uphill bushwhack to get to the actual top a few minutes away.

Whether you visit it on the way up or down, don't miss Sunset Rock, located on a yellow spur trail off the Escarpment Trail just S of Lookout Rock. After you've soaked up the view, look behind you (W), where you'll see a way to climb down to the continuation of the blue-marked Escarpment Trail. A rocky, sloping, and steep crack and ramp meet the trail below. Strong, agile, and careful hikers can take this shortcut, but do so clearly at your own risk.

The routes average 7 to 8 mi round-trip and a little under 1500 ft of ascent.

One of the lesser used but still interesting routes to Stoppel Point starts at the parking area (N42° 14.303', W74° 06.993') between Colgate Lake and Lake Capra. (You can also use this parking area to hike West Stoppel Point. See page 90.) To reach the trailhead, drive on CR78, Colgate Rd., out of East Jewett. Begin your hike from the easternmost parking area. Follow the yellow trail, which crosses an open field with an interesting view of the surrounding Blackhead Range. The trail enters the woods and skirts private land N of Lake Capra.

After crossing the small East Kill on the eastern side of the lake, the trail crosses one woods road then turns into another woods road. It climbs gradually towards Dutcher Notch (N42° 14.910', W74° 04.557'). The notch is located a bit over 4 mi from the parking area at an elevation of 2500 ft. The summit is a little more than 2 mi up Stoppel Point's N ridge via the blue-blazed Escarpment Trail to your right (S).

After climbing S for the first couple of hundred feet above Dutcher Notch, the grade moderates and the trail travels through a beautiful mixed hardwood forest. Following a half mile of very level hiking, the trail starts climbing again, reaching Milt's Lookout at an elevation of around 2800 ft. Linger here for views of Stoppel Point, the Hudson River Valley, the Taconic Range, Green Mountains, and other Catskill peaks.

Continuing up the ridge you may see the remnants of a 1983 plane crash just off the left side of the trail. The summit of Stoppel Point is just a few minutes

Stoppel Point from the Escarpment Trail. Mark Schaefer

beyond. As noted earlier, the trail does not cross the actual summit and reaching the top involves a few minutes of bushwhacking to the wooded summit. This hike is around 10+ mi round-trip and 1700 ft of ascent.

For those interested in a much fuller day of hiking, there is an excellent route to Stoppel Point on a yellow-marked trail from Stork's Nest Rd. (N42° 15.326', W74° 02.587'), located on the northern side of the mountain. Stork's Nest Rd. can be reached from a variety of roads that intersect with CR31. This is a low-elevation trailhead, and the trail gets steeper and steeper the closer it gets to Dutcher Notch on Stoppel's NNW ridge. Round-trip from the trailhead is over 8 mi with a little under 3000 ft of ascent.

Onteora Mt., 3220'   Hunter Quad
(East Kill Mt.)
Catskill 67 Rank: 25
View: 2, Interest: 3, Difficulty: 2, Bushwhack: 2

HIGHLIGHTS AND SUMMARY: Most of the mountain is private property, with the exception of some DEP land on its lower NNW flank. Onteora Mt. is visible from many surrounding mountains and is a bushwhack from any direction. With the exception of a large red spruce near the summit and a few other conifers, most of Onteora's woods consist of deciduous trees. The ice and wind storms of 2006 and 2007 ravaged the woods, and the top 400 ft of the mountain has some residual branches in places, making it difficult to navigate in a straight line. There are bears in the area and a lot of deer and porcupine sign. In winter or early spring there are nice views of Roundtop, Kaaterskill High Peak, West Stoppel, Parker, East Jewett, Plateau, and the Blackhead Range, but only peek-a-boo views from mid-springtime onward. BEST TIME TO HIKE: Best time to climb is any season.

There is a private club on one side of the mountain and you can see its golf course from the summit. To hike from the club, you need to be a member, resident, or guest. Hiking from any other direction also requires permission from the landowners. Any bushwhack would be 4 mi round-trip or less, and under 1500 ft ascent.

Burnt Knob, 3180'   Freehold Quad
Catskill 67 Rank: 31
View: 5, Interest: 4, Difficulty: 3, Bushwhack: 1

HIGHLIGHTS AND SUMMARY: The trail over Burnt Knob comes very near, but does not go over, the summit. Peakbaggers will want to take the five-minute 'whack through open woods to the high point. There are a couple of wonderful camera opportunities from the shoulder of Burnt Knob and its

open view spots just below the summit. Springtime wildflowers and autumn scenery draw attention on this nice, short hike.
BEST TIME TO HIKE: It's a great mountain in any season.

Follow CR40 out of Hensonville, then take CR56 to its end and the trailhead. The parking area (N42° 15.332', W74° 06.902') is the same as for Acra Point (see page 89). Walk W back down the road one minute to the red-marked trail. The trail crosses the Batavia Kill and starts climbing alongside a stream for under a half mile, passing through stands of conifers and deciduous trees.

The trail climbs 700 ft in 1 mi to the col between Burnt Knob and Acra Point. It's an easy ascent with few obstacles. In the col the trail intersects with the blue-marked Escarpment Trail, where there are three trail signs. Acra Point is right (E) 0.7 mi and Burnt Knob left (W) 1.5 mi. The other sign points back to the car. The Burnt Knob signage is incorrect as it is only approximately half the posted distance to the summit.

Turning left in the col, the trail picks up 100 ft of elevation as a warm-up and then gets steeper for the next 200 ft of ascent. A few minutes from the col look for a large ledge on your right. In mid-May there is a small cluster of red columbine growing at its base. On a nice spring day, trout lilies, trillium, spring beauties, and shin hobble blossoms provide distraction all the way to the summit.

As the trail turns SW on Burnt Knob's shoulder, it switches back and forth. It provides a great northern view before it swings S, popping you out on a ledge with a grand vista of the Blackhead Range. This is another classic Catskill vantage point. It also provides a look across the col at the summit of Acra Point. You'd be hard-pressed to find a nicer place to enjoy the views, take a breather, or have your lunch.

The trail continues SW and then NW underneath Burnt Knob's summit. The highest point is a 0.15 to 0.2 mi bushwhack from the trail, depending on where you begin the short 'whack. At any point from the last lookout you can simply 'whack up the ridge to the top or continue on the trail along Burnt Knob's S or NW side until you find a section of open woods that looks appealing.

My preference is to hike about another 0.25 mi of relatively flat walking past the ledge until the trail starts curving NW. The woods appear to be more bushwhacker-friendly here, and it's a short hop NNE to the summit. Nearing the top, keep walking until you arrive at what feels like the highest point. While there is no distinctive top, the open woods allow you to recognize the high point when you're there. In summer, enjoy the small birch and cherry trees amidst the fern glades. It's just a delight.

To descend, head back down the way you climbed. If you followed my preferred short 'whack, keeping Black Dome in front of you will get you to the trail in three minutes time. Or proceed E along the beautiful ridgeline, cutting down to the trail wherever it looks best. To return to your car, hike back to the col and then down to Big Hollow Rd.

Burnt Knob can also be climbed by coming over Windham High Peak, and can be linked with Acra Point and the Blackhead Range.

Burnt Knob by itself is about 3.5 mi round-trip and just over 1000 ft ascent. If you add Acra Point, it's 5.5 mi and about 1350 ft of climbing. Bring your camera on the hike and enjoy all that this great peak offers.

East Jewett Range, 3140' Hunter Quad
Catskill 67 Rank: 35
View: 3, Interest: 3, Difficulty: 3, Bushwhack: 3

HIGHLIGHTS AND SUMMARY: East Jewett Range is a bushwhack and private property peak ready to charm those who obtain permission. The mountain is home to a variety of birds and animals and is a wildflower delight in the spring. Many bears call this area home.

BEST TIME TO HIKE: This hike is best when the leaves are off the trees.

With the village of Hunter on its southern flank, Onteora Mt. to the E, and the Blackhead Range to the NE, East Jewett Range is a peak everyone notices but few know much about. With the exception of a few areas of public property, most of the mountain is privately owned and requires landowner permission to hike. Ice storms have ravaged the summit plateau and it's not an exaggeration to describe parts of the top as devastated. Many of the trees have either lost their tops or have blown over. Lower on the mountain the woods are easy to navigate and woods roads crisscross the peak in some areas. The slopes of East Jewett Range

View from Acra Point. Tony Versandi

are sheathed in a deciduous forest, but its summit has a conifer cap, making it easy to see when viewed from a distance. From all but one direction, approaches to the mountain are gradual, with steeper climbing near the summit.

In the "leaf" months the views are scarce and screened. From late autumn through early spring, there are places to see: the Blackheads, Hunter, Onteora, Pine Island, Rusk, Roundtop, Plateau, and West Kill mountains. Bushwhacks can vary from 2 to 4 mi and 1200 ft to 1500 ft of ascent.

Acra Point, 3100' *Freehold Quad*
Catskill 67 Rank: 39
View: 5, Interest: 4, Difficulty: 3

HIGHLIGHTS AND SUMMARY: This is one of the best hikes anywhere for the effort, with nice views along the ridge. There are wildflowers in springtime and spectacular scenery in autumn. The woods are open, deciduous forest with little blowdown. The open ledge located below the summit is one of the finest in the Catskills. The peak is a photographer's delight. Bookah's Bump, a point along the ridge, is a worthwhile diversion.

BEST TIME TO HIKE: The best time to hike is any season of the year.

For the quickest and shortest route to the summit, drive to the end of CR56, Big Hollow Rd. (N42° 15.332', W74° 06.902'). Park and walk back W one minute to the beginning of the red-marked trail to the Burnt Knob–Acra Point col. This is the same trailhead used for Burnt Knob (see page 87). The trail ascends gradually about 700 ft to the col. It is well marked and passes through stands of conifers and open deciduous forest. This is also an easy access point to the Escarpment Trail, allowing hikers to combine the trip with other peaks.

At the signed trail junction in the col, bear right for a 0.7 mi trail hike to the summit. The trail climbs a leisurely 350 ft over that distance, allowing a pause midway up for an excellent look at the Blackhead Range. The open ledge is the perfect location to eat lunch, take in the views, and enjoy a break. Besides the Blackheads, you can see Windham High Peak, Burnt Knob, and, on the other side of the trail, more distant views toward Albany. The trail to the summit is wooded, but the views are excellent when the leaves are off the trees. Mark Schaefer reports being able to glimpse Massachusetts' high point, Mt. Greylock, and has seen Vermont peaks, including Glastonbury, Equinox, and Killington on a clear day.

A slightly longer but more rewarding hike is to take the red trail SSE from the parking area toward Blackhead Mt. Bear left at the first trail junction onto the yellow-marked Batavia Kill Trail. After passing the Batavia Kill lean-to, take another left onto the blue-marked Escarpment Trail at the next intersection. This trail climbs Acra Point's long southern ridge.

In the springtime, small, gurgling waterfalls beg to be photographed. On an early spring day there are almost continuous views through the leafless trees, and the surrounding woods are carpeted with trout lilies, spring beauties, trillium, and other wildflowers. The blossoms of shin hobble display their white finery everywhere. The ridge walk is one of the best these mountains offer. Be sure to check the view spots off to the sides of the trail.

About 0.7 mi before the summit of Acra Point, the trail passes to the E and 100 ft under a small rise called "Bookah's Bump." On a nice day take a few minutes to 'whack up to the top of this 3060 ft sub-summit. The woods are covered with wildflowers, and large birch and cherry trees growing on the open slopes keep you company. From the top of Bookah's Bump you can see Acra Point and the Blackhead Range. If time allows, this is a beautiful detour on a nice day. Bookah's Bump has enough height to be a Catskill 100 peak, but it lacks enough elevation above the col with Acra Point.

After rejoining the trail, continue hiking N through birches and maples, eventually reaching the wooded summit of Acra Point. To reach the open ledge mentioned earlier, continue over the top and down a little ways. To complete a through-hike, continue W to the next col and then S on the red trail back to your car. The loop covers 4.75 mi and 1050 ft of climbing. Add Burnt Knob and it's an additional 1.2 mi and 420 ft of ascent.

West Stoppel Point, 3100'   Kaaterskill Quad
Catskill 67 Rank: 46
View: 3, Interest: 3, Difficulty: 2, Bushwhack: 3

HIGHLIGHTS AND SUMMARY: West Stoppel is one of those untouched peaks with no development, a wilderness feel from the moment you step into the woods, and bushwhacker-friendly routes from any direction. The woods are mostly deciduous, with some occasional conifers. They are home to many four-legged residents. It's also a good area for birders. The views are restricted in leaf season, but much improved when the trees are bare. West Stoppel's slopes are alive with wildflowers in springtime.

BEST TIME TO HIKE: This is an enjoyable hike any time of year, but autumn through early spring is best.

To reach the trailhead, drive out of East Jewett onto CR78, Colgate Rd. (N42° 14.115', W74° 08.730'), to the last trailhead on the road (N42° 14.303', W74° 06.993'). The parking area is large, with a field behind it and Blackhead and Black Dome dominating the view. Your options from this parking area are many. (This parking area can also be used to access Stoppel Point. See page 85.)

The most direct route is to walk across the road from where you parked (S) into the woods and cross the East Kill, a branch of which drains Lake Capra. In the winter, it is a simple hop, skip, and snowshoe crossing if there is a blanket of snow on the stream. You might need to remove your boots or use garbage bags (see glossary for details) during periods of higher water. Once across the stream, head SE, aiming right for West Stoppel. You can also 'whack toward the col between West Stoppel and its western sub-summit and then follow West Stoppel's gentle western ridge to the wooded top. This route is about 3 mi round-trip with 1000 ft ascent.

The forest on West Stoppel is largely beech, with some birch and maple and a sprinkling of conifers. The summit plateau is long and flat, and you'll undoubtedly walk around before being satisfied that the stand of tall conifers frames the summit. During leaf season, the beeches do an excellent job of hiding most of the views. In winter there are nice looks at the Blackhead Range, Stoppel Point, Kaaterskill High Peak, and Roundtop. You can also see Colgate Lake and Lake Capra from the summit, as well as the ridge between West Stoppel and Stoppel Point.

A variation of this route is to hike the yellow-marked trail to Dutcher Notch behind the parking area, passing N of the private property surrounding Lake Capra. At almost any place beyond the private property E of Lake Capra, begin your bushwhack by hiking S toward West Stoppel. The woods are open as you drop 60 ft from the trail, and the slope is gradual as you gain the first 350 ft of ascent in 0.4 mi towards the peak. This easy bushwhacking will be repaid when the slope gets steeper, and steeper still. There is about 300 ft of calf-burning ascent coming from this direction before the slope eases in the last 200 ft to the top. The route provides an excellent way of quickly picking up elevation, but there are ferns and nettles along the small rivulets draining the NE side of the mountain. This is approximately 6.25 mi round-trip with 1400 ft ascent.

You can also 'whack from Stoppel Point's western ridge. (See Stoppel Point section for routes to the summit.) Leave the top of Stoppel Point and lose 600 ft toward the Stoppel–West Stoppel col on a very gradual slope. The woods are a little tight for a few minutes, but then open up nicely on the way to the col. There is some blowdown along the ridge. From the col, start climbing W, then SW at 3000 ft. You'll also run into some blowdown on West Stoppel's NE ridge, but the mild gradient of the climb compensates for it. It's 2 mi and 300 ft ascent to reach West Stoppel from Stoppel Point.

There is also another route. As you drive E along Colgate Rd., look for a parking area just before you reach the Colgate Lake outlet and dam (N42° 14.308', W74° 07.280'). Cross the road from the parking area, then go over the dam on its walkway and onto a road that passes along the W side of the lake. Follow this road about 0.4 mi until you are above and directly S of Lake Capra's western end. You can then bushwhack S toward West Stoppel or its western summit. Depending on the route, it's a little over 3.5 mi round-trip.

Nearing the summit of Acra Point. Joanne Hihn

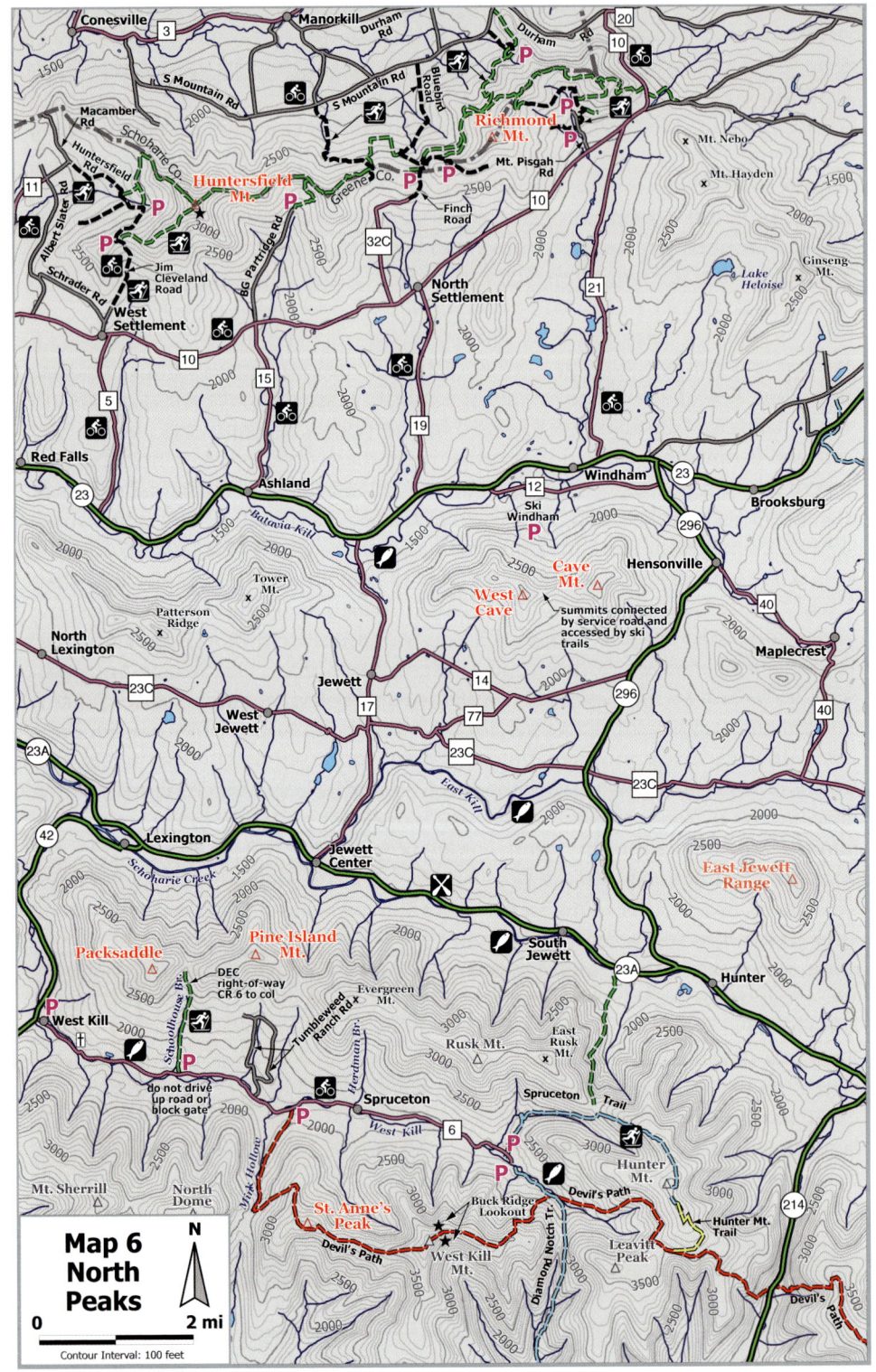

North Peaks

MAP 6

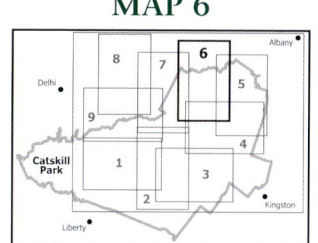

Huntersfield Mt.
St. Anne's Peak
  (West West Kill)
Richmond Mt.
Pine Island Mt.

Cave Mt.
Packsaddle Mt.
  (Lexington Mt.)
West Cave Mt.

The seven mountains in this region offer an interesting mix in terms of terrain, woodland travel, views, and challenging hiking. They include trailed summits, bushwhacks, two peaks with ski trails, and a pair, Pine Island and Packsaddle, that are bushwhacks with beautiful, open woods at their lower elevations, but "prickery" summit ridges. The views from Huntersfield, the Caves, and, depending on route, the open ledges on the West Kill–St. Anne's ridge are beauties. While some of the summits are wooded and provide limited views from the top, almost all offer scenic rewards along the hike. The region has easy trailhead access with county and town roads surrounding all the peaks.

If climbing St. Anne's, Packsaddle, or Pine Island mountains hasn't used up your energy, Spruceton Rd. (aka CR6) from its beginning to the top of Arbor Rd. is an excellent cycling route. It begins with rolling hills and finishes with a steady uphill climb to the top. The mountain bike rides up the roads to the Huntersfield and Richmond trailheads are steep and all uphill, a workout for the strongest riders. The menu of potential secondary roads in the region is only limited by your imagination and your maps.

Anglers have a wide variety of waters to select from. The Schoharie, West Kill, Little West Kill, Batavia Kill, and East Kill creeks are some of the better known fisheries. Paddlers can kayak on the Schoharie Creek in times of high water; otherwise it's pretty bony in many places.

Huntersfield Mt. lean-to. Mark Schaefer

Huntersfield Mt., 3423'
Ashland Quad
Catskill 67 Rank: 7
View: 4, Interest: 4, Difficulty: 2, Bushwhack: 3

HIGHLIGHTS AND SUMMARY: Schoharie County's high point has an interesting variety of trail and bushwhack hikes, varying from long to very short. When seen from a distance or above, the peak appears to be a huge X, with four ridges converging on the center. The superlative views from the lean-to just below the top compensate for the wooded summit. Through the conifer forest below the N ridge is a quick and peaceful route, and the mountain remains largely unknown for a great peak so close to the Capital District. Huntersfield and its neighbor, Richmond Mt., are among the farthest N of the Catskill 100 summits. Only Utsayantha, Churchill, and the two Moresville Range peaks are farther N.

A wide variety of birds and other wildlife make Huntersfield a delight for birders and naturalists. The summit and lean-to are known habitats for gray comma butterflies in April, red admirals in summer, and fall commas in autumn. There are barred owls in the woods on the N side of the mountain and porkies in the conifer forest. For campers, the lean-to near the summit is an excellent way to make a relaxing hike even more laid-back. It's also the location of the trail register.

BEST TIME TO HIKE: This is a good peak to hike any time, but the road through the Huntersfield State Forest is unplowed in winter with no place to park from the S and "no parking" signs to the N. However, the broken trail left by snowmobilers makes the road an excellent cross-country ski route.

You can approach Huntersfield from several routes. Note that the roads in this area (and in other areas of the Catskills) sometimes change names or are named differently on different maps. It's a good idea to consult several maps when locating the trailheads for the various routes, and when deciding how to get to them.

The first route can be reached from either the N or the S. For the northern approach, take CR11 to Marv Rion Rd. to the trailhead. For the southern, take Jim Cleveland Rd. off of CR10. Both roads were regraded in 2008 and are in excellent condition. In clear and dry conditions they can be easily driven in most cars. The scenic drive is unique and worth the effort all on its own. As your car keeps climbing, you'll be amazed there is a road so high that is in such good condition. There are two parking areas in this region, and the woods all around are open.

Make your way to the trailhead at the height of land at 2800 ft (N42° 20.962', W74° 21.933'). This is the highest trailhead for Huntersfield and is reachable by both roads. This is not an official DEC trail, although it does begin on a good woods road. The woods road heads E and climbs easily for the first 300 ft, then turns NE. The climbing becomes more gradual and then a little steeper as the trail gains Huntersfield's first bump. Continuing on the woods road, the trail takes a very small dip before resuming the climb of 225 ft to Huntersfield's wooded summit. You might run into some old DEC markers here, the remnants of an old trail that ran over the range of adjacent peaks. You can tell you're on top as there is a metal pole in a tree and a USGS survey marker. No one seems to know the purpose of the pole or who placed it there.

While there are no views from Huntersfield's actual summit, a lean-to just below the summit and its wooden bench provide expansive views SE toward Patterson Ridge, Tower Mt., Cave and West Cave, Hunter, Windham, and the Blackhead Range farther in the distance. There is another excellent view spot nearby that faces Ashland Pinnacle and Richmond Mt. For the sharp-eyed, look SW for the 3500 ft peaks Bearpen and Vly. The route from your car is an easy 2.6 mi round-trip and 625 ft ascent. This hike leaves plenty of time to return to your car and drive E to the Richmond trailhead if you're interested in summiting both peaks while in the area.

A slightly longer route for Huntersfield begins lower down on the northern part of the same access road at a parking area (N42° 21.411', W74° 21.791') located at approximately 2260 ft elevation. Follow a trail through completely open forest, where it crosses a stream and gains a quick 200 ft in elevation. The trail then crosses a drainage and joins a serene woods road at the bottom of a mature pine forest plantation. The woods are quiet and peaceful with soft footing. There are plentiful deer and turkey sign nearby and birdcalls in the quiet woods in spring. Unfortunately, the 2007 ice storms devastated the trees in the forest and the woods are in difficult condition.

Stay on this trail until it curls S onto Huntersfield's NW ridge, where the trail again changes character. The woodland becomes deciduous with some grassy areas and an old stone fence, with occasional views as you climb. It's not hard to imagine this spot one hundred years ago, when it was probably an open pasture or hayfield. This section of the hike up Huntersfield's NW ridge is the most inviting part of an already interesting hike. As noted in the previous description, there are no views from the actual summit.

You can make this into a loop hike by following the trail/woods road from the summit down the mountain's SW ridge until you reach the high trailhead described in the first route. Then walk the scenic road downhill a short distance to your car. The loop is about 4.5 mi and 1175 ft ascent. Up and back from the lower trailhead is just under 2.25 mi round-trip.

For another, longer, trail hike, park your car at a trailhead located on the N side of the mountain off South Mountain Rd. in the Ashland Pinnacle State Forest. This side of the mountain holds snow very late into spring and the hike is a round-trip of 6.3 mi.

You may wish to try another route to Huntersfield. Take B.G. Partridge Rd. (N42° 20.056', W74° 19.853') N from CR10 and follow it into Huntersfield State Forest. There are marked trails that climb N toward the ridgeline. In summer they may appear a little overgrown, but take some care to follow the markers and after 500+ ft of climbing they will plunk you down a little over a mile E of Huntersfield's summit. It is about 0.4 mi from the parking area to the ridge and another 1.2 mi to Huntersfield.

Please note that the prickers on the E side of Huntersfield are terrible, partially due to the clear-cutting done here. The frequent rerouting of trails on the mountain sometimes leads to confusion, and routes from this direction are best left to those very comfortable in this kind of setting.

St. Anne's Peak, 3420' Lexington Quad
(West West Kill)
Catskill 67 Rank: 9
View: 2–4, Interest: 3, Difficulty: 3, Bushwhack: 1

HIGHLIGHTS AND SUMMARY: There are two trails to St. Anne's Peak. Either will go over the summit, but a 3 minute bushwhack takes you to the high point. The ridge walk from the popular 3500 ft summit of West Kill Mt. is a beautiful and scenic trail and makes the combo a great day hike. It's smooth and easy on the feet, and an excellent place to see birds, wildlife, and wildflowers. Hike quietly and you are liable to encounter deer or send a bear racing away.
BEST TIME TO HIKE: The best time for this peak is during autumn foliage season, with spring a close second.

Since this lightly hiked peak is located immediately W of West Kill Mt., you can climb St. Anne's by itself or hike them both. To climb West Kill Mt. first, it would be a good idea to leave a car at the Mink Hollow trailhead—unless you want to walk the ridge all the way back over West Kill Mt. Then drive to the trailhead at the end of CR6, Spruceton Rd. (N42° 10.936', W74° 16.167'). Follow the blue trail markers on a rocky woods road until you soon reach the photogenic Diamond Notch Falls. Cross the stream and take a right on the red-marked trail towards West Kill Mt., being careful not to mistakenly follow the blue markers towards Diamond Notch.

The trail gradually climbs up and across a spur of West Kill Mt. It's a little rocky in spots, with only a couple of steeper sections before the spectacular Buck Ridge lookouts. The view spots are on both sides of the trail and among the most scenic in the Catskills. The northern lookout offers great views of Rusk, Pine Island, and Packsaddle, and a peek at waiting St. Anne's. The southern lookout has expansive views that include Silver Hollow and Tremper mountains. Most hikers take a break here for photography or lunch. The wooded summit of West Kill Mt. lies another 0.2 mi beyond.

The route to St. Anne's (West West Kill) begins with a moderate downhill hike from the summit of West Kill. This part of the trail is more lightly used and passes through a nice deciduous forest. There are occasional views, but they are much better with the leaves off the trees. The trail stays on the ridge, which

widens the closer you get to the col between the two mountains. It's 1 mi to the col from West Kill's summit and the trail is soft, free of erosion, and, in many places, lightly covered with a bed of spruce and fir needles. The woods are mostly birch, maple, and other hardwoods, with some shin hobble (witch hobble). In springtime, wildflowers are prevalent along the ridge and the shin hobble's white flowers stand out when in bloom. In the autumn, this is one of the most delightful foliage walks anywhere in the Catskill Mountains.

On the way to the large col dividing West Kill and St. Anne's, there are a few ups and downs, including a small hill that rises about 60 ft before dropping 200 ft into the final col. From here, it's 0.3 mi and 200 ft of rocky and steeper climbing to St. Anne's Peak. The summit is wooded and viewless and the trail appears to just miss the highest point. You can cruise over the top or do some exploring. The more "elevation-obsessed" among you may discover that the true height of land is a 3 minute walk N and E off the trail. It's up to you whether you want to look for it. As you descend St. Anne's, the trail from the northern ridge to the St. Anne's–North Dome col becomes very rocky.

You can also climb St. Anne's from the Mink Hollow trailhead (N42° 11.517', W74° 19.498'). The trail gradually climbs the first 0.3 mi, descends a little, and then resumes its climb as it parallels the stream that drains Mink Hollow. This is a good place to filter water or for your dog to cool off. Continue on the red-marked trail through the wet area to the col between North Dome and St. Anne's. The trail to St. Anne's turns sharply left and climbs steeply up St. Anne's western face until it gains the northern ridge. From here, it's a gentler ascent to the wooded summit.

The trail from the North Dome–St. Anne's col is much rockier than the one coming from West Kill. It calls for a little care with boot placement. To avoid the steep western face of St. Anne's, the trail heads NE to get onto the mountain's northern ridge.

The route over both peaks from either direction is just over 7 mi. You'll have about 2100 ft of climbing via West Kill and an additional 300 ft ascent of both peaks if you park at Mink Hollow. Climbing St. Anne's by itself from Mink Hollow is a round-trip of just over 5 mi and 1600 ft of ascent.

Along trail to St. Anne's Peak. Joanne Hihn

Richmond Mt., 3220'

Ashland Quad

Catskill 67 Rank: 26
View: 2, Interest: 2, Difficulty: 2, Bushwhack: 2

HIGHLIGHTS AND SUMMARY: Richmond is an interesting bushwhack hike from high trailheads. The woods are deciduous and easy hiking except for some blowdown, beech whips, and prickers. The hike gradients are easy with the exception of routes from the S. The open canopy, berry bushes, and solitude provide hikers with a profusion of spring wildflowers, birds, and animal sightings. Richmond is a modest day hike by itself. The more ambitious can combine it with neighboring Huntersfield Mt. Richmond is the northernmost of the Catskill 100 summits in the eastern Catskills, and can be easily bushwhacked from many directions.

BEST TIME TO HIKE: This peak is best late autumn through early spring.

The most direct route up Richmond is from CR32C, Bluebird Rd., on the W side of the mountain. Drive to a parking area (N42° 21.687', W74° 17.349') at just under 2700 ft. It's a high trailhead by New York State standards, and one of the highest in the Catskills. Begin your hike by crossing the road from the parking area, onto a woods road 50 ft away that climbs uphill. You can also drive the road in a 2WD car in dry, summer conditions. For those who want to shorten the hike by driving farther, look for a place to pull off the woods road (without blocking it) near the beginning of the 'whack described below.

Walking or driving, pass the large boulders blocking a turn into a quarry and follow the road around the northern side of the 200 ft high hill located directly across from the parking area on CR32C. The road climbs a couple of hundred feet to a col between the small hill and the beginning of Richmond's SW summit ridge. When the road starts sharply downhill, you've just passed the beginning of the 'whack.

Keep to the right (SE) side of the ridge crest to avoid private property to the N. The route along the ridge passes through a beech forest and the short size of most trees gives the impression it was previously logged. The ridge has a significant amount of storm damage and dense sections of beech whips. When not receiving a filleting from the blackberry prickers or stepping over blowdown, you can receive your annual dose of face slaps from the small beech whips and saplings growing on the ridge. There are a couple of easily climbed rock bands along the 400 ft climb from the col.

The summit is wooded and unremarkable, but has a beech tree with initials carved in the bark. Like cairns, flagging, or other human signs, summit marking is unusual on the Catskill 100 trailless summits and is strongly discouraged by any who love these peaks. In the summer, the leaves hide the views, but in other seasons you can catch glimpses of Ginseng, Tower, Cave, West Cave, Hayden, Windham, and Hunter mountains from the ridge. If you look in the right direction you might see the tops of North Dome and Sherrill mountains in the distance.

The Blackhead Range is also visible from ledges on the S side of the summit ridge.

It's 1.75 mi and 600 ft of climbing from the parking area to the summit. In winter the highway department keeps CR32C clear (though not always up to the parking area), making Richmond a possible destination for those with 4WD vehicles.

Richmond can also be hiked from either of two parking areas on Mt. Pisgah Rd. Both of these are unplowed in winter. The road intersects with CR10 (N42° 21.889', W74° 14.850') a few miles E of CR32C. The lower parking area (N42° 22.176', W74° 15.008') on Mt. Pisgah Rd. is in the Mt. Pisgah State Forest and located almost directly E of the summit. The upper parking area is also on State Forest land, NE of the summit and much higher and closer to the peak. Hikers can get from one to the other through a new clear-cut area. Depending on road conditions, it might be advisable to park in the lower parking area. As in the other route, the deciduous forest has suffered from blowdown, but patient bushwhackers can easily make the ridge and follow it SW towards Richmond.

This route does offer limited views in winter. It's just over 2 mi and 1000 ft of climbing from the lower parking area to the summit and just under 5 mi to continue over Richmond to the parking area on CR32C and the beginning of the first route.

Please note that the aqua-marked Long Path has been rerouted away from the ridgetop and farther down the mountain. Some of this is the result of ice storm damage and the clear-cutting DEC deems necessary to clear the fallen trees. At the time of publication the rerouting of the trails was in transition, and while the Long Path is between 250 ft to 400 ft below the summit, the two bushwhack routes above are better bets.

You may also try another route from the N, from Durham Rd. (N42° 23.520', W74° 16.216') just S of Steenburg Mt. (N42° 23.675', W74° 16.493'), which is just outside the northern border of Map 6. The trail skirts a 300 ft hill to its E, passes through a reforestation area, and gains 1200 ft in 2.5 mi to the summit through the State Forest.

Routes from CR10 to the E received significant ice storm damage and are in uncertain condition. Whatever your route to Richmond, you're likely to agree that it will take the area years to repair itself. In the meantime, some of these short hikes may take more time than you would anticipate when looking at the map.

Pine Island Mt., 3140'   Lexington Quad
Catskill 67 Rank: 37
View: 3, Interest: 3, Difficulty: 4, Bushwhack: 3

HIGHLIGHTS AND SUMMARY: Pine Island Mt. is a bushwhack peak. Wear long sleeves and pants, and hand and eye protection are recommended from late spring through late autumn. The berry bushes mean that deer, bear, and birds enjoy the peak as much as you will. Pine Island is one of five peaks in a row located N of CR6, Spruceton Rd. From W to E, they are Packsaddle, Pine

Island, Evergreen, Rusk, and East Rusk. Pine Island and Packsaddle are usually climbed as a pair. Evergreen and East Rusk, while completely worthy of their own names, do not have enough height above adjacent cols to be on the usual peakbagger's lists. Rusk is a well-known trailless 3500 ft mountain. BEST TIME TO HIKE: It's easiest to hike when snow covers the blackberry prickers on the summit ridge or in early spring. Its western ridge is a nice 'whack in springtime or winter, when the brambles are less of an annoyance than in summer.

The first of three routes up Pine Island Mt. is reached from CR6, Spruceton Rd. The hike begins on an unpaved road that starts at a metal gate (N42° 11.933', W74° 21.240'). This is a DEC right-of-way and generally parallels the Schoolhouse Brook drainage. Keep on the right-of-way as it is private property on both sides until 2150 ft. You can park a small car on the side of Spruceton Rd. three seasons of the year a short distance away. Do not block the gate, park near it, or drive through it as it serves as access to a private home just up the hill. When the gravel road turns right beyond the gate, keep left to avoid the driveway and private property. The road turns into a woods road at this point and passes two ponds.

As you climb higher, beautiful stone fences appear. It's private property on both sides of the road until about 2150 ft. The Schoolhouse Brook drainage is on your left and it peters out as it nears the Pine Island–Packsaddle col. In summer, the woods road is very overgrown in the upper part and you may lose it from time to time. No matter though, as the route to the col is obvious.

The Packsaddle–Pine Island col has tall, straight hardwoods, with good visibility across it. Take a short breather and contemplate the final hike to the summit. There is a well-defined woods road that heads right (E) up Pine Island's western ridge. It's fairly easy to follow but doesn't stay on the ridge crest for the 1 mi and about 530 ft of climbing to the summit. Long pants and sleeves, as well as gardening gloves, are always in style as the ridge walk has a well-deserved and notorious reputation as a scratchy hike with acres of thorny problems. There is some blowdown on the ridge and the summit is wooded, but there are screened views when trees are bare. Pine Island from Spruceton Rd. is 1500 ft of ascent over its 5 mi round-trip.

Winter bushwhacking. Moonray Schepart

A second route to Pine Island also originates on CR6. Look for the southern edge of DEC property across the road from the Mink Hollow trailhead (N42° 11.517', W74° 19.498'). Scoot across West Kill Creek, then through overgrown fields and woods on a rectangle of public property. Travel NNE up Evergreen Mt.'s SW ridge. At approximately 3100 ft, contour NW along the shoulder of Evergreen Mt. or go over Evergreen before heading W from its summit to the Evergreen–Pine Island col. It's another 500 ft of climbing to hit Pine Island from the col. Expect just under 2100 ft of ascent and 3 mi one-way to Pine Island over Evergreen's summit.

A third route to Pine Island originates high on its southern flank. Follow CR6 until reaching Tumbleweed Ranch Rd. (N42° 11.666', W74° 20.030'). Turn onto Tumbleweed Ranch Rd. and bear right at the first turn. As the road continues to climb, continue to bear right until you reach Arbor Rd. Follow Arbor Rd. to its end (N42° 12.678', W74° 19.872'), where you'll find a large turnaround. Head uphill into the woods on the remnants of an old woods road.

The road is easy to follow for the first 0.3 mi, but gets more indistinct as you climb. It disappears after it gains about 300 ft. The slope gets much steeper above so follow the rule of up (see glossary). The summit is less than a mile from where you parked, and your calves will earn every inch of the last 450 ft to the summit.

The woods are all deciduous with the usual mix of blowdown, and in spring you'll be treated to areas of purple and painted trillium, spring beauties, and other seasonal wildflowers. For me, trilliums are the wildflowers that say, "Welcome to spring!" With leaves on the trees, there are not many views from the wooded summit, but you can see Packsaddle, Evergreen, North Dome, Sherrill, St. Anne's, and West Kill by looking around. Hitting the summit, you are treated to Pine Island's pricker fest for a short while when you top out. The route is about 1 mi and a little under 1000 ft of climbing.

You can discover other routes to Pine Island from the N. All will require permission from landowners.

Cave Mt., 3100' Hensonville Quad
Catskill 67 Rank: 41
View: 5, Interest: 4, Difficulty: 2, Bushwhack: 1

HIGHLIGHTS AND SUMMARY: Cave Mt. is one of the Ski Windham peaks. Besides being a winter playground for skiers, it's also an excellent place to observe birds, other wildlife, and wildflowers. Cave Mt. and its neighbor, West Cave, are technically "bushwhacks," as there isn't a hiking trail, but anyone can follow the ski slopes to the tops. Find yourself a perch on one of the slopes in the off-season and you may be rewarded with the sight of fawns or bear cubs wandering out on the grassy slopes. Right after the ski center closes, the slopes are a great place to hike on rock-hard artificial snow. Pick a sunny day, slather on the sunscreen, and go "glacier climbing" in the

Northeast. Friends of mine play a game to see who can find the most coins that have fallen onto the snow under the ski lifts.

BEST TIME TO HIKE: This is a good hike any time of year, but early autumn or spring is best.

Cave and West Cave mountains are usually combined and climbed from Ski Windham, formerly known as the Cave Mt. ski area (N42° 17.989', W74° 15.256').

During cold weather, call ahead (800-754-9463) to find out whether the mountain is open for skiing. During the ski season, an inexpensive snowshoe pass gets you on the peak. Out of season, park, alert the staff, pick a ski trail, and off you go.

You won't have a wilderness experience on a ski mountain, but that's made up for by the views and animal sign: deer, bears, coyotes, and birds, especially on the open slopes bordered by forest. In the spring and early summer the observant hiker can see deer and fawns, and shouldn't be surprised to see a mama bear with her cubs on the grassy runs. The summit of Cave Mt. appears to be a good-sized rock in the woods beyond the top of one of the ski lifts—a perfect place to sit and enjoy lunch.

Cave Mt. and its shorter sister, West Cave, are easily climbed together. Follow an easy 1 mi walk along an unpaved maintenance road that dips between the two summits. Unless the weather obscures the way, you can see the other peak as you stroll across. The upper ski trails offer interesting views; Roundtop,

View from Cave Mt. Mark Schaefer

Shultice, Irish, and Moresville Range peaks can be seen from the Why Not Trail. From different places on Cave Mt., Huntersfield, Ashland Pinnacle, Richmond, Richtmyer, Pisgah, Nebo, Zoar, Hayden, and Ginseng are visible.

Depending on the route, it will be under 3 mi and 1400 ft ascent to climb Cave Mt., and 5 mi and just under 1700 ft ascent by including West Cave.

Be alert hiking during the big game hunting season as ski area employees and others sometimes hunt the ridgetop and southern side of the mountain. Remaining on the open slopes is a good idea, particularly if hiking with a dog.

Packsaddle Mt., 3100'
Lexington Quad
(Lexington Mt.)
Catskill 67 Rank: 43
View: 2, Interest: 2, Difficulty: 3, Bushwhack: 3

HIGHLIGHTS AND SUMMARY: Packsaddle is a bushwhack and pleasant hike from Schoolhouse Brook, or a little more challenging from NY42. There are brambles to play with above the col, but they are fewer and less dense than along the ridgetop of its neighboring summit, Pine Island Mt. A hiker on Packsaddle will come across bear scat and deer sign. In the spring, the sound of birdcalls accompanies you on your hike.

BEST TIME TO HIKE: The best time to hike is any time of the year, but spring, autumn, and winter are best.

See the section on Pine Island Mt. for information on locating the trailhead and parking details. The most practical route starts as described in that section, along a DEC right-of-way up Schoolhouse Brook. Stay on the right-of-way, along a woods road, until reaching public property at 2150 ft.

The woods road passes through a reforestation area that was likely the result of an 1891 forest fire on the E side of Schoolhouse Brook. The fire began at an elevation of about 2100 ft and spread farther up the mountain, according to Dr. Michael Kudish in *The Catskill Forest, A History*. It's been suggested that the DEC easement from Spruceton Rd. to the col may have been obtained in order to accomplish the reforestation. The woods road is overgrown in summer on its upper end, but the woods are open enough that it doesn't really matter.

Continue through the Packsaddle–Pine Island col, and on its far side, pick up a woods road that heads W up Packsaddle. You should be able to stay with it almost all of the way up the 500 ft and 0.5 mi to Packsaddle's wooded summit. The blackberry canes can be diabolical on the summit ridge in summertime, so be prepared to dance the "Pricker Polka" if you wear shorts and a tee shirt for the hike. You can avoid the worst of them by keeping slightly to the N above the col until right under the summit. The views from the summit are screened during summer, but visuals improve after the trees drop their leaves. It's 2.25 mi and a 1475 ft ascent from your car on the Spruceton Rd. via this route.

A second route to Packsaddle can be done as a through-hike connecting Packsaddle's SW ridge with the Schoolhouse Brook route. Park near DEP signs just N of the intersection of NY42 and CR6, near the hamlet of West Kill, and walk into the woods near where West Kill Creek crosses NY42 (N42° 12.713', W74° 23.214'). Look for DEP signage adjacent to the highway, where a tributary of the creek tumbles down Packsaddle's SW flank.

The lower section of Packsaddle Mt. is a gradual climb, in a forest of open hardwoods, but it's lumpy, with lots of uneven rocks two-thirds of the way up the peak. In summer there are large areas of nettles and some blown-over trees. There is one section of about 400 ft with steep climbing on rocky ground. In the last 300 ft of climbing, the sparse hardwoods are replaced by deciduous trees growing much closer together. An ascent of 1600 ft and 2 mi of hiking gets you to the summit, where you can reverse your route or head to the Packsaddle–Pine Island col and down to the Spruceton Rd. via Schoolhouse Brook.

There are some nice looking routes from the N, but all of them cross private property. Regardless of your route, Packsaddle is wonderful hiking. The quiet traveler may see deer, bear, or porcupines, and lots of birdlife. I remember a hike here with friends, one of whom is a wonderful naturalist. When two of us were discussing what animal had left a particular scat, we asked her to join the debate by suggesting we needed a "turd" opinion.

West Cave Mt., 3040' *Ashland Quad*
Catskill 67 Rank: 56
View: 5, Interest: 4, Difficulty: 2, Bushwhack: 1

HIGHLIGHTS AND SUMMARY: West Cave is almost always climbed with Cave Mt. (See the section on Cave Mt. for trailhead details.) West Cave is technically a bushwhack, but it's a simple hike up the open ski slopes where you can select your own level of difficulty. In spring, the observant hiker may see deer and bears with their young out in the grassy ski runs. The views and photography are great. As you drive along NY23 near Windham, you'll see West Cave and Cave mountains looming above and connected by a ridge. You can begin your hike right from the Ski Windham parking area.
BEST TIME TO HIKE: Although you can easily climb any time of year, immediately after the ski area closes might be the best, followed closely by autumn and early summer.

An excellent way to climb West Cave is to keep all the way to the right-hand ski slope above the parking lot, hiking just outside the property lines of the big homes lining the slope. This is the Wonderama Trail. Keep the trees on your right. As the trails split off further up the mountain, you can choose the gradient and degree of difficulty on the ski run of your choice. You'll discover that you can rest your knees by switchbacking whenever the slope is too steep.

As you climb higher, a number of other ski trails intersect. You'll find a large sign showing the names and where they go. Midway up, a good choice is the Wedel Trail. It's steep in its upper reaches, but gets you to the summit quickly. If you descend this way, Wonderama and Wedel trails are noted on the signboard at the top of the slope.

Climbing is a pleasure right after Ski Windham closes for the season. Hiking in the spring is easy as you walk on top of the dense and compacted artificial snow covering the ski runs. The snow remains rock hard until it melts. Before then, you can experience a "glacier climb" on a bright sunny day. Under early spring conditions, hiking poles and crampons or MICROspikes® (see glossary) are strongly recommended. Hiking in the winter while the snow guns are working is an experience unto itself. The roar of the guns and the snow they throw makes it feel very much like you're on an alpine peak in a whiteout. On the way up, keep looking back to enjoy excellent views towards the N. Once the climbing is done, walk a short ways to the height of land and the top of West Cave. There is a ski lift terminus and shed right at the top. The lift is the actual summit of the mountain.

The upper Wraparound ski trail heads towards Cave Mt. Without snow, it looks like an ATV/service road. It connects the two summits and is an easy way between them. To climb Cave Mt., follow this ski trail for a brief descent and your route becomes an ATV track and dirt road. You can follow the flagging, paint blazes, or the road for the easy ascent to Cave Mt.

West Cave is one of the easiest ascents of the Catskill 100 peaks. You can stop frequently as the views get better and better the higher you go. The woods are very friendly, nice and open with virtually no blowdown. There's even a memorial stone bench at the top of the Wedel Trail, an excellent spot to take a break and drink in the views before the short stroll to the actual summit. You will get a stellar look at the entire Huntersfield range to the N, which includes Huntersfield and Richmond (Catskill 100 peaks), Ashland Pinnacle, Mt. Nebo, Mt. Hayden, and Ginseng Mt. It's about 1.25 mi and 1350 ft of climbing to the summit, and a 5 mi, 1700 ft day if you combine the hike with Cave Mt.

Ski slope approach to West Cave Mt. Alan Via

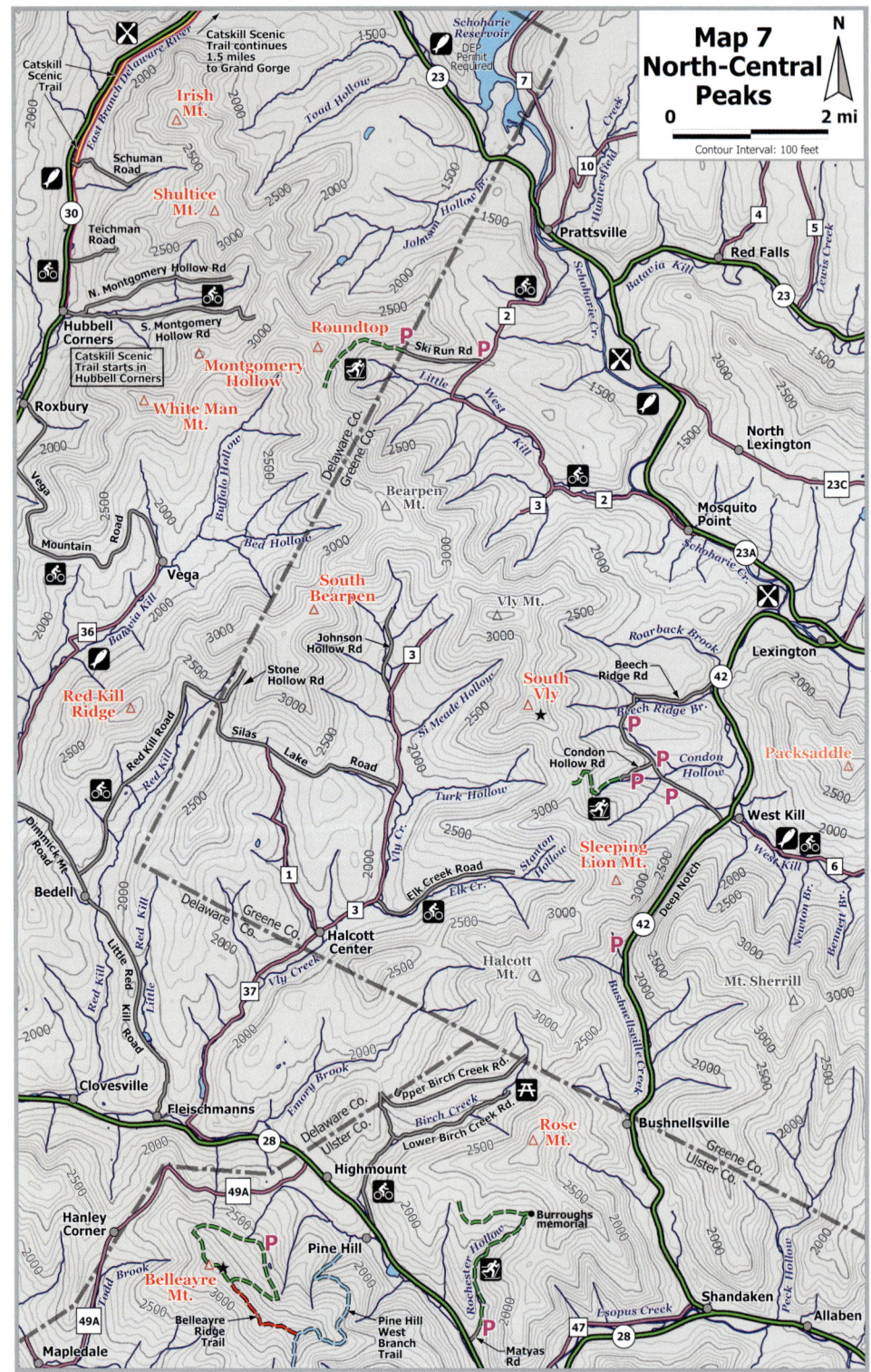

North-Central Peaks

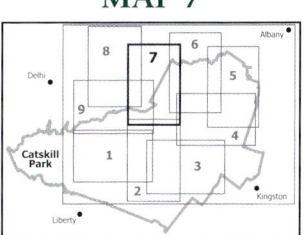

MAP 7

- Roundtop (Ontiora or Little West Kill) (Prattsville Quad)
- Belleayre Mt. (Belle Ayr)
- South Bearpen
- Sleeping Lion (NE Halcott)
- South Vly
- Shultice Mt. (Schultice)
- White Man Mt. (Hack Flats)
- Red Kill Ridge (Butternut Mt.)
- Rose Mt.
- Irish Mt.
- Montgomery Hollow (Walt's Knob)

Ten of the eleven summits we'll discuss in this region are bushwhacks in whole or in part, but there are woods roads routes to many. Several are over private property, requiring permission to hike part or all of the mountain. Roundtop, Belleayre, Sleeping Lion, and South Vly have routes open to anyone.

The mountains are bounded by excellent state and county roads; town roads provide additional trailhead access. As a group, the summits are mostly wooded, with Belleayre being an exception. The peaks are mostly a mix of fields and deciduous trees in the lower reaches and deciduous forests up top. Ice storms and caterpillar damage have opened canopies and there are sections of blackberry prickers that sometimes make winter travel a better option. Flat ridges on a number of the mountains often necessitate a hunt for the high point. Many porcupines call this area home, so be aware if you hike with your pooch.

The 26-mile Catskill Scenic Trail (see glossary) is an excellent ride for those with mountain bikes or hybrids, as are North and South Montgomery Hollow roads, Vega Mountain Rd., Beech Ridge Rd., Elk Creek Rd., and others in between. Red Kill Rd. is one of the most scenic places for a Catskill bike ride, as are the nearby town roads.

Fishermen can try their luck in the Schoharie Reservoir (DEP permit required), West Kill, East Branch Delaware River, and Schoharie Creek. There are also countless small trout streams draining many of the valleys. Paddlers can put in on the Schoharie Creek and Delaware River.

Thistle on Belleayre Mt. Mark Schaefer

Roundtop, 3440'
(Ontiora or Little West Kill)
Catskill 67 Rank: 6
View: 1, Interest: 2, Difficulty: 2, Bushwhack: 2

Prattsville Quad

HIGHLIGHTS AND SUMMARY: This is one of the three Roundtops on the Catskill 100 list of peaks. It's located directly N of the taller Bearpen Mt., a Catskill 3500 ft summit. All routes are bushwhacks, but woods roads to the summit make the first route fairly easy. Blackberry prickers flourish on the upper reaches of the peak and there are interlaced canes in places. The short bushwhack from the col has a high pricker-to-mileage ratio. Roundtop is not a hike where the views require packing your camera.
BEST TIME TO HIKE: The best time to hike is between late autumn and early spring.

Locating the trailheads for the hikes can be challenging. Drive S out of Prattsville on CR2. Pass a number of intersections until you reach Ski Run Rd., a little less than 3 mi S of the village. In winter, park at a scenic spot where CR2 intersects Ski Run Rd. (N42° 17.458', W74° 26.983'), but otherwise drive up Ski Run Rd. to the Bearpen State Forest parking area. Just beyond the State Forest parking area, the continuation of Ski Run Rd. climbs steadily for 2 mi and 1200 ft up to the North Bearpen–Roundtop col (N42° 17.259', W74° 29.352').

When DEC acquired the summit of Roundtop and the surrounding property, it became part of the Bearpen State Forest. At one time, the col had been the site for a camp, humorously named the Ben Dover Hunting Club before it was razed. While the cabin is a funny memory, the col is a good place to take a break and "assess" your surroundings. At the col turn right (N) and follow the old ATV path landscaped on both sides with aggressive berry prickers. From the col it's 0.4 mi and 250 ft to Roundtop's wooded top, covered by deciduous trees and bejeweled with pricker canes.

Looking at a map, it might occur to you to take a shortcut by heading into the woods between 2600 ft and 2700 ft and striking directly for the summit. I'd advise against it as you'd be trading a little trail mileage for the opportunity to shred your gear and be answering post-hike questions like, "Where did you get all of those scratches?"

The road and bushwhack from the beginning of Ski Run Rd. is a little under 6 mi round-trip and 1450 ft ascent. The hike is slightly shorter from the State Forest parking area.

Routes from George Lawrence Rd. or the ridges from Bearpen or Montgomery Hollow mountains all pass over private property. They can be feasible hikes if you introduce yourself to the property owners and ask for permission.

Blackberry bushes abound on the upper slopes of Roundtop. Mark Schaefer

Belleayre Mt., 3420'
(Belle Ayr)
Catskill 67 Rank: 8
View: 5, Interest: 3, Difficulty: 2

Fleischmanns Quad

> HIGHLIGHTS AND SUMMARY: There are trails and ski run routes with spectacular views up and down the mountain as well as along the summit ridge. There is a great abundance of birds and other wildlife and a good chance to have the summit all to yourself in the snowless months. Belleayre has mountain biking trails and events, as well as a summer music festival.
> BEST TIME TO HIKE: While you can hike any season, the three non-winter months are the best to enjoy all this peak provides.

There are too many variations up and down this ski area mountain to cover them all in detail. The mountain is located on Galli Curci Rd., off CR49A (N42° 08.525', W74° 30.635'). CR49A turns off of NY28 near Highmount, between Pine Hill and Fleischmanns.

My preferred routes for climbing Belleayre are the ski trails or grassy access roads, because you're out in the open with good views over your shoulder at every turn. During winter you'll need a lift ticket and you should avoid any ski trails. The Belleayre staff or ski patrol will shoo you out of any areas being used by skiers or snowboarders.

You can start your hike farther down the mountain or, if your time is limited, drive up to Overlook Lodge (N42° 07.883', W74° 30.371'), a parking area at 2500 ft located near the base of quad lift number 7. Park your car, say hello to the friendly workers, and then hike slightly uphill and left past Overlook Lodge. Look for the beginning of a dirt service road that ascends the mountain on the E side of the ski area. In the ski season, the service road serves as the Discovery Way and Cathedral Brook runs, although you may not know that until you see a sign on the summit ridge.

When there is no snow, this hard-packed dirt and grassy service road climbs the NE slope of the peak. At every turn you'll enjoy N-facing views. When you reach the summit ridge the road levels out and is grassy in summer months. As you walk along the ridge, an opening in the trees to your left leads SE to the former site of a fire tower. Looking at a map, it's easy to get the impression that the tower location is the summit. This is actually a side trip that heads away from the summit, which is 1.4 mi NNW from the old tower foundation. If you decide to check the old tower site, you'll notice intersections for Rider Hollow, Cathedral Glen, and Lost Clove trails and a lean-to in the col before the climb to the tower.

Retrace your steps toward where you first reached the summit ridge and continue over a few small rises that provide excellent long-range views towards Rose, Halcott, Bearpen, and Vly mountains to the N. An excellent place for lunch and to break out the camera is the open clearing at Sunset Lodge. It's a small building

located at 3325 ft. The lodge is the terminus of the large ski lift and is open in the winter. From here it is a ten-minute stroll along the grassy ridgetop to Belleayre's 3420 ft summit (N42° 07.719', W74° 31.155').

To return to Overlook Lodge, you can select any number of leg-numbing ski trail descents. A more enjoyable route is down Deer Run. This access road/ski trail descends the NNW shoulder of the mountain as it curves down towards Sunset Lodge. Deer Run is the other route up the mountain that I would recommend.

Belleayre is a satisfying hike in the autumn as the trees on the nearby slopes and in the distance are aflame with fall color. In the spring and early summer, the mowed ski runs and berry bushes attract birds, bear, and deer, each with their young. The animal scat is evidence of their presence. When hiking quietly in the early or late hours, it is not uncommon to see wildlife on the open slopes. Ski area employees may suggest you keep your dog on a leash in the early spring because of the fawns and cubs out on the grassy ski runs.

One of the nicest times to hike Belleayre is right after the end of the ski season. The ski runs are deep with natural and manmade snow, heavily compacted from the previous months' activities. Once the skiers have departed, the conditions are often perfect for walking on top of the snow. Pick a sunny early spring day and you can be hiking or snowshoeing in a tee shirt and shorts on 6 ft of hard-as-cement snow. If you choose a steep trail, consider bringing crampons or MICROspikes® for traction.

From Overlook Lodge, hiking to the tower site, back over the summit, and down Deer Run is 5.25 mi and 1200 ft ascent. You can add another mile and 500 ft of climbing by starting at the lower lodge.

Belleayre Mt. ski run in summer. Tony Versandi

South Bearpen, 3410'
Catskill 67 Rank: 11
View: 1, Interest: 1, Difficulty: 4, Bushwhack: 4–5

West Kill Quad

HIGHLIGHTS AND SUMMARY: All routes are bushwhacks and the highest summit is just beyond DEC land on private property. It's probably poor form to begin by offering faint praise for a mountain, as each peak has its own interest and charm. But you really have to look for them on this one. There is a saying that revenge is a dish best served cold. South Bearpen is a peak best climbed in the cold, when snow covers the undergrowth.

Pricker canes make this peak a challenge and one climbed mostly by bushwhackers hiking the entire Catskill 100 list. The berry bushes are the reason for lots of birds, bears, and deer in the area. There is excellent mountain and road biking on the surrounding roads.

BEST TIME TO HIKE: The best time to hike is winter and early spring, before the prickers can pop up and arm themselves for summer.

This mountain has three separate summits, all measuring between 3403 ft and 3410 ft. While there are sizable areas of public property on the peak, the highest summit is on private property. Obtain proper permission, or hike from the W to the 3403 ft SE summit on DEP and DEC property from Stone Hollow Rd. and call it a mountain—it's just 7 ft shorter!

South Bearpen's upper ridges are guarded by large areas of dense pricker canes and their thorns exact a toll for those who travel there. Even the many woods roads that crisscross the mountain are overgrown with waist- to head-high thorn bushes from late spring onward. There are also vast areas of beautiful ferns. These make walking less like a visit to the Red Cross, but they camouflage the rocks and blown-down branches underneath. In wintertime, the pricker canes are either bent over or buried, and the nettles gone to purgatory.

If the vegetation and appearing and disappearing woods roads aren't challenge enough, the multiple ridges can test your land navigation skills. In snowy conditions a peak like South Bearpen is far easier as you can see where you are going and the undergrowth has disappeared. The woods on the mountain are exclusively deciduous, and in areas of mature trees the prickers are less of a problem. In winter there are views of Sleeping Lion, Halcott, Vly, Belleayre, and Rose mountains, and with a little luck you might see Balsam Mt. in the distance. The berry bushes attract wildlife and the mountain is home to bears

Beech trees show porcupine activity. Joanne Hihn

and deer. From pretty much any direction, expect hikes of 4 to 7 mi and 1500 ft to 1800 ft of climbing.

Sleeping Lion, 3408'
(NE Halcott)
Catskill 67 Rank: 12
View: 2–3, Interest: 3, Difficulty: 4, Bushwhack: 4

West Kill Quad

HIGHLIGHTS AND SUMMARY: All routes are bushwhacks and many are steep and interesting. The woods are generally open and deciduous with an abundance of wildlife. The high proportion of beech trees is attractive to the large porcupine population and the berry bushes provide a great food source for birds and bears. Go in the springtime for a woodland with wildflowers blooming, birds chirping, and turkeys gobbling. Before setting out, take the pronunciation test. To pass for a local or experienced Catskill hiker say, "Hawk-it," or the less used localism, "Haw-cut" Mt.
BEST TIME TO HIKE: This is a good hike any time of year.

One favorite route to Sleeping Lion (NE Halcott) is via its slightly taller and southern neighbor, Halcott Mt. (a Catskill 3500 peak), and the connecting ridge. Park in the parking area (N42° 11.053', W74° 24.889') usually used for Halcott Mt. on the W side of NY42 in Deep Notch. Pick your way up Halcott Mt. on your own route, or jump on one of the herd paths that will lead you to its canister.

Meadow near Sleeping Lion. Joanne Hihn

This route allows you to pick up a "two-fer" by first climbing Halcott Mt. Along the way, look for a beautiful grove of large cedar trees.

From the top of Halcott, stay on the ridgeline between the two peaks, dropping a little more than 500 ft in a very gradual descent to the col. The last half mile of Halcott's NE ridge before the col is wide; if you are not attentive to your bearing, you won't be the first to find yourself on your way toward Stanton Hollow or back to NY42. The woods are deciduous and, if the leaves are gone, you can look back and see where you came from and ahead at Sleeping Lion. The views and photography improve measurably after autumn. Travel is much easier after late autumn, as well, when the nettles are gone.

It's a bit over 400 ft to the summit of Sleeping Lion from the col, and a tad steeper than the slope you just descended on the way from Halcott. Porcupines are plentiful on the peak, evidenced by the chewed beech trees. The summit of Sleeping Lion is wooded and undistinguished, but you'll encounter a few herd paths made by hikers walking the ridge to the summit.

From the summit you have a couple of options to get back to your car. The shortest is to backtrack to the col and head straight downhill, though you will be crisscrossing some drainages where the hiking becomes challenging. Another option is to climb 150 ft towards Halcott and then follow the intervening ridge SSE back to NY42. Though there is a small amount of extra elevation gain, the SSE ridge that begins SW of the col is a less steep descent and has almost no drainages to cross, in comparison to the 'whack to NY42 from the col.

Climbing both peaks and returning down the S ridge is a bit over 4.5 mi with close to 2400 ft ascent. By hiking back part of the way to Halcott, you'll add 0.25 mi and make it a 2550 ft day. Unless you have strong bushwhacking skills, take the longer way home. This is also a good idea in wet, snowy, or slippery conditions.

A more adventurous way up or down Sleeping Lion is from the S, hiking up and intersecting the southern ridge at any point. But spend some time looking at a map before you start out and don't expect many areas where you can catch your breath from this direction. From the NY42 parking area, look for the ridge between your car and the summit. If you follow this as a descent route, take care to stay well W of the edge of the ridge. The middle of the ridge is very steep. However, the farther E you venture, the cliff-ier and rockier it gets, and it can be treacherous. You don't want to venture out onto Sleeping Lion's eastern face only to find you can't descend or reclimb. Look up from Deep Notch and this will be apparent.

Another nice route to Sleeping Lion is from Condon Hollow Rd. Follow the road up to the DEC parking area (N42° 13.015', W74° 24.790'); avoid the snowplow turnaround in cold-weather season. Start walking a dirt road that becomes a woods road at the last house. The road climbs and switches back up to the col between a southern summit of South Vly and the farthest N bump of Sleeping Lion. This route is longer than the others. It traverses numerous bumps along the way to Sleeping Lion—many of which aren't apparent on topographic maps—but you're likely to have the hike to yourself. The nettles and prickers will make its 6

Near South Vly summit. Joanne Hihn

mi round-trip and 1500 ft ascent feel longer than it is.

You might like to try a bushwhack from the parking area on Beech Ridge Rd. (N42° 12.842', W74° 24.077'). This is a little under 4 mi round-trip and 1600 ft of ascent.

South Vly, 3360'   West Kill Quad
Catskill 67 Rank: 15
View: 3, Interest: 2, Difficulty: 2, Bushwhack: 3

HIGHLIGHTS AND SUMMARY: South Vly can be climbed by a variety of routes, all of which involve a certain degree of bushwhacking. Pricker canes up high and blowdown make this a good winter hike. South Vly lacks stupendous summit views but the abundant deer, bear, porkies, and birdlife provide other diversions along the way.

BEST TIME TO HIKE: South Vly can be climbed any time of the year, but late autumn through early spring is best for views and ease of travel.

To reach the start of the first bushwhack, drive from where either end of Beech Ridge Rd. intersects with NY42. One end is near the village of West Kill, the other is S of Lexington. Venture Out's Catskill map or DeLorme's *New York State Atlas and Gazetteer* will help you locate the trailhead (N42° 13.121', W74° 24.487') at Condon Hollow. Park at the intersection in winter. The rest of the year you can drive up Condon Hollow Rd. a short distance to a public parking area located at about 1950 ft (N42° 13.015', W74° 24.790').

Beyond the parking area, Condon Hollow Rd. becomes a woods road. It climbs nearly 1000 ft into the col between South Vly and Sleeping Lion (NE Halcott), turning into Turk Hollow Rd. on the other side. Automotive archeologists should look for the old wrecked car on the N side of the col.

As you hike, consider your options. You can hike to the col and climb the mountain along its SE ridge. Or you can jump into the bushwhack off the woods road at just under 2700 ft and head straight at South Vly's SE ridge a little earlier. While the earlier departure is doable, there is a lot of blowdown in the woods on the E side of South Vly from near the road's hairpin turn. Any potential time savings might be more than used up by dueling with fallen treetops, beech whips, and steeper terrain.

Once in the col, it's a bushwhack up South Vly's SE ridge, where you get to play dodge 'em with beech whips and blowdown. Stay on the ridge, up and over the intermediate sub-peak, then hike another 0.6 mi to South Vly's wooded top. The 'whack from the col is over a combination of DEC and DEP property. The route is not a trail, but is an obvious path with occasional blazes along the DEP/DEC boundary. This is a good hike for long pants, a long-sleeved shirt, and eye protection, as berry canes and beech whips will be "Vlying" for your attention. You can skip the obstacles by hiking the peak in winter.

At 3210 ft there is an interesting opening on the summit ridge. Friends have speculated about its origin, with ideas ranging from natural causes to a log landing cleared to bedrock. I personally favor the idea that aliens chose the location for their saucer landings. Don your aluminum foil hat, as it is a good spot for looks at Halcott, Packsaddle, and Sleeping Lion. In another 100 ft you top out on the wooded summit. The usual advice about where *you* feel the summit is located applies. For my money, the huge rock is the highest point on the summit ridge. Look around as there are good views from its vicinity in winter. The route is 5.5 mi round-trip and 1700 ft ascent.

A second route connects South Vly to a bushwhack from Sleeping Lion (NE Halcott). Leaving the summit of Sleeping Lion, descend its very gradual NW ridge. Along the way pass over three rises. Keep E of the third rise, the lowest along the descent but with the most gain and closest to the Sleeping Lion–South Vly col, to avoid a small rectangle of private property before continuing the slow drop into the col. It's about 1.6 mi and 550 ft of elevation loss down to the col. And while the route is a longer hike and bushwhack than the Condon Hollow approach, it does allow you to pick up two trailless Catskill 100 summits on one hike, staying on public land all the way. Sleeping Lion to South Vly is 2.7 mi and 1000 ft of climbing.

A map gives the appearance that you can climb South Vly by traversing the ridge from the taller Vly Mt. to its N. A bushwhack from Vly would follow the ridgetop, but there is a large gap in public property along the route requiring permission from the landowner. The same caution applies to climbing from Si Meade Hollow from the W.

If you aren't worn out with route options, there's another. For those who would prefer a complete bushwhack to the summit instead of gaining much of the elevation on Condon Hollow Rd., look for a small wedge of DEP land (N42° 13.590', W74° 24.917') that abuts Beech Ridge Rd. SE of the summit. You can bushwhack from your car directly NW up South Vly's eastern flank, but it's steep and "ledgy," and has sections of dense prickers.

Shultice Mt., 3280'   Roxbury Quad

(Schultice)
Catskill 67 Rank: 19
View: 3, Interest: 3, Difficulty: 3, Bushwhack: 3

HIGHLIGHTS AND SUMMARY: Shultice Mt. is located between NY23 and NY30 in Delaware County, 3 mi SSW of Grand Gorge. The mountain is a bushwhack and private property. Permission from the landowners to hike is required. Deer, porcupines, and bears are active on the peak, as is common on Delaware County mountains. All hikes pass through a mix of open deciduous forest, overgrown farm fields, and woods roads, with the usual prickers higher up on the mountain and long-distance views from near the top.

BEST TIME TO HIKE: The best time to hike is right after the autumn hunting season through mid-spring.

With landowner permission, there are hikes from North Montgomery Hollow, Teichman, and Johnson Hollow roads, with routes under 4 mi round-trip and 1400 ft ascent. For hikers less interested in climbing to the summit or seeking permission to hike, look for a large section of DEP land that extends high up along Shultice's western side. Quiet hikers can enjoy the wide variety of birds and other wildlife this mountain offers in this sizable DEP parcel. Avoid the area during the hunting seasons.

White Man Mt., 3140'   Roxbury Quad
(Hack Flats)
Catskill 67 Rank: 38
View: 3, Interest: 2, Difficulty: 3, Bushwhack: 3

HIGHLIGHTS AND SUMMARY: White Man Mt. is a bushwhack peak entirely on private property and inaccessible without permission to hike. The woods are deciduous, but the toll for passage is blackberry prickers from late spring until heavy frost.
BEST TIME TO HIKE: The best time to hike is when the prickers and leaves are gone.

The mountain is located directly E of Roxbury and NY30, with town roads on all four sides. When hiking White Man Mt., it's a good idea to dress for pricker cane success. Woods roads crisscross the mountain and there are areas that have been heavily logged. The berry bushes are an attraction for deer, bears and birds, and the beech forest is a magnet for porcupines.

In the summer, trees screen much of the summit views. In winter, other Catskill summits are visible, including Montgomery Hollow, Roundtop, Red Kill, South Bearpen, Old Clump, Meeker Hollow, and the Plattekills. Any hike will be under 3 mi round-trip and 1500 ft of ascent or less.

Red Kill Ridge, 3100'   Fleischmanns Quad
(Butternut Mt.)
Catskill 67 Rank: 45
View: 3, Interest: 3, Difficulty: 2, Bushwhack: 3

HIGHLIGHTS AND SUMMARY: Red Kill Ridge is a bushwhack from any direction and most of the mountain is private property. You can hike a half mile through open fields and overgrown meadows, passing old stone walls that were likely part of a farm forty years ago, before DEP acquired the prop-

erty. Without permission, this is as far as you can proceed, but it's a wonderful hike for those not interested in summiting and satisfied with the views from the lower slopes. There is an abundance of birds and other wildlife. The lower slopes are a great place to observe trees slowly reclaiming the old meadows.
BEST TIME TO HIKE: The spring wildflowers here are a treat, as are the autumn views E across the valley, making autumn through spring the best time to hike.

Red Kill Ridge is reached by driving N out of Fleischmanns on Little Red Kill Rd. to the hamlet of Bedell (N42° 11.707', W74° 33.000'), then onto Dimmick Mountain Rd. Take a right turn onto the very scenic and picturesque Red Kill Rd. You can gawk at the scenery up the valley for about 2 mi until reaching the first DEP signs on the left (W) side of the road. In springtime, the views across the valley are spectacular—a vision of meadows, wildflowers, forest, and 2922 ft West Settlement Creek, a Catskill 200 highest summit across the way. The drive on the local roads and the short hike on DEP land is a nice half day all by itself.

Although the Red Kill Ridge woods are inviting down low, the summit ridge is a maze of tall blackberry and raspberry prickers. Dog owners take note—the beech trees on Red Kill are porcupine nirvana, judging from the amount of bark chewing seen everywhere. Any hiking route involves a couple of miles of round-trip hiking with an ascent of 1000 ft. Combine the short DEP hike with your birding binoculars, camera, and bicycle, and make it a full day.

Rose Mt., 3090'
West Kill Quad
Catskill 67 Rank: 47
View: 4, Interest: 5, Difficulty: 3, Bushwhack: 3

HIGHLIGHTS AND SUMMARY: Rose Mt. is a bushwhack. The trip up Rochester Hollow alone, whether on skis, snowshoes, bicycle or boots, is worth the effort. The Burroughs monument and the stone fences provide a great place to ponder what Rochester Hollow looked like 125 years ago, but spring wildflowers, a trailside burbling brook, or showy autumn foliage also provide entertainment on the hike in. The summit is private property, so obtain permission or bag Rose's slightly shorter southern summit instead. This is another "porcupine peak," as the face full of porcupine quills my Lab Bookah and another

John Burroughs monument in Rochester Hollow. Alan Via

dog received will attest. If you enjoy hiking with a dog, keep a close eye on your pet. Matyas and Birch Creek roads are excellent for biking. Nearby Birch, Vly, and Esopus creeks provide post-hike fishing opportunities. The recreation area on Birch Creek Rd. is a great place to relax after a hike.

BEST TIME TO HIKE: The best time to hike is any season, but spring, autumn, and winter are tops.

The trailhead is located on Matyas Rd., which is located on the N side of NY28 between Pine Hill and Big Indian (N42° 06.860', W74° 27.293'). Drive up Matyas Rd. to the isolated DEC parking area (N42° 07.071', W74° 27.100') located in the Shandaken Wild Forest. I am not exaggerating when I describe the woods road up through Rochester Hollow as beautiful. It ascends gradually, is well graded, and is very easy hiking.

In spring, a tributary of Birch Creek that drains Rochester Hollow shows off its many small waterfalls, and wildflowers festoon its banks and both sides of the trail. You can see trout lilies, trillium, spring beauties, and columbine, to name just a few. In summer, the mature trees along the woods road provide shade, and ferns cloak the ground on both sides. The autumn woods are spectacular here as well. The woods road through Rochester Hollow must have taken years to construct as it's edged with rocks and boulders. There are also rock drainage ditches and water diversions. When the leaves are off the trees you can see all the details of the opposite slopes, and the summit ridge of Rose eventually reveals itself in the distance.

The woods road climbs 700 ft as it curves its way 1.85 mi to a hairpin turn in Rochester Hollow. At 2150 ft, the road turns abruptly W and a small stone monument (N42° 08.247', W74° 26.394') surrounded by a decades-old fence waits for hikers. The monument was erected in 1921 by a local school to honor John Burroughs, and the abandoned farmstead was reforested in his honor. Behind the monument there are old stone cellars, and intricately laid stone fences, tall

Bookah on Rochester Hollow woods road. Mike Cruz

and straight, march their way up through the mountain's hardwood slopes.

A hike, ski, or snowshoe to the monument and back is a nice half-day outing. Otherwise, the bushwhack begins here through Shandaken Wild Forest land all the way to 2700 ft. The woods on the southern side of Rose Mt. are completely open and easy bushwhacking, a mix of maple, birch, cherry, and beech, largely without blowdown. If you have received landowner permission to continue above 2700 ft, there is a woods road on the ridgetop that leads close to the summit plateau. Otherwise, stay on DEC land, climb Rose's 2901 ft SE summit, and call it a wonderful day.

In the summertime, the summit plateau is grown over with prickers, nettles, and dense greenery. In winter or early spring, it is a very easy 0.5 mi stroll across the summit plateau to the nondescript top. While summertime views are subtle, hikers can see Balsam, Belleayre, Deep Notch, Halcott, Fir, Big Indian, North Dome, and Sherrill from different places on the peak after leaves have fallen.

While you're in the area, take a drive along the NW side of the mountain, turning off NY28 in Pine Hill onto Birch Creek Rd. (N42° 08.065', W74° 28.653'). Almost immediately, you will see DEP land on the E side. After a short distance, bear right on Lower Birch Creek Rd. You'll pass another long stretch of DEP property on this scenic road. At the road's end is a Shandaken Wild Forest parking area (N42° 09.523', W74° 26.729'), with rest facilities, tables, and a stocked fish pond. This is a wonderfully relaxing destination for picnicking, fishing, swimming, or birding, at the site of an old farmhouse under the watchful gaze of Halcott Mt. You can hike a ways up Rose Mt. from this side on DEC property, but it's private property above 2600 ft.

Hiking routes are between 5 and 6 mi and 1700 ft of climbing or less.

Irish Mt., 3060' Roxbury Quad
Catskill 67 Rank: 51
View: 2, Interest: 2, Difficulty: 3, Bushwhack: 3

HIGHLIGHTS AD SUMMARY: Irish Mt. is in Delaware County, midway between Grand Gorge and Roxbury, immediately E of NY30. All hikes to Irish's summit are bushwhacks and most of the mountain is on privately owned land. Obtaining landowner permission to hike beyond DEP property is paramount. DEP land is situated along the rail trail bordering NY30, but private land stands between it and the summit.

BEST TIME TO HIKE: The best time to hike is December through mid-May.

There are woods roads all over the mountain, some overgrown. The forest consists of maple, birch, beech, and ash. Irish Mt. is another porcupine haven, if the chewed beeches and scat are a measure. My Lab received a muzzle full of quills playing tag with a porky on DEP land here. While Labs make great hiking companions, they'll never pass a Mensa test. A local resident related how his two beagles roamed around his home for nine years without incident. His two Labs, however, repeatedly tangled with porcupines. Bird activity, deer rubs, scrapes, and bear sign are everywhere.

The higher elevations on the mountains have pricker patches that will generate oohs and aahhs from friends and family who'll question your sanity when seeing your post-whack souvenirs. The top is thickly wooded, and before autumn the views from Irish are limited. Even with bare trees, the views are not greatly improved, but Shultice, Old Clump, Narrow Notch, SW Moresville Range, and Grand Gorge are visible.

Whether you obtain permission to hike beyond public property or remain on DEP land, it's a good idea to carry a pair of needle-nose pliers and know how to remove quills from your four-legged hiking partner. Most hikes will be 3 to 4 mi round-trip and under 1500 ft of ascent.

Montgomery Hollow, 3040'
(Walt's Knob)
Catskill 67 Rank: 54
View: 3, Interest: 2, Difficulty: 3, Bushwhack: 3

Roxbury Quad

HIGHLIGHTS AND SUMMARY: Montgomery Hollow is a private-property bushwhack peak located just E of Roxbury and Hubbell Corners, and S of South Montgomery Hollow Rd. The local name for the mountain is Walt's Knob, named for Walter Meade, a Catskill wildlife photographer from Roxbury. Meade's photographs have appeared in *Kaatskill Life* and *The Conservationist*. The Walter Meade Gallery is located near Roxbury. The summit isn't named on some maps but is immediately NE of an area called Hack Flats on the USGS quad.
BEST TIME TO HIKE: Avoid the hunting season, but the best time to hike is from late autumn to very early spring.

Because the mountain is entirely on private property, stop by and introduce yourself to one of the local landowners. With permission in hand, there are good routes for Montgomery Hollow from many directions. The peak is crisscrossed with woods roads and the forest is completely deciduous. As with its neighboring peaks, come ready to duel with pricker bushes high on the mountain.

The W side of the peak has seen some recent logging and the open forest canopy is a boon to deer, bear, and birds, and hikers shouldn't be surprised to see porcupines waddling around in the woods. Although the summit is wooded and the views screened, at least eight other Catskill 100 summits are visible from the mountain or its slopes. Any routes will be under 4 mi round-trip and under 1400 ft ascent.

Trillium. Alan Via

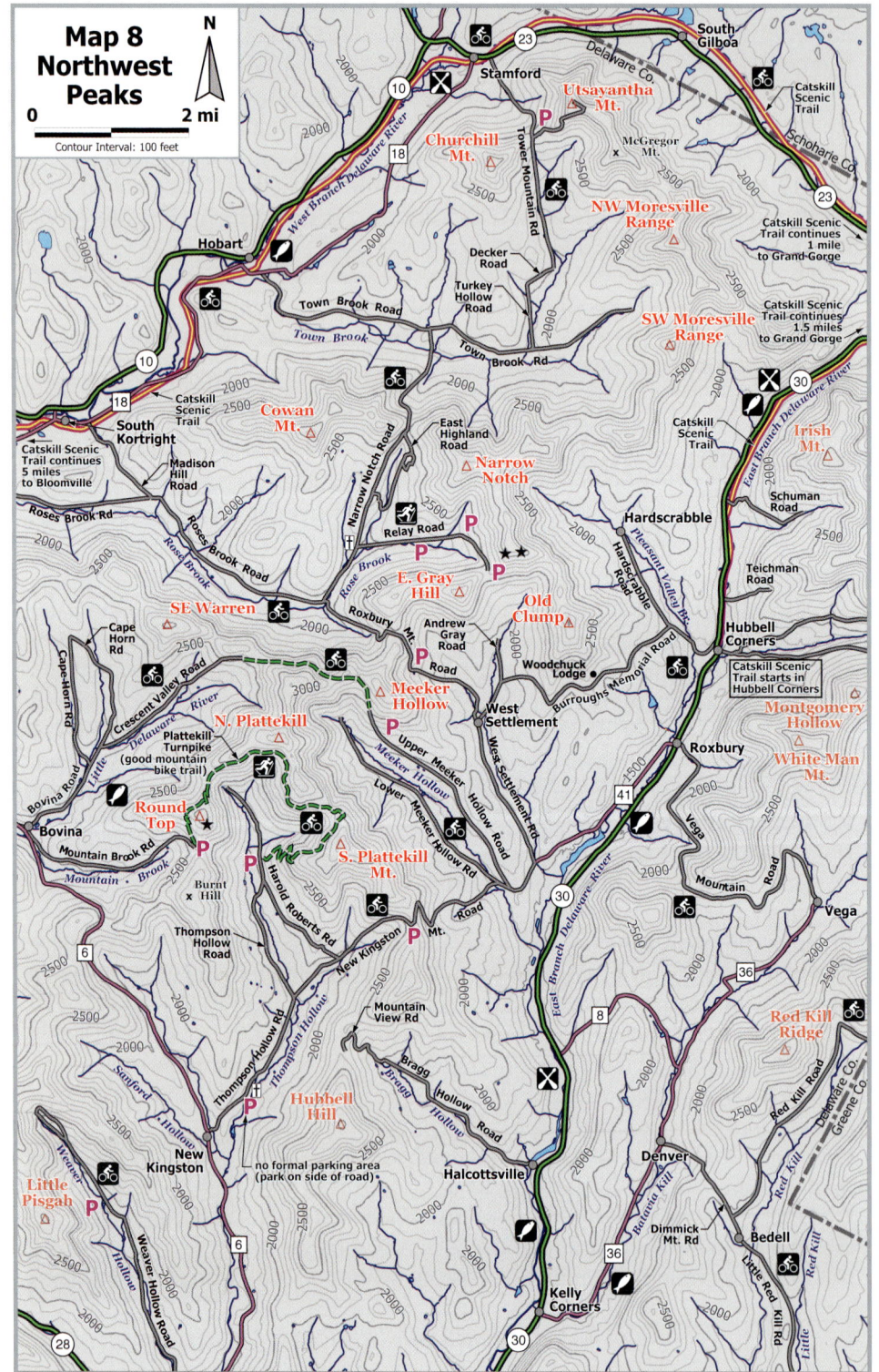

Northwest Peaks

MAP 8

North Plattekill Mt.
South Plattekill Mt.
Moresville Range NW Peak
Narrow Notch Mt.
Utsayantha Mt.
Cowan Mt.
Churchill Mt.
Round Top (Hobart Quad)
Moresville Range
 SW Peak
Southeast Warren
Old Clump
East Gray Hill
Meeker Hollow Mt. (Kenyon Mt.)

Of the thirteen Catskill 67 peaks we discuss in this region, one is a ski area, another has a road to its summit and tower, and eleven are bushwhacks. Many of the untrailed peaks have woods roads that reach their tops, or come close. Seven of the peaks are on public property and one of the six mountains with private property can be accessed by patronizing the local B&B.

All the peaks have good access and scenic roads to the trailheads; some trailheads are easier to locate than others. Most of the summits are wooded, but almost all have good views along the way. Hikers are likely to see porcupines, deer, bears, coyotes, and birds.

For cyclists, the Catskill Scenic Trail is near all the peaks in the region; in some cases the drive to the trailhead parallels the mountain bike/hybrid path. The Plattekill Turnpike (see glossary) is a wonderful mountain bike ride connecting routes to three of the peaks. For fit mountain bicyclists, Utsayantha Mt. can be cycled from Stamford right to the summit, and dozens of scenic roads to and around the trailheads could provide a season's worth of rides.

Anglers have the East, West, and Little Branches of the Delaware River, and small streams in any of the mountain valleys. Paddlers can try out their paddling skills on the West Branch of the Delaware River when water levels are acceptable.

Cross-country skiers have miles of trails to follow on the Catskill Scenic Trail and the Plattekill Turnpike. The Plattekill Turnpike is a birder's delight in springtime.

Plattekill Turnpike on North Plattekill Mt. Alan Via

North Plattekill Mt., 3340'   Hobart Quad
Catskill 67 Rank: 18
View: 5, Interest: 3, Difficulty: 2, Bushwhack: 3

HIGHLIGHTS AND SUMMARY: North Plattekill has a ski area on one side and is a bushwhack from other directions. The southernmost peak is the higher of the two summits on this mountain. The northern peak exceeds 3000 ft but there is not enough of a drop between it and its "official" and slightly higher southern twin. The Plattekill State Forest is a haven for birds and other wildlife, and the blackberry bushes provide fodder for birds and bears. Visit the beautiful old Catskill graveyard nearby, at the photogenic O.S. Baptist Church, located (N42° 15.898', W74° 35.705') on CR41, SW of Roxbury. Known as the Old Yellow Church since it was built in 1833, this is an interesting place to visit after your hike.

BEST TIME TO HIKE: Warmer weather months allow better access to some of the trailheads, but early spring, autumn, and winter allow hikers to avoid the worst of the prickers.

The most direct route to North Plattekill is from Lower Meeker Hollow Rd. Drive to Ski Plattekill (N42° 17.329', W74° 39.147') and ask a staffer where you can park. The climbs from the ski area are varied; select a slope or degree of steepness you prefer, put on your pack, and head uphill. There are also mountain bike trails you can hike. Any up and down combination of routes from the ski area will be between 2 and 2.5 mi round-trip and about 1100 ft of ascent.

North Plattekill can also be climbed from the end of the drivable part of Upper Meeker Hollow Rd. (N42° 16.898', W74° 37.860'). The road becomes a DEC right-of-way just past Stone Tavern Farm. The people who own the farm are cordial and run a summer music camp. Stop by, say hello, and allow them to show you where to park to keep from interfering with the camp operations. Stone Tavern Farm is also a B&B and its location makes it an excellent base for hiking in the area.

The road beyond the farm is drivable to a point, depending on the season, but it quickly becomes a rough woods road the farther you travel. The public right-of-way passes through private property, so stay on the road until it enters public property near the E and N sides of North Plattekill. As you near the height of land on the continuation of Upper Meeker Hollow Rd., the road starts curving W. There is a fork in the road. Unlike Yogi, you should "bear" left and the road will lead you up to the N peak of North Plattekill. You can enjoy the views along the way, and then continue with a woods road up to the next and highest summit. Expect the usual construction and repair common to ski area summits during the off-season. When done as a through-hike, with vehicles at the ends of both Upper and Lower Meeker Hollow roads, it's 4 mi and 1600 ft of ascent.

An interesting variation of this route is to ascend a sliver of public land that touches the woods road right-of-way ten minutes past Stone Tavern Farm. You can climb NE directly up Meeker Hollow Mt. (see description of this route on

Autumn brook near North Plattekill. Mark Schaefer

pages 142–143 in the Meeker Hollow section) and then walk a horseshoe-shaped route on DEC land from the summit of Meeker Hollow Mt. around and over North Plattekill.

Not to be overlooked is the opportunity to climb both North and South Plattekill mountains, a pair of Catskill 100 summits. This route begins from a DEC parking area (N42° 15.819', W74° 40.119') at 2050 ft, two-thirds of the way up Harold Roberts Rd., W of South Plattekill. This is one end of the Plattekill Turnpike, which climbs most of the way up South Plattekill (see section on South Plattekill, next page).

From the top of South Plattekill, follow the ridgeline N. After dropping about 400 ft to the South–North Plattekill col, you can either rejoin the Plattekill Turnpike or continue to bushwhack NW up the ridge towards North Plattekill. The turnpike follows the contour until just under the summit of North Plattekill, where you begin your 'whack 250+ ft S of the summit. This is an excellent way to hike, mountain bike, snowshoe, or ski one or both Plattekills, and you can even throw in Round Top for a triple. Although it travels just underneath the summits, bushwhacks from the turnpike are dense with blackberry canes and nettles in summertime, making this an ideal route in winter or early spring. This route is a 7 mi round-trip with 1800 ft ascent.

Although the ridge from South to North Plattekill appears a feasible route, there is some dense vegetation in places. The turnpike provides a nice break and gets you a good way N until the last 300 ft to North Plattekill. There are some logging paths between the turnpike and the summit, but many are overgrown with prickers.

A final route is via the turnpike near Round Top from the end of Mountain Brook Rd. (See page 135 in section on Round Top for access and beginning of the route.) From the N side of Round Top, the turnpike drops slightly then heads toward North Plattekill. You can follow the previous route from the turnpike to the summit.

The top of North Plattekill is very scenic, but it resembles the summit of many small ski areas in the off-season. There are ski trails and outbuildings along the ridge, as well as the top of one of the lifts. The views are great over the tops of the runs toward Meeker Hollow, Cowan, East Gray, Narrow Notch, SE Warren, White Man, and the Moresville Range peaks. Otherwise, there are limited views in the woods on the way to the summit.

Bring your binoculars for birds, animals, and long-range views, and don't forget the camera.

Wildlife is abundant in the Plattekill region. Barbara Via

South Plattekill Mt., 3260'

Hobart Quad

Catskill 67 Rank: 20
View: 3, Interest: 3, Difficulty: 3, Bushwhack: 3

HIGHLIGHTS AND SUMMARY: South Plattekill is one of three Plattekills on the Catskill 100 Highest list and is a bushwhack from any direction. It's located a few miles W of NY30 and 2 mi SE of the slightly taller North Plattekill. South Plattekill is shown on USGS topographic maps as Plattekill Mt. but called South Plattekill by Catskill 100 Highest hikers to differentiate it from its slightly more lofty northern sister. It can be climbed from many different directions, all of them on public property.

The Plattekill Turnpike is a great way to travel through the Plattekill State Forest. Whatever your mode of travel—bicycle, skis, snowshoes, or on foot—this high-elevation unpaved road gets you places quickly. In summer there are long sections of the turnpike without shade or water, so come prepared on hot, sunny days. While the views from the summit of South Plattekill are better when the leaves are off the trees, the views from the turnpike are excellent. The profusion of berry canes means lots of opportunities to observe wildlife and birds. The beech trees support a healthy population of deer, bears, and porcupines.

BEST TIME TO HIKE: Best and easiest time to hike the peak may be before or after the pricker season.

For the first route, drive to a small parking area (N42° 15.102', W74° 37.848') at 2600 ft, at the height of land on New Kingston Mountain Rd. The NW side of the road is DEP land and the bushwhack begins through a fairly dense deciduous forest. At 2900 ft, catch the small wedge of DEC land that abuts the DEP land to stay on public property. The DEC wedge widens as it encompasses South Plattekill's SE ridge. The bushwhack up the ridge is fairly easy hiking. You'll go over a small subsidiary bump and then climb the remaining 350 ft in another half mile to the summit. In places the trees and saplings grow close together so views from the bushwhack are scarce and sight navigation is difficult. The rule of up gets you to the wooded summit. Climbing South Plattekill from the parking area is about 3 mi round-trip and 1000 ft of ascent.

There is a small colony of summer and hunting camps along a dirt road that parallels the start of the route. If you happen to run into a property owner at the trailhead, you might just get lucky and be allowed to walk the road, gaining 400 ft of easier hiking and fantastic views from this private road.

Another route begins at a DEC parking area (N42° 15.819', W74° 40.119') two-thirds of the way up Harold Roberts Rd. The parking area sits on a small wedge of DEC land on one end of the Plattekill Turnpike. The turnpike, an unpaved access road, climbs to the col immediately N of South Plattekill. It has a moderate gradient as it is designed for vehicles. From the col, it's another 350 ft of ascent to the summit along South Plattekill's N ridge. As on the previous route,

Typical Catskill woods road and stone wall. Mark Schaefer

the deciduous forest gets a little tight from the col to the summit. The round-trip from the parking area is around 3.75 mi and 1400 ft ascent.

A third trek to South Plattekill combines the hike with North Plattekill. To double up, 'whack S off the top of North Plattekill. (For routes up North Plattekill, see previous section, page 124.) Although the forest is deciduous, there are sections of overgrown woods roads that meander along the ridge, in and out of biting pricker canes. There are screened views along the ridge.

Unless you opt for a winter hike, count on wearing long pants and sleeves. The top 300 ft of North Plattekill's S ridge has logging slash and prickers, best avoided on a hot summer day. The best time of year for this route is late autumn through early spring, when snow has covered the prickers or before they've grown new fangs in mid-May. Bushwhacking from North Plattekill, it's approximately 2 mi and almost 500 ft of climbing to reach South Plattekill.

South Plattekill can also be 'whacked from four different sections of DEP property located on Lower Meeker Hollow Rd.

Moresville Range NW Peak, 3240'   Roxbury Quad
Catskill 67 Rank: 22
View: 3, Interest: 3, Difficulty: 3, Bushwhack: 3

HIGHLIGHTS AND SUMMARY: The Moresville Range peaks (NW Peak 3240 ft and SW Peak 3040 ft) are two of the most northerly of the Catskill 100 summits. They are located almost midway between the villages of Hobart, Stamford, and Grand Gorge. Because the summits are not on public land, take the time to meet the landowners and obtain permission to hike. Stay away during the deer and turkey hunting seasons.

NW Moresville Range is covered by a beautiful deciduous forest and many types of birds and animals call the area home. The wind farm proposed for the ridgeline would impact bird migration, visuals, and wildlife throughout the area.

BEST TIME TO HIKE: Can be hiked any time of year, but the best views are when the leaves are off the trees.

NW Moresville has an easily located summit, situated on the NW end of a ridgeline running between both of the 3000 ft Catskill 100 peaks in this group. The 3160 ft peak in the middle of the range (N42° 22.001', W74° 33.513') does not have enough of an elevation change between summits to "count" as a Catskill 100. There are screened views along the ridge towards Irish, White Man, Narrow Notch, Old Clump, Churchill, Cowan, Meeker Hollow, Plattekill, and many other peaks. The views in winter along the ridge are even better, with some exceptional view points.

As on a number of other summits in Delaware County and elsewhere, there are areas where the pricker bushes can be annoying. Either put up with the scratches or hike in wintertime.

NW Moresville Range's population of deer and porcupine is evident from the chewed trees, rubs, scrapes, scat, and tracks. Don't be surprised if you spot an eagle overhead flying toward one of the reservoirs.

The Moresville Range ridgeline is under consideration for a wind farm. Should the project begin to move forward, access during the engineering and construction phases might be challenging. Access might be near impossible when the project is completed. Any 'whacks will be 3 to 4 mi in length and between 1200 ft and 1500 ft of ascent.

Narrow Notch Mt., 3220' Roxbury Quad
Catskill 67 Rank: 24
View: 4, Interest: 3, Difficulty: 3, Bushwhack: 3

HIGHLIGHTS AND SUMMARY: Narrow Notch Mt. is a bushwhack peak. It is named for the deep col immediately W of the summit at the height of land on Narrow Notch Rd. A drive up the road and through the skinny notch between the ridges of Cowan and Narrow Notch mountains shows that any other name would be inappropriate. Porcupines, deer, bears, and birdlife are abundant. If you like local history, or just connecting some of the names on local gravestones with local landmarks and peaks, the ancient Relay Rd. and Nesbitt cemeteries are worth a look around. Relay Rd. is an unpaved dirt road that gets a little rougher as you climb. A drive to the trailhead on a gorgeous day will have you slowing down to take in the scenery. Open meadows and the slopes of other peaks highlight the 500 ft drive up to the trailhead.
BEST TIME TO HIKE: Any time of year, except getting to the Relay Rd. trailheads in winter might be difficult.

The surest route for Narrow Notch is from Relay Rd. (also sometimes called Morse Rd.), which intersects Narrow Notch Rd. (N42° 19.179', W74° 38.646') S of the "notch." Be sure to take a few minutes to check out the Relay Cemetery at the road junction. Walking into an old graveyard in the mountains is a step back in time. Try to connect the gravestone names with local features and imagine the family histories. Midway up the road is the Nesbitt Cemetery, sited near what was probably an old farmstead high up on Relay Rd.

There are three DEC parking areas. One is located just inside the Relay State Forest boundary and the second another 0.5 mi farther. The final one is your destination, a large parking area located in the col (N42° 18.904', W74° 36.692') between Narrow Notch and East Gray Hill. There may be logging going on in the area.

From the parking area in the col, hike NE on a well-defined woods road that starts out gradually and then gets steeper over the next quarter mile. Just before you reach Narrow Notch's southern summit, there are two great view spots.

From these vantage points you can see a number of the Catskill 100 peaks, including the Plattekills, Old Clump, White Man, Cowan, Irish, Shultice, Round Top, and Southeast Warren. You also look at East Gray Hill, directly across the col where your car is parked.

Once past Narrow Notch's first summit, stay with the woods road as it hugs the ridgetop, checking map, compass, or GPS to avoid straying onto private property on the E and N sides of the ridge. There are intersecting woods roads so vigilance is important. At approximately 1.5 mi from the parking area, Narrow Notch's ridge takes a sharp dogleg W and starts to climb. To keep on public property, leave the woods road and sidehill NW at around 2960 ft until the gradual and short climb to the completely wooded summit. Keep to the western and southern sides of the summit to remain on DEC property.

There are some brambles along the ridge but the deciduous forest has little blowdown and the woods road keeps you mostly unscathed. Narrow Notch's ridge is a good spot to watch for birds and four-legged fauna of all sorts. In addition to a good chance you'll walk near a waddling porky, this is a hike to see deer or a bear. Although the summit is mostly viewless, there are screened views along the ridge and the two view spots at the southern end of the ridge are extraordinary. The round-trip from the Narrow Notch–East Gray Hill col is about 1100 ft ascent and just under 4 mi.

You can also ascend Narrow Notch from where the Relay State Forest borders East Highland Rd., between 2300 ft to 2400 ft. There is DEC land bordering the road (N42° 19.845', W74° 37.880') and a bushwhack from this side is a short hike. It's just under a mile and a little over 900 ft to the summit. You may intersect some woods roads, but they don't lead you to the top. The lower section of the hike passes through overgrown pastures with an easy grade for the first 300 ft. The next 350 ft is steeper, then the slope eases off as you near the top.

You can also combine Narrow Notch with a hike up East Gray, starting at the Relay State Forest parking area. See the section on East Gray, page 140.

Utsayantha Mt., 3214' *Stamford Quad*
Catskill 67 Rank: 27
View: 5, Interest: 4, Difficulty: 1

HIGHLIGHTS AND SUMMARY: Utsayantha is the northernmost of the Catskill 100 summits and its NW ridge towers over the village of Stamford. There is an unpaved road and a short trail to the summit. The mountain used to be privately owned but the summit was donated to the village of Stamford by a local philanthropist. In 2003, the village decided to develop the summit into a tourist attraction and fix the deteriorating summit structures and fire tower. The summit now has a restored fire tower, a cell tower, and another building with a deck and picnic tables. In 2011, the building was in the process of being renovated; it was once a gift shop for Stamford

hotel guests ascending the mountain by horse and buggy. The summit has three hang-gliding platforms maintained by the Utsayantha Flyers Organization (UFO). The local volunteer fire department sometimes has to rescue flyers who get tangled up or injured.

The views from the tower and the historical information at the summit kiosk add up to a great day. You won't have a wilderness experience, but the mountain is an excellent vantage point for photography and birding and the short hike leaves lots of extra time for other activities. Bring a good map and see how many named mountains you can see on a clear day. Utsayantha sits on a ridge that extends over McGregor Mt. to the southern end of the Moresville Range. You'll understand why the proposal for wind towers on the Moresville Range is controversial when standing on Utsayantha.

BEST TIME TO HIKE: Best time to hike is autumn, but any season will do.

The trailhead to Utsayantha is reached by turning S off of NY23 (Main St.) in Stamford onto Mountain Rd. (N42° 24.458', W74° 36.626'). Mountain Rd. turns into Tower Mountain Rd. as it climbs 600 ft out of Stamford to a parking area at 2500 ft in the Utsayantha–Churchill Mt. col (N42° 23.581', W74° 35.960'). In the winter, the town plows the rough road up to a snowplow turnaround farther up the mountain. I wouldn't recommend trying to drive the summit road past the col or snowplow turnaround; it gets steeper and in wet, snowy, or icy conditions can be treacherous. Even on a perfect day, leave your car in the col and enjoy the 0.85 mi, 700 ft climb to the summit. You can either walk the unpaved road to

View from Utsayantha Mt. tower. Tony Versandi

the top, or look for a lightly marked trail on the left side of the road 300 ft below the top.

Except in winter or bad weather, don't expect to have the mountain to yourself, as locals and tourists often come to enjoy the exceptional views and summer breeze. The tower affords a 360 degree view, and on a clear day you can see a large swath of the Catskill Mountains to the S and SW. Local hiker Jim Bouton reports that he has seen the Adirondacks from here. If climbing the tower stairs makes you queasy, the views from the hang-gliding platforms are a good substitute.

For many years hikers used a trail that originated on private land near the village and climbed 1300 ft up the mountain's NW ridge. A change in ownership has affected access and the current owner does not want the trail described. This could change in the future, but for now the route is closed.

Cowan Mt., 3100' Hobart Quad
Catskill 67 Rank: 42
View: 2, Interest: 1, Difficulty: 2, Bushwhack: 2

HIGHLIGHTS AND SUMMARY: Cowan Mt. is located a few miles SSE of Hobart. All routes are bushwhacks and the peak is entirely on private property. The USGS has mislabeled the summit's location, placing "Cowan Mt." on its 3080 ft NE sub-summit. The actual top is 0.45 mi SW and a 20 ft contour line higher. The summit of Cowan is wooded and largely viewless, but when the leaves are off the trees you'll catch glimpses of Old Clump, Narrow Notch, East Gray, Southeast Warren, Churchill, and Utsayantha mountains. Large areas of Cowan Mt. are undergoing transition for logging, second-home development, or both. Logging activity is always ugly for the first couple of years, with stumps, skidder paths, and associated disturbances. At the same time, hikers are guests.
BEST TIME TO HIKE: You can climb Cowan any time of year, but the best time would be from late autumn through early spring.

As in much of the northeastern and western Catskills, old farms in this region are disappearing and the overgrown fields and woodlands are being sold for second-home development. While New York City's DEP is often vilified for what is perceived by some as land confiscation, that aggressive agency is unquestionably preserving the mountains, forests, and streams for future generations, as well as protecting the Catskill watershed.

The woods on this mountain are all deciduous and there is an extensive series of woods roads, including one over the summit. The top 100 ft of Cowan has large areas of tall, aggressive blackberry canes. Armor up during the warm-weather months. Also keep your eyes open for one of the many porcupines that live here. My dog, Bookah, "made friends" with a baby porcupine on the summit.

There is a private home development on the northern side of the mountain and many camps on the roads that ring the S and SE side of the peak. It would be prudent to avoid asking for permission to hike near the hunting season.

Depending on the direction, bushwhacks can be anywhere from 800 to 1500 ft of ascent and 2 to 4 mi round-trip. The best time to hike is mid-December through early springtime.

Churchill Mt., 3060' Stamford Quad
Catskill 67 Rank: 50
View: 2, Interest: 1, Difficulty: 2, Bushwhack: 2

HIGHLIGHTS AND SUMMARY: Churchill is best known as the peak just across the road from Utsayantha Mt. Located on the opposite side of Tower Mountain Rd., S of Stamford, Churchill Mt. is on private property and is a bushwhack from any direction. With permission from the landowner, it's a short, easy hike. You can climb it on the same day you climb Utsayantha. Summit views are lacking, and the blowdown and prickers make this a peak-bagger's mountain.

BEST TIME TO HIKE: Although this is a short hike, easily climbed any time of year, for a good, close-up view of Utsayantha the best time to hike is when the leaves are off the trees.

Although Churchill is conifer-free, its woods have broken branches and storm blowdown, and there is a significant amount of prickers to deal with on any 'whack to the completely wooded summit. When the leaves are off the trees, any views are mostly dominated by Utsayantha. Although there is no clear, discernable summit, a "stroll" through the prickers around the top will convince you that you have undoubtedly been over it. Only a sense of exploration or peak-bagging zeal would motivate most to climb this scratchy, viewless peak.

Almost any route would be 2 to 4 mi round-trip and 1300 ft or less of ascent.

Round Top, 3060' Hobart Quad
Catskill 67 Rank: 52
View: 3, Interest: 3, Difficulty: 1, Bushwhack: 1

HIGHLIGHTS AND SUMMARY: This is one of three Roundtops (or, in this case, Round Tops) on the Catskill 100 list. It's a short and easy bushwhack with a road to just below its summit. The peak can be climbed by itself or in combination with the Plattekills. Unfortunately, there is a new, illegal ATV path to the summit. A friend and I removed a couple of gallon bags of orange flagging. The DEC ranger investigated, and although they tried to apprehend the ATV users who established the path, they were not successful, largely because of the amount of illegal ATV use and shortage of DEC

Map 8 Northwest Peaks 135

enforcement personnel.
BEST TIME TO HIKE: This is a nice hike anytime, but winter access means a longer walk to the trailhead.

To locate the trailhead, look for Bovina, a tiny crossroads in rural Delaware County located SSW of Hobart. Mountain Brook Rd. (N42° 16.065', W74° 43.569') is an unpaved road leading right out of "downtown" Bovina. The road narrows as it climbs past posted land and hunting camps situated close to the road on both sides. As the road ascends Round Top's SW flank, it gets much steeper. It passes onto DEC land just before ending in a large DEC parking area (N42° 15.951', W74° 41.086') in a col between Round Top and 2900 ft Burnt Hill. In dry weather, hikers should have no problem driving to the parking area. Look for a red metal gate just beyond the parking area, with a DEC sign stating that the road beyond is closed to any motorized traffic except snowmobiles. At 2660+ ft, this is one of the highest trailheads in the Catskills.

This is one end of the Plattekill Turnpike, an unpaved road that passes 300 ft below the summit of Round Top. (See section on South Plattekill, earlier in this chapter, for additional details on the turnpike.)

Walk up the dirt road beyond the gate, climb 300+ ft along Round Top's western flank and turn E as you come around and onto Round Top's northern ridge. The turnpike levels out here. Look on your right (SE) for what was previously a faint herd path and is now the ATV track that ascends Round Top's NW ridge.

Bookah breaking trail for Tom near summit. Alan Via

Following this, the "bushwhack" up the ridge to Round Top's wooded summit is short and easy and passes through a beech, maple, and cherry forest with a few prickers. Unfortunately, the ATV path, located on Plattekill State Forest land, did away with the bushwhack, killing the fun of route-finding and sense of discovery for everyone not sitting on an ATV.

The woods in the area are filled with rabbit, porcupine, deer, and coyote sign. In springtime you are serenaded by warblers and other courting birds. From the gate to the summit, you climb a little over 450 ft in a round-trip of about 1.75 mi.

Round Top can also be climbed up its southern ridge, but it's a little steeper and you won't have a dirt road taking you most of the way. You also won't have to slog over an ATV path. Near the same parking area (described above), look NE through a small stand of conifers. There is an old pasture worth exploring for its excellent views of distant peaks and nearby Burnt Hill. This is the way to go if you're 'whacking Round Top's southern ridge—walk through the old pasture and just head uphill to the top.

On the summit, views are scarce, but you can see Round Top's two Catskill 100 Highest neighbors in early spring or winter.

There are other routes to Round Top from other directions, but all cross private property. See the sections on North and South Plattekill for information on routes to those peaks, which could be combined with Round Top via the Plattekill Turnpike.

Moresville Range SW Peak, 3040' Roxbury Quad
Catskill 67 Rank: 55
View: 3, Interest: 3, Difficulty: 3, Bushwhack: 3

HIGHLIGHTS AND SUMMARY: The Moresville Range peaks (NW Peak 3240 ft and SW Peak 3040 ft) are two of the most northerly of the Catskill 100 summits. They are located almost midway between the villages of Hobart, Stamford, and Grand Gorge. Only Utsayantha and Churchill are farther N. At 3040 ft, SW Moresville Range is 200 ft shorter than its northern brother and untrailed. The peak is on private property and permission is required to bushwhack from any direction.

BEST TIME TO HIKE: The best time to hike is any time of year.

Please see additional information on the mountain's location in the section on Moresville Range NW Peak earlier in this chapter.

Although the NW Moresville Range summit is noted on the USGS topographic maps as "Moresville Range," the SW Moresville Range's summit is not. Take note that the 3160 ft sub-summit (N42° 22.001', W74° 33.513') located between the NW and SW peaks is not a Catskill 100 mountain. It does not rise enough from the connecting col to qualify. The summit of SW Moresville Range is the next peak SSE of it. This can be confusing and is best understood by looking at a map.

The peak has woods roads all over it, and although there are few summertime views from the deciduous summit of SW Moresville Range, the views from the col immediately to the N are extraordinary. Deer, bears, porcupines, and other wildlife call the range home.

Any of the bushwhacks to the summit are likely to be 3 to 4 mi round-trip and 1100 ft to 1400 ft ascent. Because the summits are on private property, spend time getting acquainted with the property owners and avoid the deer and turkey hunting seasons. If the wind farm proposed for the Moresville Range is approved, future access will be difficult.

Southeast Warren, 3020'   Hobart Quad
Catskill 67 Rank: 59
View: 2, Interest: 2, Difficulty: 3, Bushwhack: 3

HIGHLIGHTS AND SUMMARY: SE Warren is a private-property peak, a nice hike for birders and nature observers, and, like many other Catskill summits, home to porcupines, deer, and bear. A short hike with woods roads, this is a peakbagger's mountain. Guests at Highlanders View Bed and Breakfast, located less than 1000 ft below the summit, can obtain permission to climb the peak. Ski Plattekill is next door, and there are more than a dozen other Catskill 100 summits just minutes away.

BEST TIME TO HIKE: With a lack of views and abundance of prickers, SE Warren would be best in winter or early spring.

Southeast Warren woods road. Alan Via

Southeast Warren is located in Delaware County, about 3 mi S of Hobart, and is entirely private property. Be sure to review maps before planning a hike here as the original USGS map has mislabeled the highest summit in the range. They placed the name of Mount Warren on the mountain's NW peak, which is 140 ft lower. This little bit of cartographic homework will keep you from climbing the wrong peak.

The simplest way to access this mountain is to make reservations or stop by in person at Highlanders View Bed and Breakfast (N42° 18.001', W74° 40.825'), a charming and friendly inn located near the end of the picturesque Crescent Valley Rd. The owners are cordial and the B&B couldn't be in a nicer setting, making it a great place to spend a weekend—plus, their guests can hike the mountain.

Drive N of Bovina on Bovina Rd., past a couple of side roads, and turn right onto Crescent Valley Rd. (N42° 17.030', W74° 42.511'). Continue until you see the Highlanders View B&B sign. From near the Highlanders' driveway, walk along a woods road that passes an old dwelling as it heads uphill. The road climbs steadily and passes old stone fences on its way through hardwoods.

As you climb toward the summit ridge, the road nears a stream gully that might tempt you to strike NE for the summit. By staying with the woods road to the ridgeline, you avoid extensive areas of prickers and nettles that call the SSE slope of the mountain home. In some areas the brambles are merely chest high, but closer to the ridgeline you may have to decide whether to confront 6 ft pricker canes or take your chances with dense nettle gardens. Stay on the woods road and avoid the worst of it! At the ridge, follow an old path that heads NW 250 ft toward the nearly flat summit. The summit rises higher toward its western edge.

Take your revenge on the prickers and climb SE Warren when 3 ft of snow has them buried, though in the winter, the plateau is a heavily used snowmobile trail. It's about a 2 mi round-trip from Crescent Valley Rd. near the Highlanders View sign and under 1000 ft ascent.

Old Clump, 3000'   Roxbury Quad
Catskill 67 Rank: 62
View: 2–4, Interest: 3, Difficulty: 3, Bushwhack: 3

HIGHLIGHTS AND SUMMARY: This is one of the best names for a mountain anywhere. It's a bushwhack, and the summit is private property. Catskill Mountains historian Mark Schaefer suggests the name "Old Clump" might date back to 1795, when naturalist John Burroughs' paternal grandparents settled on the slopes of the mountain. The people of Roxbury attempted to rename the peak Burroughs Mt. after John Burroughs, who grew up and lived near Roxbury for many years. No visit to the area is complete without stopping by Woodchuck Lodge (N42° 17.643', W74° 35.187') to view the plaque on Boyhood Rock and Burroughs' grave site, located on Burroughs

Memorial Rd. The trip is well worth the time, and it's a place to reflect on what his writings did to protect these mountains for further generations.
BEST TIME TO HIKE: To avoid the pricker-laden top portion of the peak, hike during winter or early spring.

Wildlife abounds and the peak is at its showiest best during autumn or in spring, when the early wildflowers are blooming and before the blackberry canes develop their annual bite. Old Clump is another Delaware County peak that is misplaced on USGS map quads. In this case, the cartographers didn't just mislabel the high point, they hung the name on a 2920 ft bump located 2.5 mi W, with a Catskill 100 summit, East Gray, in between. The erroneously named Old Clump is the summit directly E of the intersection of Narrow Notch and Roses Brook roads. The correct Old Clump is 1 mi N of the Burroughs Monument on Burroughs Memorial Rd. (N42° 18.174', W74° 33.280'), approximately 2 mi W of Hubbell Corners. You wouldn't be the first to climb the "wrong" Old Clump.

The good news is that you now know where this elusive mountain is located. The bad news is that the summit and most of the mountain is on private property. Hikers satisfied with hiking to just below the summit can stay on DEP land to almost 2700 ft on Old Clump's W side.

To reach the trailhead, drive NE out of West Settlement (N42° 17.288', W74° 36.865') onto Andrew Gray Rd. through a checkerboard of DEP land. A gate across the road with posted signs marks a short rectangle of private property that blocks hundreds of acres of DEP land 0.2 mi beyond on the remnants of Andrew Gray Rd.

Park your car without blocking the gate and walk W onto DEP land. As you near a small tributary of Roses Brook and a stone wall, keep on the DEP side of the private property signs. Circle around the private property to rejoin Andrew Gray Rd. on DEP land. As the road starts a gradual turn NW, start your bushwhack on the right. Hike uphill towards Old Clump, enjoying the woods right up to the private property boundary beginning about 300 ft below the summit. The woods are deciduous, with a forest of pricker canes the higher you climb.

A second route begins at the DEC parking area (N42° 18.904', W74° 36.692') located at the end of Relay Rd. (See page 130 in Narrow Notch section for details.) There may be signs of recent logging activity here. Head NE out of the parking area as if you were climbing Narrow Notch Mt. After about 0.25 mi and 250 ft of climbing, look for an old woods road on your right, heading E. There is a great place for views and photos nearby. Take this road E for approximately 0.6 mi.

In the col between the southern end of Narrow Notch Mt. and Old Clump, turn S at an intersection of woods roads, climbing towards Old Clump's northern ridge. At this point, leave the woods road and sidehill S, keeping W and downhill of the private property boundary. As with the previous route, this pathway is for those who are content getting most of—but not all—the way to the summit. As with the other route, you'll have your hands full fending off prickers and can only proceed to the summit with prior permission from the landowners.

While I love Old Clump's name, the views are not spectacular except from the shoulder of Narrow Notch.

If you hike when snow is on the ground, the prickers are less likely to bite and the bushwhacking becomes generally easier. Old Clump and its surroundings are home to deer, bears, coyotes, and porcupines. Travel quietly for a chance to see or photograph the four-legged inhabitants. Any route to the peak will be 4 mi or less and under 1200 ft ascent.

East Gray Hill, 2980' Roxbury Quad
Catskill 67 Rank: 65
View: 3, Interest: 2, Difficulty: 2, Bushwhack: 2

HIGHLIGHTS AND SUMMARY: East Gray Hill is a very short hike on an old woods road that is technically a bushwhack. Birds and other wildlife abound, and it's a great place to encounter bears during the berry season. Be sure to check out the Relay Rd. and Nesbitt family cemeteries on the way to the trailhead.

BEST TIME TO HIKE: The hike to this peak is definitely most enjoyable in late autumn, winter, or early spring, when prickers are still napping.

The best way to climb East Gray Hill is from Relay Rd. (sometimes called Morse Rd.). A landmark for the turn off Narrow Notch Rd. is the beautiful Relay Cemetery (N42° 19.179', W74° 38.646'). See page 130 in the Narrow Notch section for information on how to get to Relay Rd. and the parking area.

From the DEC parking area in the East Gray Hill–Narrow Notch Mt. col (N42° 18.904', W74° 36.692'), walk SW about 100 yd on a woods road towards the base of East Gray's NE ridge. The road might be muddy or overgrown, depending on the amount of logging taking place. Where the woods road turns away from the ridge, hike across a grown-over area and pick up East Gray's NE ridge. In summertime, the very overgrown woods road is choked with blackberry canes and other summer "trip-ery." One Catskill 100 Highest completer describes it as a "pricker bush farm." From late autumn until mid-spring, when the vegetation is buried or gone, it's much more congenial to hike and easier to follow. Regardless of season, the woods road gets fainter and fainter as it gets higher, until it fades out. At any point, apply the rule of up and simply pick the best way up the NE ridge.

In summertime, where the woods road peters out, the raspberry prickers get jealous and join the blackberry canes. Although it is only 0.5 mi and just under 400 ft from the parking area to the summit, the last quarter mile in midsummer can be a nightmare if you don't pick your way carefully. Adding to your navigational pleasure is enough calf- to knee-high hidden blowdown to satisfy the most diehard bushwhacker. The mileage and ascent aren't the challenge of climbing East Gray from this direction; it's finding a route with the least blowdown and brambles. If you stay to the N side of the ridge crest as you near the summit, the prickers are less ominous.

East Gray's summit is wooded, but there are great views when the leaves are off the trees and many of the Catskill 3500 and Catskill 100 peaks are visible in the distance.

A second and longer 'whack begins from the S. To reach the trailhead, drive NE out of West Settlement (N42° 17.288', W74° 36.865') onto Andrew Gray Rd. through a checkerboard of DEP land. A gate across the road with posted signs marks a short rectangle of private property blocking hundreds of acres of DEP land 0.2 mi beyond on the remnants of Andrew Gray Rd.

Park your car without blocking the gate and walk W on DEP land. As you near a small tributary of Roses Brook and a stone wall, keep on the DEP side of private property. When the private property ends, you have two choices. You can either circle back E to rejoin Andrew Gray Rd. where it continues on public land and follow it up to the East Gray–Narrow Notch col, climbing the peak by the previous route. Or you can continue your bushwhack by climbing East Gray's SSE ridge, the most direct way to the top. The lower part of the ridge is a hike through overgrown fields, with steeper terrain midway up.

Sounds like fun, right? In warm weather, the southern, open woods of East Gray present waist-level prickers. Their density, height, and ferocity increase as you gain elevation. The SSE ridge is shorter, and may be preferable from winter through

Nesbitt Cemetery. Alan Via

early spring when you'll miss much of the excitement and subsequent storytelling. Whichever option you select, the summit is just over 1 mi away with 1050 ft of ascent.

East Gray is a short hike from the Relay Rd. trailhead and a little longer coming from the S.

Meeker Hollow Mt., 2980' — Hobart Quad
(Kenyon Mt.)
Catskill 67 Rank: 66
View: 2–3, Interest: 3, Difficulty: 2, Bushwhack: 2

HIGHLIGHTS AND SUMMARY: Meeker Hollow Mt. is known by locals as Kenyon Mt., after the Kenyon family who resided in the West Settlement and Meeker Hollow areas in the mid-1800s and earlier. This small gem is situated in a picturesque setting. I see deer running around every time I visit. Beautiful stone fences lace the mountain, as do some woods roads. Hike on a nice spring morning and enjoy the background music of birds while gazing at wildflowers on the forest floor. Hikers can enjoy the hospitality of the Stone Tavern Farm B&B, or go horseback riding after a hike. Take your pick of different routes.

BEST TIME TO HIKE: An enjoyable hike anytime of year. Spring wildflowers and birds, summer ferns and greenery, autumn leaves, or the stark woods of winter.

For the most direct route, drive CR41 to the intersection of Upper and Lower Meeker Hollow roads (N42° 15.490', W74° 36.376') and then follow scenic Upper Meeker Hollow Rd. to the Stone Tavern Farm. Although it's a public road to the farm and DEC right-of-way beyond, stop to say hello. I met the owners the first time I hiked there, discovered the best place to leave my car, and received information on the mountain.

Stone Tavern Farm is a bed and breakfast, as well as a summer camp and nice place to stay when hiking the Delaware County peaks. Although you can drive the unpaved road beyond the farm, it's simply not advisable. There are small cabins alongside the road so be certain you don't block the road or cabin driveways.

The road quickly deteriorates beyond the cabins, getting rougher as it climbs. There are tall hardwoods shading the road, a stand of stately conifers on your right, and picturesque old stone fences. When you reach DEC markers and yellow blazes near 2400 ft, start your bushwhack NE into the woods for the remaining 600 ft to the top. The forest is predominantly beech, but there are beautiful birches, as well as large cherries and oaks. Some blackberry bushes mix with easily climbed rock bands on this side of the mountain, but this is otherwise an easy 'whack. When reaching the summit ridge, it's a good idea to walk around as Meeker has a "your call" high point.

When leaves are on the trees, the scenery from the wooded summit is limited, but early winter into spring provides constant views from the upper half of the mountain. Dominating the view is a close-up of North Plattekill across the valley. You can also see White Man, Irish, Shultice, South Plattekill, East Gray, Old Clump, and other peaks.

Be alert for porcupines. I'm amazed at the number of beech trees the porkies have stripped of their bark. The quiet hiker has a good chance to see some of the large deer population. From the car, it's a little under 3 mi round-trip and just under 1000 ft of easy climbing to the summit.

If you ask the Stone Tavern Farm owners, you may get directions to a lightly marked private trail just past the conifers. This trail gains elevation quickly. If you run out of markers, follow the rule of up on your way to the summit.

For another variation of the above route, hike Upper Meeker Hollow Rd. to about 2800 ft. Where the road turns W towards Plattekill Mt., 'whack N a short distance, skirt Meeker Hollow's NW summit on its W then N side, then follow the ridge SE to the summit.

A favorite route begins on Roxbury Mountain Rd. (called Roses Brook Rd. and West Settlement Rd. at different locations) at the northern edge of DEP property (N42° 17.848', W74° 37.758') on the NE side of the mountain. There is an old woods road here whose camouflaged beginning hides a beautiful 0.5 mi walk through a mixed hardwood forest decorated with beautiful old stone fences. Walk the woods road to a metal gate that marks the beginning of private land and pasture near 2150 ft. Remember this location in case you decide to return the same way. At the gate, begin your bushwhack by hiking SW through hardwoods until you get onto Meeker Hollow's SE ridge. The gradient is moderate and the 'whacking easy, until the last 300 ft of nearly continuous blackberry prickers. The angle of the slope gets easier the higher you climb. Keep climbing up and over the wooded summit to the northernmost part of the last contour.

You can return the same way down the ridge to the gate and walk the woods road to your car, or continue E at the gate on DEP land, hiking through a delightful deciduous woods along a stone fence and pasture. You'll reach an overgrown field, hop a narrow stream, and reach the road below where you left your car earlier in the day. The round-trip is about 2.5 mi and just under 1000 ft ascent.

Or consider a through-hike, a nice Catskill 100 sampler, by leaving a car at the Meeker Hollow trailhead, going up one side of the peak, and down the other.

Melissa, frog wrangler, Meeker Hollow Mt. Alan Via

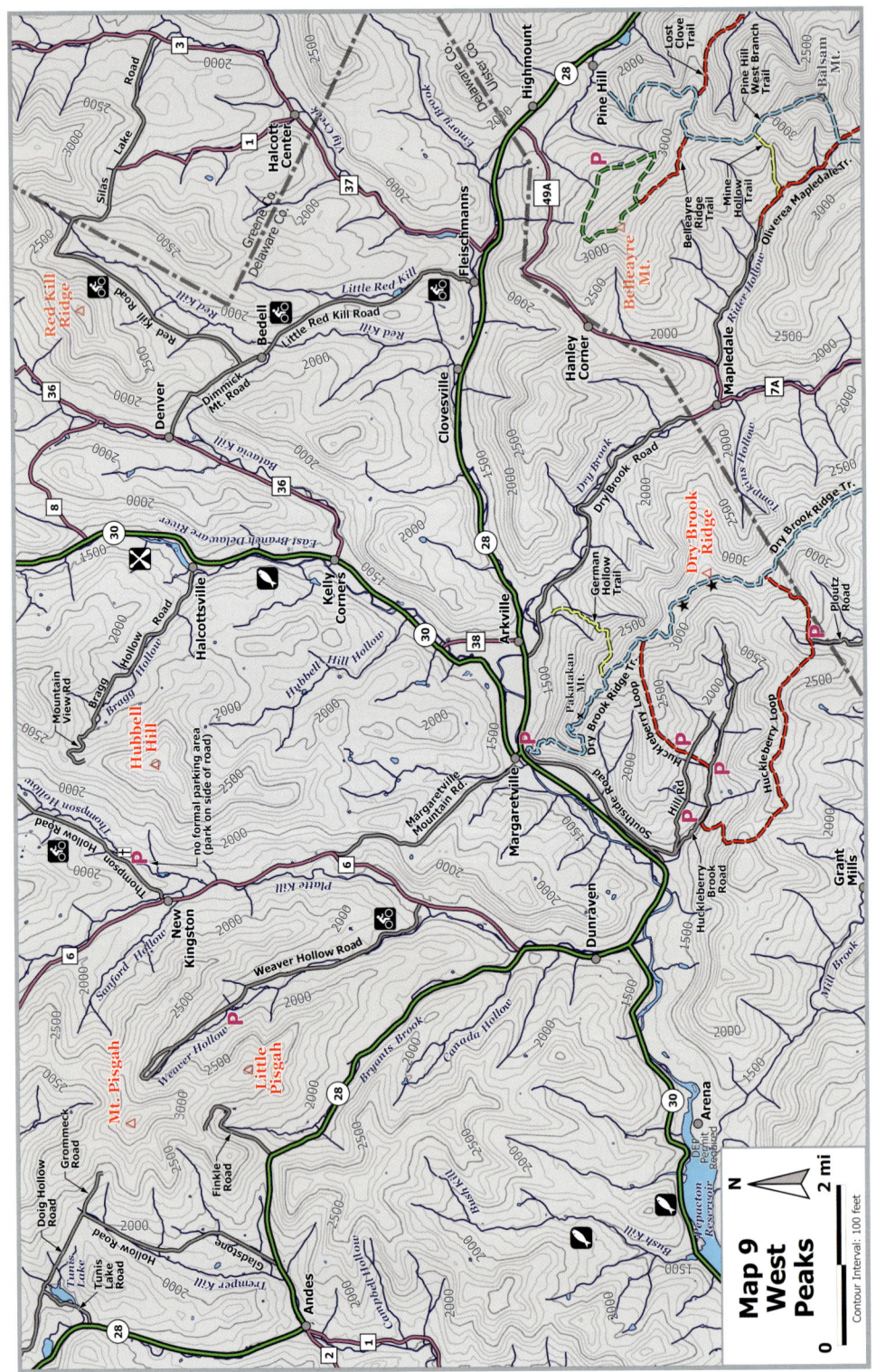

West Peaks

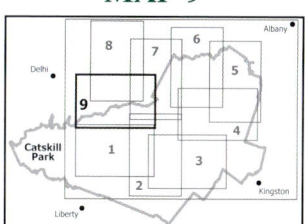

MAP 9

Dry Brook Ridge
Mt. Pisgah
Little Pisgah
Hubbell Hill

One of the four peaks in this region is trailed, another is a closed ski area, and the remaining two are bushwhacks. Only Mt. Pisgah, the site of the former Bobcat Ski Center, is on private property. The mountains consist mostly of deciduous forests with fields or overgrown meadows at their bases. There are excellent views from Dry Brook Ridge and Mt. Pisgah, and beautiful fern glades and grown-over fields on parts of Hubbell Hill. There is easy road access for all peaks. As on other mountains in the area, you have to put up with a few sections of pricker bushes near the summits, except on Dry Brook Ridge.

Fishermen have the Pepacton Reservoir (DEP permit required), various branches of the Delaware River, and many, many smaller streams to sample. Paddlers have the Delaware River. Mountain bikers can pedal the Plattekill Turnpike and Catskill Scenic Trail. Throughout the region, hundreds of miles of roads await both road and mountain bikers. Weaver Hollow, Thompson Hollow, New Kingston, Upper and Lower Meeker Hollow, Roses Brook, and Roxbury Mountain roads will be cycling favorites.

Old Man of the Forest, Little Pisgah. Alan Via

Dry Brook Ridge, 3460'
Seager Quad
Catskill 67 Rank: 2
View: 4, Interest: 3, Difficulty: 2, Bushwhack: 2

HIGHLIGHTS AND SUMMARY: The mountain misses the magic 3500 ft elevation by a mere 40 ft. The trail over its summit ridge misses the highest point and the peak has bushwhack options. The Huckleberry Loop trails are scenic, and the peak offers options for shorter day hikes. The Dry Brook Ridge Trail is the longest but best tour of the mountain. Dr. Mike Kudish, Professor Emeritus, botanist, and forestry expert, says there are bogs along the ridge. One has peat 700 years old, the other has peat approaching 3700 years. Other trail guides provide more extensive trail descriptions.
BEST TIME TO HIKE: The best time to hike is any time of year, but the mountain is spectacular in autumn and during wildflower season.

There are numerous ways to climb the second highest Catskill 67 peak. One is to park on Southside Rd. (N42° 08.572', W74° 38.962') across the Delaware River from Margaretville, and take the blue-marked Dry Brook Ridge Trail. The Dry Brook Ridge Trail passes through a mix of hardwood and conifer forest.

The trail climbs steeply for the first 500 ft, levels off, then resumes its climb, switchbacking for another 500 ft to the summit of Pakatakan Mt. Along the way watch for remnants of a bluestone quarry, and sections of oaks, cherries, and maples. After another flat stretch, the trail climbs gradually up Dry Brook Ridge's NNW ridge. This trail intersects two others, one from German Hollow and the other the Huckleberry Loop Trail.

Near 3200 ft, look to your right (W) for a short unmarked path leading to great views of Barkaboom Mt., Mill Brook Ridge, and other peaks. After soaking up the views, continue along the wooded summit ridge, passing another W facing view spot that looks out over a steep drop-off. The marked trail does not pass over the true summit, which is a two-minute bushwhack E. As on a few of its trailed Catskill 100 brethren, such as St. Anne's, Giant Ledge, and others, you can consider the trail's high point to be your summit, or you can step off-trail to the "actual" high(est) spot. As anyone who has hiked with me will attest, my reputation for

Fern glades on Dry Brook Ridge. Joanne Hihn

being hardheaded about locating the actual highest point is well deserved.

Another trail to Dry Brook Ridge begins at the end of Ploutz Rd. (N42° 05.640', W74° 37.217'). The trail gradually ascends Dry Brook Ridge's SW and then southern ridges, gaining a little over 1200 ft on a round-trip of 3.5 mi. It intersects the Ridge Trail a bit over 1.25 mi from the summit, near its 3440 ft sub-peak. Early in the hike you'll see old stone walls, open hardwood forest, and ferns in season. The trail switchbacks and gently ascends to the summit ridge. Although the woods are less open as you near the ridge, there is plenty to look at as you hike.

The Hill Rd. (N42° 07.059', W74° 39.049') parking area is at the other end of the Huckleberry Loop Trail and is located at 1900 ft. You can hike NE to intersect the Ridge Trail NW of the summit.

With open and inviting woods, Dry Brook Rd. offers some bushwhacking opportunities. Most require permission from property owners to reach public land.

Mt. Pisgah, 3345'
Catskill 67 Rank: 16
View: 5, Interest: 3, Difficulty: 2, Bushwhack: 2–4

Margaretville Quad

HIGHLIGHTS AND SUMMARY: The mountain is not on public land and the best route has always been from the now closed Bobcat Ski Center. According to a Delaware County history and genealogy website, the peak received its name from a stagecoach traveler who was being jolted around on a wilderness road. Spying the tall peak, he was apparently reminded that "they, like the children of Israel, were wanderers in the wilderness and often in view of the mount, it should be called Pisgah." The mountain puts on a gorgeous display of wildflowers in the springtime and deer, coyotes, bears, and birdlife abound.

BEST TIME TO HIKE: The best time to hike this peak is in the warmer weather months, but winter climbs are possible.

The most direct way to hike the peak is from the former Bobcat Ski Center (N42° 13.646', W74° 44.886'), which is located between Andes and Margaretville. Driving N on NY28 from Margaretville, turn onto Gladstone Hollow Rd. (N42° 11.646', W74° 46.238') just E of Andes. Then turn right onto Grommeck Rd.

The ski area has been closed since about 2000, so be sure to ask permission before you hike. Routes to the summit are walks uphill on ski trails of various distances and gradients. Since the parking area is located at an elevation of approximately 2400 ft, it is just under 1000 ft of ascent to the summit and,

Trout lillies. Joanne Hihn

depending on the directness of your route, between 2 and 3 mi round-trip. The top of Mt. Pisgah is wooded, but there are fantastic views of the surrounding valleys, hills, and mountains of scenic Delaware County. After enjoying the views from the top of the ski runs, simply retrace your steps or descend on the access road back to your vehicle.

With permission from landowners, there are also routes from Weaver Hollow Rd. or from the S (see the section below, on Little Pisgah).

View from Mt. Pisgah. Joanne Hihn

Little Pisgah, 3020'

Margaretville Quad

Catskill 67 Rank: 58
View: 3, Interest: 3, Difficulty: 3, Bushwhack: 2

HIGHLIGHTS AND SUMMARY: Little Pisgah is a small bushwhack peak NE of Margaretville and immediately S of Mt. Pisgah (see previous section). The mountain is a short bushwhack with one public property route from its NE side. The woods are deciduous and a little rocky in places and if you don't see a porcupine while you're hiking, you'll certainly notice the white branches of the beeches whose bark they've stripped. What I most enjoy about this hike is the extraordinary display of Dutchman's-breeches, trout lilies, trillium, spring beauties, and other wildflowers, accompanied by bird serenades in springtime. Old stone fences mark the edges of meadows in the lower part of the route and it's a pleasure to walk through the former pastures and look back at the views of the surrounding peaks and valley. Bring your mountain bike for some excellent but hilly riding along Weaver Hollow Rd.

BEST TIME TO HIKE: You can hike this peak any time, but avoid the hunting season.

The best route and the only one on public property is from the DEP parking area (N42° 12.349', W74° 42.639') on Weaver Hollow Rd. To find the trailhead from Margaretville, drive NW on Margaretville Mountain Rd. until making a sharp left turn onto CR6. Proceed S on CR6 and then turn right onto Weaver Hollow Rd. The drive to the DEP parking area on Weaver Hollow Rd. is a jewel, one of the most scenic in the Catskills, with open meadows, old farms, and long-distance views down the valleys. The DEP parking area is on the left side of Weaver Hollow Rd. at 1900 ft and is used by hunters and fishermen. If possible, leave the peak for sportsmen to enjoy during the hunting seasons.

The bushwhack to Little Pisgah begins anywhere along Weaver Hollow Rd. near the parking area. Pass through beautiful meadows on the lower part of the

Hubbell Hill ferns. Alan Via

mountain and jump a small stream that's easy to cross if there hasn't been snowmelt or recent periods of heavy rain. After a couple of hundred feet of elevation gain, the fields give way to small hardwoods. Look over your shoulder to enjoy the gorgeous scenery and the beautiful stone fences in these lower woods. Old woods roads crisscross the area, and with a combination of luck and good judgment, these will gain you some elevation.

At about 2400 ft the gradient of the bushwhack gets steeper for the next 300 ft, but it lessens the last 0.3 mi to the summit. There are some wooded ledges midway up and just below the top, but nothing to be concerned about. The woods are deciduous; beeches and maples predominate. With such a short bushwhack, you're on Little Pisgah's wooded summit in no time. Your arrival will be fairly uneventful owing to a lack of views in summer. You'll celebrate it nonetheless, having passed through areas of prickers and blowdown in the last 200 ft of climbing. For my part, the journey is more interesting than the summit on this mountain. You've read it before—this is another of those Catskill 100 peaks where "your guess is as good as mine" marks the exact summit. Here's a hint: large rock. Don't wander too far when you reach the summit, as private property is just beyond.

When the leaves are off the trees there are views of Hubbell Hill, Dry Brook Ridge, Mt. Pisgah, the Plattekills, and Roundtop.

For those who share the woods with hiking dogs, keep them close unless they ignore porcupines. It's a generally easy 1050 ft of ascent and about a 2.5 mi round-trip bushwhack, depending on your exact route.

Hubbell Hill, 3000'   Margaretville Quad
Catskill 67 Rank: 61
View: 3, Interest: 3, Difficulty: 3, Bushwhack: 3

HIGHLIGHTS AND SUMMARY: Hubbell Hill is one of those interesting bushwhack peaks where beautiful meadows, stone fences, and open fern glades are scattered at different places around the mountain. There are lots of birds and wildlife, making Hubbell Hill a good destination for photographers and birders. The summit plateau is wooded and the screened views during leaf season are more than made up for by attractive woods, meadows, and occasional views of surrounding peaks when the foliage is gone. With the exception of one large DEP and DEC parcel on its western side, Hubbell Hill is surrounded by private property. Fortunately, this parcel provides a public property access.

BEST TIME TO HIKE: This peak is nice any time of year, but post hunting season through spring is best.

To reach the small DEP road frontage on Thompson Hollow Rd., drive N on CR6 from NY28/30 to New Kingston (N42° 12.819', W74° 40.909'), turning right

and driving another 0.75 mi on Thompson Hollow Rd. Look for DEP signs and park on a small rise (N42° 13.185', W74° 40.507') uphill from the beautiful old Archibald Cemetery. Walk downhill, keeping the cemetery on your right and remaining on a narrow strip of DEP land until you reach the 10 ft wide stream that drains Thompson Hollow. In times of snowmelt or after periods of rain, getting across the stream with dry boots can be a challenge. We once took an hour looking for a dry crossing after a period of rain. Unless you enjoy hiking with wet boots, wade the stream barefoot, carry water shoes, or use a trick I've employed while bushwhacking (see "garbage bag crossing" in glossary).

The narrow strip of DEP land widens considerably on the other side of the stream, encompassing the entire western side of the mountain. After crossing the stream, look for an old woods road; stay with it for 0.5 mi through fields. It's indistinct at times through the overgrown fields, but is easy to follow once it enters the hardwood forest. The road climbs to within 500 ft of the top, and when it begins to turn in the wrong direction, leave it and 'whack toward the summit. Once on Hubbell's summit plateau, the high point appears to be on the N end of a 0.1 mi wide contour. Depending on the season, the summit ridge may be easy or it may be a pricker plantation. In winter or very early spring, the blackberry canes are covered or flattened. Keep your eyes open and travel quietly; there are bears, deer, porkies, and coyotes on Hubbell Hill.

From Thompson Hollow Rd., the ascent is approximately 1300 ft with a round-trip of about 3 to 4 mi. Routes are about the same from other directions.

Open meadow on the slopes of Hubbell Hill. Alan Via

APPENDIX 1:
Bushwhacking Basics

Some of the 67 peaks have trails, woods roads, or ski trails to the summit, but many are untrailed. This section is for readers who would like to try bushwhacking or those who have started and are ready for a little more. Experienced bushwhackers are welcome to skim through or skip this part.

New bushwhackers shouldn't expect to toss their gear and this guide in their packs, jump in the car, and head for the trailless peaks. If you are interested in off-trail travel, let me share some information that might point you in the right direction.

Don't bushwhack alone. Some experienced soloists will strongly disagree, but if you're looking to get started in land navigation, off marked trails, don't go alone. A broken bone, an eye injury, a serious fall, an allergic reaction, or a dislocated shoulder is a serious problem on a well-used trail. Though I sometimes ignore my own advice, I know that if I suffer the same injury during a 'whack, I could have a true emergency. In my view there are many things that can go wrong, especially for those new to off-trail travel. Carefully evaluate the risk before venturing out alone, because your rescuers won't have a trail to follow and there is little chance another bushwhacker will happen by.

Learn from experienced bushwhackers. You can hire a guide to take you bushwhacking, but an easier alternative is to find experienced off-trail hikers to team up with. Come prepared, then watch and listen to what they do and how they do it. You might just get a turn out front for part of a trip. I don't know any bushwhackers who wouldn't share their experience and enthusiasm with new hikers who want to leave trails behind. See the glossary for a list of hiking groups that have organized trips.

Familiarize yourself with map and compass. It's often said that hikers should always carry a map and compass. That's the easy part. You really need to learn how to use those tools. Buy and study topographic maps (the ones with contour lines). Sit on a summit or open mountain ledge with your map on your lap and rotate it until the map's orientation is facing the same direction as your gaze. Match the map features with the scenery to get an idea of what a ridge, valley, summit, pond, and col look like on a map. When experienced map readers pick up a topographic map, it's like they are looking out from that mountain. They look at a map and see what you're seeing from that summit, absent the clouds and vegetation. Read a book, take a seminar, and then practice, practice, practice.

For every hike, get out your map the evening before and study it. Look at the trailhead and your destination and mileage, and the elevation gains and losses. Pencil in your directions of travel on the map and then use your compass to calculate the bearings and reciprocal bearings. Carry the folded map in the field or make a copy. And bring more than one map on a bushwhack, to accompany the backup compass you have in your pack.

Think you don't really need a map and compass? Who needs them in the digital age? That "analog" route-finding system is old tech, low tech, no tech—and mostly old hikers do that, you may think. Yep, that's me. I really do drag out my topographic map the night before a hike and do my "homework." Even if I've been on the hike many times before or someone else is leading the bushwhack, I draw the compass bearings on the map—because things go wrong. Electronic equipment fails, batteries wear out, extra batteries get left at home, the GPS falls on a rock, or the thick woods snatch the GPS off the shoulder strap of your pack. Now what? Are you thinking, "Don't worry, I'll just be sure there are two other GPSs in our group"? I hope this really isn't the answer to why you don't need to learn map and compass skills.

I carry a GPS and use it extensively in the field. I like the model I have enough to have a backup one at home. But when I do my map homework the evening before, I also plan a route on a computer topographic map and download the route to my GPS. In the woods, I then can see exactly where we're bushwhacking without having to get out the map—but the maps are sitting there in my pack and pocket, ready to go when I need them. By constantly honing and practicing your skills, you won't be over-relying on a GPS and letting your "analog" skills go stale. During a hike I can use the GPS map display to pick up a compass bearing to a desired location and dial the bearing into my compass. The GPS can ride in its pouch while I follow the magnetized compass needle to the next destination.

Research hardware and software before buying. The rapid growth of technology prevents me from making a GPS model recommendation that might be out of date in a year. Instead, look for a high-sensitivity receiver with the capacity to store a large number of digitized maps.

The latest family of Garmin GPS receivers has a "custom mapping" feature, which means that any USGS topographic map or aerial photograph can be uploaded and then viewed on the display screen of the GPS, so what you see on the GPS display matches your paper map. This is an incredibly valuable bushwhacking tool, especially in the Catskills.

You'll want to obtain mapping software for both the GPS and your computer. I have no reservations about suggesting the excellent state-specific National Geographic mapping software for your computer. This software allows you to display maps on your monitor, plan routes, and download routes to your GPS. Back home after your hike, you can upload the tracklog of where you walked onto the computer map. This allows you to visualize your hike and relate the terrain you saw in the woods to the map displayed on your monitor. This is very useful feedback, and the tracks can be saved and used to repeat the route on a future hike.

Plan a time to turn around—even if you don't reach your destination—and leave notification. As you gain experience, you'll get better at translating inches and contour lines into how long a bushwhack is likely to take. Estimate a return time and let a trusted contact know that you'll either be home or will call by a certain time. To prevent a rescue from being mobilized and needlessly worrying friends and family, never crowd or pass the contact time. If you care about your contact's peace of mind, you won't want them agonizing over whether to wait "just another hour or two" before alerting the authorities. If a rescue ever does have to be mobilized, you can greatly aid the process by leaving a copy of your route drawn on a topographic map, with your return or call time indicated. Your expectation will be that your backup will make a phone call by the noted time; your responsibility is to get out of the woods to prevent that.

Alan Via

HIKER'S AND BUSHWHACKER'S EQUIPMENT

There are readers for whom any list will describe too much or too little to carry. Much of that depends on the experience level of the hiker. Nonetheless, here are some suggestions for those just getting started. I'm certain you will add or subtract from these lists.

Equipment List for Day Hikes
boots or other footwear with hiking-appropriate soles
adjustable hiking poles
daypack, containing:
  rain/wind shell
  water bottles or hydration system
  headlamp (flashlight provides light but a headlamp frees up both hands) and extra batteries
  first aid kit (include personal medication and pain reliever)
  map
  compass
  knit or fleece cap and gloves
  food and trail snacks
  whistle
  watch
  change of clothes
  small multi-tool
  closed cell foam pad
  SmartWool® socks or equivalent
  trail and/or topographic map and compass
  fire-starting kit with waterproof matches
  small roll of toilet paper (bury after use)

Optional Additions
  camera
  insect repellant
  GPS
  gaiters
  sunscreen and sunglasses
  sweatband or bandanna
  lightweight work or gardening gloves
  baseball cap

Additions for Longer Hikes
extra food and water
more supportive footwear
extra clothing in waterproof bag
change of socks

Additions for Bushwhacking
very durable and larger daypack
goggles or glasses
extra headlamp and batteries
leather gardening gloves
GPS
long-sleeve shirt and long pants
full-length insulated pad and bivy sack
extra clothing and gloves
extra compass and topographic maps (and the know-how to use them)

Additions for Winter
larger pack
backcountry/climbing snowshoes, with adequate snowshoe crampons
insulated water bottle cozy
hot drink/soup
small shelter tarp
MicroSpikes®
hiking poles with snow baskets
heavier weight GORE-TEX® or soft-shell parka
complete change of clothes
extra gloves, socks, and mittens
tall or winter gaiters
long underwear
synthetic pants or shell pants
repair kit with tools for snowshoe repair
very robust fire-starting kit
cold-weather boots and winter socks
heavyweight mitten shells/gloves
face mask/goggles

APPENDIX II:
A Subjective Look at the Peaks

I believe many of us who are ardent hikers love lists of peaks based on a variety of criteria. Such lists set our goals, our anticipations, our challenges. Here's mine for the Catskill 100, but I certainly invite you to create your own.

Most Challenging
Little Rocky (cliffs)
Mill Brook (bushwhack
   from Mill Brook Rd.)
Olderbark (cliffs)

Least Challenging
Belleayre
Cave
Churchill
East Gray
Huntersfield
North Plattekill
Overlook
Mt. Pisgah
Round Top (Hobart)
Silver Hollow
Utsayantha
West Cave
Winnisook

Best Names
Barkaboom
Cradle Rock Ridge
Little Rocky
Old Clump
Olderbark
Sleeping Lion (NE Halcott)
Woodpecker Ridge

Nicest Views
Acra Point
Ashokan High Point
Beaver Kill Range
Belleayre

Burnt Knob
Cave Mt.
Giant Ledge
North Plattekill
Overlook
Mt. Pisgah
Red Hill
Roundtop (Kaaterskill)
Stoppel Point
Utsayantha
Van Wyck
West Cave

Summits with High Points Slightly Off the Trail
Burnt Knob
Dry Brook Ridge
Giant Ledge
Sand Pond
St. Anne's
Stoppel Point
Willowemoc

Easiest Woods for Bushwhacking
Beaver Kill Range
Denman
High Falls
Hodge Pond
Plattekill
Roundtop (Kaaterskill)
Van Wyck
   (from Woodhull)

Scrappiest
Churchill
Cowan
Montgomery Hollow
Packsaddle
Pine Island
South Bearpen
Southeast Warren

Wilderness Feel
Beaver Kill Range
High Falls
Olderbark
Wildcats (East and West)

Least Interesting
Churchill
Cowan
East Gray
Sand Pond
South Bearpen
Southeast Warren

APPENDIX III:
Tandem Peaks

Acra Point–Burnt Knob
Beaver Kill Range–High Falls
Beaver Kill Range–Willowemoc
Beaver Kill Range–Willowemoc (Beaver Kill Ridge)–Sand Pond
Cave–West Cave
Churchill-Utsayantha
Denman–Red Hill
East and West Wildcat
Hodge Pond–Mongaup
Hodge Pond–Mongaup–Willowemoc (Beaver Kill Ridge)
Huntersfield-Richmond
Irish-Shultice
Mill Brook–Woodpecker Ridge–Cradle Rock Ridge
Montgomery Hollow–Roundtop (Prattsville Quad)
Montgomery Hollow–White Man
Narrow Notch–East Gray
Narrow Notch–Old Clump
North Plattekill–Meeker Hollow
North Plattekill–South Plattekill–Round Top (Hobart Quad)
NW Moresville Range–SW Moresville Range
Overlook-Plattekill
Packsaddle–Pine Island
Mt. Pisgah–Little Pisgah
Sand Pond–Willowemoc
South Vly–Sleeping Lion
Stoppel–West Stoppel
Winnisook-Spruce
Woodhull–Van Wyck

Glossary

Asian longhorned beetle: This invasive insect likely hitchhiked into the U.S. in a wooden pallet. Scientists believe the 0.75 to 1.50 inch beetle has the potential to be one of the most devastating insects that has ever threatened our woodlands. Its hosts of choice are sugar maple, birch, and ash, but other deciduous trees are also in jeopardy. Millions of trees have already been killed in the eastern U.S. and unless some means is found to counteract the threat, the potential damage to the Catskill forest is almost unimaginable. Transportation of firewood has the potential to spread this pest even faster.

ATVs: In their proper place, all-terrain vehicles are useful farming, logging, and property maintenance tools. They do little damage on hard dirt roads and trails designated for their use. On many routes, ATV "trails" allow easier hiking progress, but at what price? If you hike more than just a few of the routes in the book, you're certain to encounter illegal ATV trails slashed across public property. Not satisfied with riding on private property, illegal users are blazing and flagging paths across land that belongs to all of us. If you see an ATV where you shouldn't, note the plate numbers of the ATV or the truck hauling it and report it to the local ranger. Please remove the illegal flagging on public property used to make illegal ATV routes more permanent.

bark road: Roads were cut through the woods of the Catskills in the 1800s by bark peelers to access eastern hemlock trees. The bark was used to tan hides into leather in tanneries in Hunter, Tannersville, and elsewhere. Bark was generally light to transport, so bark roads often go straight up; there was little need for switchbacks. Bark stripping helped wipe out many of the old hemlock woodlands. The old bark roads are seen and used by many Catskill hikers.

beech whips: Short, face-high beech saplings. Where present in numbers, they tend to be fairly close to each other and the tips of the buds are sharp. Their height and leaf density can hamper visibility, and their points can scratch your arms—and do more if a tip hits your cornea. Wear glasses or goggles in areas with whips.

black bears: There are between 2500 and 3000 in the Catskills, a large increase from the estimated 230 in the 1970s. At that time, the public wanted to see bears more frequently, so the opening date of the bear-hunting season was delayed. This provided pregnant females an opportunity to den up before hunters entered the woods. The start of the hunting season has recently been moved to an earlier date in order to control the now-large population.

  Seeing a bear or evidence of its presence may provide either a thrill or anxiety, depending on the individual hikers' point of view. If happening upon a bear gives you concern, rest assured that your scent and footfalls, conversation, or other noise you make while hiking will almost guarantee that bears know where you are and highly unlikely you will see one. Bear attacks are extremely rare, but they do occasionally happen; any interaction (photographing, observing) should be from a distance. Though not generally dangerous, do not approach a cub or attempt to pick one up. If hiking with a dog, be careful he doesn't decide to investigate the "big furry dog" or its "puppy."

blowdown: Refers to blown-over trees or fallen treetops or branches. Blowdown can turn an otherwise easily traveled route into a more difficult one. Over a couple of days in April 2007, devastating ice storms followed by high winds wreaked havoc on the Catskills. The storm made a mess of mountainsides in large areas. Many feel this was the worst damage seen in thirty years. On many mountains, formerly open woods are now strewn with downed treetops and branches that slow travel. In August 2011, Tropical Storm Irene also caused widespread devastation in the Catskills, including damage to roads, bridges, and trails.

bogs: Dr. Mike Kudish discovered that tree fossils preserved in high-elevation peat bogs could be used to reconstruct forest history and that the age of the peat can be determined by radiocarbon dating. Because of his research, Catskill forest history has been pushed back to 14,000 years. You'll see some occasional references to bogs in some peak chapters.

brush hog: A piece of power equipment that is used to cut through brush, small trees, and bushes to clear a path. Think of it as a lawnmower for the woods. It's often used by property owners to clear paths or keep old woods roads from becoming overgrown.

bump or **bumplet:** Hikers often refer to small ups and downs along a ridge as bumps. A bump is less than a peak and is often a sub-summit; a little effort is required to hike over it. A "bumplet" is a little smaller, and my humble attempt at a humorous variation.

bushwhacking: Hiking off-trail, usually with the benefit of map and compass, often supplemented by a GPS. For years, bushwhacking meant only map and compass; it is only recently that it started to include digital equipment. It is also referred to as 'whacking. See appendix on bushwhacking basics.

cairn: A pile of rocks, usually marking the beginning or continuation of a bushwhack route or the high point of a summit. The word "cairn" is thought to be of Scottish origin. Cairns were originally used to mark the route above tree line, for the benefit of travelers in bad weather. You will sometimes see cairns marking where others have begun a bushwhack. See more about cairn placement in the chapter "Respect for the Mountains, Their Stewards, and Private Property."

catching feature: A geographic landmark, feature, or object that allows you to locate yourself on a hike. These can be streams, roads, telephone lines, lakes, or other dominant map features located on the other side of your hiking objective. If you run into a catching feature, you know you've hiked past your destination. Sometimes you can follow the feature to a known point. Try to note where the catching features are located in the area you're hiking before you head into the woods. This is important homework before a trail hike, and is essential for a bushwhack.

Catskill Scenic Trail: A 26-mile cycling and cross-country skiing trail over the former track bed of the Ulster and Delaware Railroad. One end originates in a parking area E of Bloomville (N42° 19.977', W74° 48.299') and the other at Hubbell Corners (N42° 18.042', W74° 33.312'). Bring a mountain bike for this unpaved rail trail.

clove: Arthur Adams describes the origin of the word as the Dutch *kloof,* meaning a ravine, hollow, or notch in the wall of a mountain. There are a number of areas referred to as cloves in the Catskills.

col: A gap, valley, pass, or low point between two peaks, summits, or intermediate summits.

course of least resistance: When bushwhacking you make constant decisions as to the best direction to hike. Looking around, the woods may be easier to hike in one direction than another. Going right might be easier than heading left. Can you go around a ledge or climb it? Is it swampy in one direction but dry in another? Being aware of terrain and surroundings and following the course of least resistance means not being a slave to your planned route. Utilize the options the mountain presents you.

DEC: The New York State Department of Environmental Conservation controls and regulates NYS public property that is not regulated by the NYC Department of Environmental Protection (referred to as DEP).

DEP: The New York City Department of Environmental Protection was originally set up to protect the watershed and reservoirs for the New York City metropolitan area. The DEP publishes maps of and patrols the areas they control. DEP buys land or protective easements in order to safeguard the New York City watershed. DEP vehicle hangtags and permits are required to access most DEP property. To apply for a free, online, printable permit visit the DEP website.

dogleg: Often used by hikers or bushwhackers to describe an L-shaped mountain ridge that when viewed on a map looks like a dog's rear leg. The term is used this way: "Follow the ridge until it doglegs right." Look at a dog's leg and you'll instantly see the connection.

drainage avoidance: Most Catskill mountains have streams on their flanks that over the centuries have eroded into gullies. These gullies are often called drainages, and may be wet and rocky. Sometimes they are strewn with rocks and trees that have fallen into them. The moisture in these drainages is conducive to the growth of dense vegetation and stinging nettles.

While maps might suggest drainages as good routes, experienced bushwhackers generally practice "drainage avoidance," and instead travel on the ridges that parallel them. Drainages may sometimes be good routes when covered with several feet of consolidated snow.

eastern tent caterpillar: These caterpillars build silky tents in trees in springtime as homes for their larvae. The emerging caterpillars attack the leaves of deciduous trees, with cherries and apples as their favorites. Periodic infestations result in forest canopy loss and encourage the growth of sun-loving vegetation.

emerald ash borer: This 0.375 inch metallic-green foreign insect invader, sometimes referred to as the EAB, sneaked into Michigan from Asia in 2002 and made its NYS appearance in the summer of 2009. The emerald ash borer is wreaking havoc in the Midwest and scientists feel certain the large ash forests of the Northeast are in jeopardy in the coming years. The purple plastic rectangular objects, nicknamed "Barney Boxes," that you come across hanging in trees are EAB traps. They contain a natural plant oil to attract the insects and are covered with an ecologically safe glue that traps them. This gives scientists a way to see if the EAB has invaded a new territory.

fernwhacking: Hikers on the peaks of the Catskill 67 will encounter large areas of ferns, often on bushwhack routes. Some of these areas comprise many acres, and in places you hike in and out of them all day. Picking your route through these scenic, ferny areas is sometimes jokingly referred to as "fernwhacking."

In addition to their photographic appeal, ferns are welcomed by hikers as they often crowd out nettles and prickers. It is a mixed blessing when this occurs. Dense fern growth can make bushwhacking more challenging, when the ferns hide what's underneath. Autumn's first frost kills the ferns, exposing completely open woodlands right into spring.

There are two varieties of shoulder-high ferns, cinnamon and interrupted, which are very local in appearance. One of the best examples of a fern glade is on the summit of Mill Brook Ridge. See also "shinwhacking."

first-growth forest: Dr. Michael Kudish, Professor Emeritus in the Division of Forestry at Paul Smith's College, defines this as forest that has not been commercially used. There are over one hundred square miles of first-growth forest still surviving in the Catskills, in nearly fifty separate parcels. Logging, tanbark peeling, quarrying, agriculture, and forest fires each contributed to the disappearance of first-growth forests. Ridgetop and second-home "development" is their latest threat.

fishers: In the mid-1970s, DEC began a program to reintroduce fishers in the Catskills. Fishers were seen as valuable furbearers, as well as a species native to the area. They had been mostly extirpated concurrent with the elimination of much of the hemlock forests in the 1800s. DEC paid a premium to Adirondack trappers to capture fishers, and forty-three of them were released near Slide Mt. and the Shawangunk Ridge from the middle to late 1970s. Their population numbers were then followed through winter tracking.

Fishers are prolific breeders, with litters of three to four kits. Since the female breeds again while the kits are two to three weeks old, their numbers have been rapidly expanding. They will eat just about anything, including small mammals, birds, snakes, skunks, amphibians, and porcupines. When DEC still required trappers to present skinned fisher hides, about 30 percent of them had porcupine quills embedded in the face and neck areas. Once it was determined the new generation of fishers was taking hold, trappers no longer had to present the hides.

You may see a fisher flashing by in the woods, but in winter, look for their distinctive tracks: they have five-toes and a two-feet by two-footed gait.

forest tent caterpillar: They don't actually make tents, but rather silken covers. Their targets are ash, oak, and maples, though their food of preference is sugar maples. The caterpillars go through cycles and anyone who has spent time in the Catskills is aware when they are plentiful.

garbage-bag crossing: Carry a pair of kitchen-sized plastic garbage bags in your pack, the ones with handles. By pulling them over your boots, you can get across streams without having to remove your boots, freeze your legs and feet, or "rock dance." This technique also saves you the time you'd otherwise spend getting your boots and socks off and on. The trick works best in slower moving, shallow water. Try to keep your plastic bag–clad boots off of mossy or wet rocks. See the section on Hubbell Hill.

GPS: Shorthand for Global Positioning System. The GPS system was originally developed by the U.S. Defense Department to determine the precise position of military targets and personnel. GPS marries satellite and information technology hardware and software. The technology was adapted for civilian use and initially non-military GPS receivers had a built-in 100 meter error, called "selective availability." Selective availability (SA) was developed to prevent the technology from being used by adversaries of the United States. In 2000, President Clinton turned off SA. As a result, some recreational GPS units are now capable of accuracy within 10 ft, leading to an explosion of use by hikers, geocachers, and those driving vehicles.

Grid: A term originally used by the Rip Van Winkle Hiking Club to refer to the Catskill Grid, a chart that lists the 35 Catskill 3500 ft peaks vertically and each month of the year horizontally (or vice versa). "Completing the Grid" means you've climbed each Catskill 3500 peak in every month of the year. The daunting challenge of making these 420 ascents has been completed by a small handful of dedicated Catskill experts, including friends and Catskill 100 completers Ralph Ryndak and Jim Bouton.

handrails: Map features that can get you from one place to another. A stream, narrow ridge, woods road, and many other linear map features can be used to assist off-trail travel. Pick up a handrail and follow it to a known point or another handrail. If you are comfortable with maps, handrails jump out at you when you are planning a route or consulting a map in the field.

hemlock woolly adelgid: The U.S. Department of Agriculture (USDA) describes them as small, aphid-like invaders from Asia that threaten the health and sustainability of eastern and Carolina hemlocks. The hemlock woolly adelgid was first seen in the western U.S. in 1924 and in the eastern U.S. in 1951, near Richmond, Virginia. By 2005, the insect was established in portions of sixteen states from Maine to Georgia, where infestations covered about half of the range of hemlock. Areas of extensive tree mortality and decline are found throughout the infested region, but the impact has been most severe in some areas of Virginia, New Jersey, Pennsylvania, and Connecticut. In the north, hemlock decline and mortality occurs within six to ten years of infestation. Experts believe it is a question of when, not if, the adelgid will severely impact the Catskills.

herd paths: Unmarked paths that develop as a result of hikers walking the same route. Animals also create herd paths, often along the easiest routes of travel.

hiking clubs: Adirondack Mountain Club (ADK), Catskill 3500 Club, Appalachian Mountain Club, Taconic Hiking Club, Catskill Mountain Club, and the Rip Van Winkle Hiking Club all schedule guided hikes, both on and off trail. Most of these organizations have websites. The Adirondack Mountain Club has chapters all over the Northeast, all with experienced leaders. This is a great way to meet like-minded hikers and learn about new areas.

hunting seasons: There are month-long turkey seasons in spring and autumn and the firearms big game season generally begins around the third week of November. Separate seasons exist for bear, archery, and black powder firearms. It is an excellent idea to avoid bushwhacking during those times. When hiking, consider wearing blaze orange. My dog wears a blaze orange dog vest and a bell during hunting seasons.

ice storms: The deciduous forests in the Catskills are susceptible to ice storms. A huge spring storm dumped a couple of feet of heavy wet snow on the Catskills in April 2007. Up high, the storm was a snow event. At lower elevations, snow was followed by icing. The winds that accompanied the storm broke off treetops, doing more damage than long-time Catskill residents and hikers had ever seen.

More than thirteen miles of the Devil's Path had to be closed until the debris could be cleared. The Blackhead Range was devastated, and the top of Plateau Mt. appeared to have been carpet bombed. A friend who was out hiking with his dog during the storm described branches falling around him all day. While the trails have long been cleared, the broken treetops and limbs still litter the woods, changing the character of bushwhacking in large areas of the Catskills. In many of the peak chapters you'll see references to this storm, as well as another that occurred a year earlier.

Leavitt Peak: This is an alternative name for SW Hunter. There is a movement to have SW Hunter officially renamed Leavitt Peak to honor long-time 3500 Club members and early climbers Elinore and Bill Leavitt. The proposal was presented to the board of the 3500 Club. The USGS Board of Names requires a rename to receive common local currency as one step before it will approve the name.

ledges: These are the cliff bands seen all over the Catskills. They can be difficult to get over (Olderbark, Little Rocky, others), or very short and easily climbed. By being observant, you can often find ramps or other passages through them. Animal herd paths can be of great assistance and often show the way. The local wildlife know the safest and easiest way through.

logging, skidder, bark, or **ox roads:** Hike the Catskill 67 and you will cross or hike these from time to time. Logging roads were cut to provide access for tree harvesting. Skidder roads were cut or pushed through the woods to accommodate log skidders, vehicles used to drag a cut tree or log to an area where it can be further worked on. Ox and bark roads (see also "bark roads") refer to the remnants of old roads you may sometimes encounter. Oxen were often used to haul heavy loads of gear and equipment.

lumpy: Perhaps the best description of hiking conditions where the forest floor is covered with rocks of different sizes. The rocks you encounter as you negotiate your way up or down a mountain can be large or small, anchored or loose. Having to step over and around them increases hiking effort. Sometimes the rocks can be hidden by nettles, ferns, or other vegetation.

Lumpy conditions can be found on bushwhacks around Devil's Path, the Winnisook-Spruce ridge, the north side of Mill Brook Ridge, and many others. The term "lumpy" comes to us courtesy of Ralph Ryndak and it perfectly describes a bushwhack we did where 4+ mi felt like 7 mi. Ralph said it was "lumpy."

maps: See entries for Venture Out, NY–NJ Trail Conference, and National Geographic maps in the references section. USGS topographic maps are useful for route planning.

MICROspikes®: A relatively new piece of winter gear made by Kahtoola that fills a niche midway between boot crampons and instep crampons. They consist of a heavy rubber rand that you pull up over the bottom of your boot, with small, triangular spikes underneath held in place by chains, and a wire bail that covers the front of your boot. Though they don't have the bite or grip of full boot crampons, MICROspikes come on and off in a hurry, and perform well on moderately icy terrain.

MICROspikes are not a substitute in conditions calling for crampons, such as blue or water ice. They are useful where snowshoes or full crampons are too much, but wearing no traction is unwise. These are not to be confused with YakTrax®, which are barely suitable for walking on your icy driveway. The small, tubular springs that hikers discover in the woods are the remnants of expired YakTrax that were not up to the rigors of hiking.

peakbagger's mountain: In the text, this means a mountain that is attractive mostly to "listers" because of the mountain's difficult terrain, overabundance of prickers, lack of views, or another "unpleasant" feature. A "peakbagger's mountain" is one that might best be described as a less-than-fun hike for anyone other than the hardcore hiker.

Plattekill Turnpike: An unpaved road cut and maintained for fire control and ranger activities, as well as possible logging access in the Plattekill State Forest. The name was bestowed by Roxbury hiker Jim Bouton. One end can be found at the DEC parking area on Harold Roberts Rd. (N42° 15.819', W74° 40.119') and the other at the end of Mountain Brook Rd. (N42° 15.951', W74° 41.086').

From Harold Roberts Rd., the turnpike climbs to near the first col N of South Plattekill Mt., turns NW, and runs parallel to the North-South Plattekill ridge at an average elevation of between 2900 ft and 3000 ft. It then turns W as it curves under the summit of North Plattekill, following the cirque SW around and above the end of Harold Roberts Rd. The turnpike then turns S, cutting through the North Plattekill–Round Top col, passing around the W side of Round Top, and ending at the large DEC parking area and gate on Mountain Brook Rd. It passes a few hundred feet under three Catskill 100 summits, Round Top, North Plattekill and South Plattekill, and is an excellent route for hiking, mountain biking, cross-country skiing, and observing birds and other wildlife. Keep in mind that the summits of all three mountains are bushwhacks from the turnpike.

portable handrail: Don't confuse this with the map and compass handrail (see "handrail" earlier in glossary). When heading up or down steep terrain, hikers often grab a tree, rock, or root to steady themselves. The dead tree or the rock that comes loose is now a "portable" handrail, creating a situation that varies from amusing to less so if the tree falls on your hiking companion or you take a tumble.

posted signs or **posters:** Signs posted by property owners to denote boundaries and private property. There are also DEC and DEP boundary posters. Posted signs are supposed to contain the property owner's name and address. If you run into one in the woods, take down the information, turn around, and use it to ask the owner for permission the next time you hike.

prickers and **pickers:** Common and interchangeable terms used to describe stinging nettles and blackberry or raspberry bushes found on some mountains, the latter two being most prevalent in Delaware County. Nettles make their appearance from mid-spring onward, usually in wet or damp areas. They can "bite" you through some clothing, and wet synthetic clothing is notorious for being the next worst thing to bare skin.

"Pickers" is a local phrase for the blackberry or raspberry canes. The most onerous are the red-caned blackberry brambles with the sharp spines. The berry prickers often appear in small patches or can cover entire summits, and the canes may grow to over 6 ft. The barbs soften up or disappear by late autumn, and snow can pack down and cover them.

The forest tent caterpillar and, to a lesser degree, eastern caterpillar infestations of 2007 to 2009 weakened many of the hardwood trees. Ice storms magnified the damage, creating a newly opened forest canopy, which allowed more sunlight to reach the ground. Blackberry seeds sprouted rapidly, spreading this scourge. As the canopy gradually restores itself, the pricker bushes will slowly die off, their seeds waiting for another period of sunlight in which to germinate.

The shade from beech trees discourages blackberry growth underneath and selecting a bushwhacking route under beeches can provide a respite from the thorny purgatory. Dr. Mike Kudish provides this identification: "blackberry canes are red and taller than a person. Raspberry canes are more slender, gray, and usually waist high. I used to tell students that raspberries scratch people, blackberries dissect them."

primitive bike corridors: The Catskill Park State Land Master Plan calls for bicycle corridors on four trails along old roads. These will include the 3.2 mi length of Mink Hollow Rd.; 4.5 miles of Overlook Turnpike from the Overlook Mountain Wild Forest boundary to Platte Clove and Prediger Rd.; Diamond

Notch Rd. through the Hunter–West Kill Wilderness; and 2.4 mi of the Colgate Lake–Dutcher Notch Trail, formerly an old road. The plan also allows for bicycles on Wild Forest area roads open to the public, state truck trails, old wood roads, foot trails, snowmobile trails, and horse trails.

rule of up: Used by bushwhackers to describe the easiest way when there are a number of ways to proceed, none of which looks like a bad alternative. Follow the rule of up as long as it takes you in the direction you want to hike.

scooper: A local nickname for those living in Livingston Manor, once the world's largest producer of scoop shovels.

seep: A term introduced to me by Dr. Mike Kudish, botanist and flora expert. This is a hydrological term that denotes a sheet of water of higher pH and oxygenation. Seeps serve as a water source for the local fauna and flora and are often home to a wide variety of plant life that Mike refers to as "seepers." The presence of a seep often leads to an otherwise unlikely concentration of plant life in a small area. A seep differs from a spring as springs come from a point source and a seep comes from a broader area. Barkaboom and West Stoppel are among several mountains that have beautiful seeps.

shinwhacking: When dense areas of ferns or other vegetation cover rocks and blown-down branches, it's easy to trip and stumble on the hidden obstacles. When tree branches are hidden underneath the surface of a fern glade, a hiker's shins are sometime the first to discover the limb. Ouch! See also "fernwhacking."

sidehilling: When a hike or bushwhack cuts across the fall line of a slope. On a trail, sidehilling is of little concern. When bushwhacking with no flat path beneath your feet, however, you expend a lot more effort by walking across sloping terrain. It can also be tough on knees, hips, and ankles.

Sometimes the top of a ridge is harder to hike so bushwhackers sidehill underneath the crest. Sidehilling sometimes happens by accident, as when you're trying to regain a direction you inadvertently lost. Bushwhackers also sidehill to avoid drainages or to reach a col or other objective.

stone fences: The Catskill Mountains were settled long ago and beautiful stone fences mark old farmsteads. Settlers cleared woodlands for agriculture and livestock and the stones ended up as fences. They marked property or field boundaries and though the old farms or buildings are often gone, the walls remain, a scenic reminder of different times. Many of the Catskill 67 peaks are dotted with these.

switchbacks: When terrain is steep, woods roads or trails often zigzag up the slope, allowing a hiker to gain elevation with more distance but less effort. This gradual, back and forth can also be done when bushwhacking. A hiker can ascend straight up the fall line, or go left and right uphill. Switchbacking makes for a slightly longer but easier climb.

topographic maps: Maps that show contour lines, elevations, bodies of water, roads, and other man-made features. They are referred to by hikers as topo maps or quads (for the shape of map quadrangles). The quad referenced in the heading of each peak section is the United States Geological Survey (USGS) map on which the peak is located. Each quad has a specific title, named for a peak or other prominent geographic feature on that map. Most other maps derive their basic information from the USGS topographic maps.

waypoints: These are markers, either in a GPS or on a paper map. Hikers can note places, features, or landmarks they want to pass on their way to and from a destination. You can waypoint waterfalls, streams, trail junctions, interesting terrain, and summits on a GPS and then return to them at a future time.

woods roads: Unpaved dirt, grass, or clay roads constructed for logging, agriculture, quarrying, or access to private property. Woods roads in excellent condition can be driven by a vehicle. Others are rough, washed out, grown over, or rocky. They can have blowdown blocking them or be pricker or nettle infested. Many of the peaks are crisscrossed by old woods roads. When you find one heading in your direction, consider it a gift from the bushwhacking gods.

References
and Suggested Reading

This list includes all works used as references in this book, as well as a list of trail guides the reader may find useful and some suggested reading that may enhance your experience of the Catskills.

BOOKS

The Catskill Forest: A History, Michael Kudish. Fleischmanns, NY: Purple Mountain Press, Ltd., 2000.
Mere compliments don't do justice to this must-have resource. The map that accompanies it is like nothing else and the book provides information painstakingly accumulated and related in detail.

Guide to the Catskills with Trail Guide and Maps, Arthur G. Adams, Roger Coco, Harriet Greenman, and Leon R. Greenman. New York: Walking News, Inc., 1975.
The listing of the 98 Catskill 3000 ft peaks first appeared in this guide. Although out of print, the book is available from online vendors and is a treasure worth seeking.

The Catskills: An Illustrated Historical Guide with Gazetteer, Arthur G. Adams. Bronx, NY: Fordham University Press, 1977 (rev. 1990).
This book is a wonderful source of historical and geographical information. It allowed me to fill in many background gaps.

In the Catskills, Selections from the Writings of John Burroughs. Originally published 1910, Houghton Mifflin Co.
Burroughs was a prolific writer whose works covered many subjects and places. This wonderful book is a collection of eight of his essays about the Catskills. It has been reproduced in paperback versions and is easily available online.

Forest Forensics: A Field Guide to Reading the Forested Landscape, Tom Wessels. Woodstock, VT: The Countryman Press, 2010.
An excellent guide to the forest landscape and how to interpret the signs left by man or nature. A great read and assist to answering questions of why things are as they are when walking through the woods.

The Catskills: From Wilderness to Woodstock, Alf Evers. New York: Overlook Press, 1982.
Its dust jacket says it all: "lore, legends, superstitions, violence and scandal, art and commerce, flora and fauna, natural and unnatural wonders that have made the Catskills one of America's most historically rich and romantic regions." This

exhaustive book covers Catskill Mountain history from the time of the Native Americans through the 1960s and is a must read for any student of local history.

The Catskills, T. Morris Longstreth. Hensonville, NY: Black Dome Press, 2003 (originally published by the Century Co., 1918).
The author provides an entertaining account of his treks through the Catskills in 1917.

Trails with Tales: History Hikes through the Capital Region, Saratoga, Berkshires, Catskills, and Hudson Valley, Russell Dunn and Barbara Delaney. Hensonville, NY: Black Dome Press, 2006.
A good source of information on Overlook Mt.

Adirondack Mountain Club Guide to Catskill Trails, 3rd ed., edited by Carol and David White. Lake George, NY: Adirondack Mountain Club, 2005.
This hiking guide was edited by two of the most knowledgeable Catskill experts anywhere. When I mentioned at the very beginning of the book that a debt of gratitude is owed to those who have written on this subject before, the Whites immediately came to mind.

Catskill Trails: A Ranger's Guide to the High Peaks, Book One: The Northern Catskills and *Book Two: The Central Catskills,* Edward Henry. Hensonville, NY: Black Dome Press, 2000.
These two volumes cover the Catskill High Peaks region and are written from the perspective of a Forest Ranger.

Another Day, Another Dollar: The Civilian Conservation Corps in the Catskills, Diane Galusha. Hensonville, NY: Black Dome Press, 2008.
This excellent book details the history, projects, and work of the Civilian Conservation Corp in the Catskill Mountains.

Appalachian Mountain Club Catskill Mountain Guide, Peter Kick. Boston: Appalachian Mountain Club, 2002.
This excellent guide is very useful, and its accompanying tear-proof topographic map shows the Catskill Park in its entirety.

The Other 54: A Hiker's Guide to the Lower 54 Peaks of the Adirondack 100 Highest, Spencer Morrissey. Long Lake, NY: Inca-pah-cho Wilderness Guides, second edition, 2011.
The only guidebook to the lower 54 peaks of the Adirondacks, by my good friend and hiking partner.

Catskill Peak Experiences: Mountaineering Tales of Endurance, Survival, Exploration and Adventure from the Catskill 3500 Club, edited by Carol White. Hensonville,

NY: Black Dome Press, 2008.
As the title suggests, stories and tales of all sorts by members of the Catskill 3500 Club. This interesting book is hard to put down and sustained me through some periods of writer's doldrums.

MAPS

"Catskill Trails" six-map set, New York–New Jersey Trail Conference, Mahwah, NJ.
This multi-map set, available in several editions and updated every few years, has been the gold standard for Catskill hikers for many years. This series covers all 35 of the 3500 ft Catskill High Peaks and many of the Catskill 100 summits. The set is waterproof, lightweight, and easy to handle. For this book, I consulted the 9th ed., 2010; 8th ed., 2005; 6th ed., 1998; 3rd ed., 1987; and 1st ed., 1983.

DeLorme's NY Atlas and Gazetteer. Yarmouth, ME: DeLorme, 2003 (rev. 2007).
This atlas rides in my car year 'round. It covers all of New York State, grid by grid, and shows town, village, county, and state roads. It is a handy companion to the maps mentioned above.

"Catskill Region" Outdoor edition topographic map, Venture Out Maps Corp., Middletown, NY.
This superlative map of the Catskills, available in several editions, is as close to a necessity as exists for locating peaks, trailheads, and back roads. Most DEP and DEC property is shown in close detail, allowing hikers to more easily find their way, plan hikes, and avoid private property. Pick up a couple of these even if you don't plan on hiking all the mountains. They are a true masterpiece by the cartographer and will soon be out of print.

"Catskill Park" Trails Illustrated Map (#755), produced by National Geographic and Adirondack Mountain Club, September 2011.
This is a double-sided tearproof map covering the Catskill Park, but not the entire Catskill Mountains. The 3500 ft peaks are highlighted, but the Catskill 67 peaks are shown only when they are named on the USGS maps on which this map is based. Errors found on the USGS maps are also on this map.

INTERNET RESOURCES

Views from the Top, www.viewsfromthetop.com.
One of the longest running and most authoritative hiking and discussion forums on the Internet. General hiking information, trip reports, gear discussions, and trail conditions, pertaining to New York and New England states. Sub-forums on paddling and photography.

The Catskill Mountaineer, www.catskillmountaineer.com.
This website is a treasure trove of information about the Catskill Mountains. Book reviews, history, lore, region-by-region hiking trips, and a section on the Catskill Mountain's twenty-five best hikes.

The Catskill Center for Conservation and Development, www.catskillcenter.org.
One page of the Catskill Center's website is devoted to the Red Hill Fire Tower. This page is maintained by the tower restorers and stewards and provides additional information about the peak.

History of Delaware County, 1797–1880, W. W. Munsell (converted to electronic text by Bob Chagnon, John Hope, Louise Belsby, and Steve McNeill). On the Delaware County Genealogy and History website, dcnyhistory.org. Accessed 2010.

Adirondack High Peaks Forums, www.adkhighpeaks.com.
Internet forum strongly focused on the Adirondacks but with a Catskills subsection.

ORGANIZATIONS

Adirondack Mountain Club (ADK), www.adk.org.
Since 1922 ADK has worked to protect wilderness throughout New York State. The club builds and maintains trails, publishes guidebooks and maps, and actively promotes responsible recreation through its twenty-seven chapters.

Catskill 3500 Club, www.catskill-3500-club.org.
An excellent organization run by Catskill experts. Read about the club, peaks, and activities, and see the upcoming outing schedule on the website. Their quarterly newsletter, *The Canister,* can be downloaded from the site.

Michael Kudish Natural History Preserve, Inc.
Founded by Dave Turan and Kelly Keck in honor of Dr. Michael Kudish, the preserve is dedicated to educating the public in areas of Catskill flora, fauna, natural history, and clean water. It is located on Tower Rd. in Stamford, New York. The preserve distributes research, studies, and analysis related to the natural history of the Catskill Mountains, America's first wilderness. The one hundred acres of permanently protected land supports a biologically rich and diverse population of flora and fauna. The information on bogs located in the glossary came from information provided by the preserve. Visit their website at mknhp.com

Appalachian Mountain Club (AMC), www.outdoors.org
AMC promotes the protection, enjoyment, and understanding of the mountains, forests, waters, and trails of the Appalachian region. AMC is the nation's oldest outdoor recreation and conservation organization.

About the Author

Alan grew up in a small city just outside the Adirondack Blue Line. In his youth he spent much of his spare time looking for new places to fish and explore. He was always fascinated by maps and working a compass, poring over the large green areas and contour lines. His first training in land navigation was with the Boy Scouts, and then the U.S. Army. His bride, Barbara, presented him with a new compass as a wedding gift, which speaks volumes. They became newlyweds just as the backpacking boom of the early 1970s was beginning, and they outfitted themselves with Kelty frame packs, Sierra cups, Svea stoves, heavy hiking boots, and all the other regalia made popular in *The Complete Walker*.

When he was in his twenties, Alan joined the Adirondack Mountain Club (ADK). He considers himself fortunate to have come under the mentorship of some extraordinary trip leaders, including Werner Baum, Carlo Chizzolin, and George Hallenbeck. With their guidance, he learned to enjoy a walk in the woods without a fishing rod or shotgun and to appreciate a satisfying hike for its own sake. Before long he was leading trips into the mountains on his own.

During his fourteen-year tenure as chair of the Outings Committee of ADK's Albany Chapter, Alan was responsible for assembling, on average, over two hundred trips a year. He's been an active committee chair for ADK for twenty-four years and was named ADK's Distinguished Volunteer of the Year in 2006.

Alan became an Adirondack 46er in 1976; a member of the Catskill 3500 Club in 1982; a New England 111er in 1985; and both a winter 46er and 35er. More recently, he became one of a very small group to have completed the one hundred highest peaks in both the Adirondacks and Catskills. Never one to leave a group of peaks unhiked, Alan hopes to soon finish the New England Hundred Highest and is currently hiking the Vermont 100 and the NYS 3k peaks.

Despite his enjoyment of the mountains of the Northeast, his love of higher terrain has led him to the Canadian Rockies and the mountains of Colorado, Washington, Oregon, Arizona, and California.

—*Neil Woodworth*

Author and Bookah, High Falls Ridge. Joanne Hihn

Adirondack Mountain Club

INFORMATION CENTERS
The ADK Member Services Center in Lake George and the ADK Heart Lake Program Center near Lake Placid, at the head of the Van Hoevenberg Trail, offer ADK publications and other merchandise for sale, as well as backcountry and general Adirondack and Catskill information, educational displays, outdoor equipment, and snacks.

LODGES AND CAMPGROUNDS
Adirondak Loj, on the shores of Heart Lake, offers year-round accommodations in private and family rooms, a coed bunkroom, and in cabins. It is accessible by car, and ample trailhead parking is available.

Jim Bullard

The Adirondak Loj Wilderness Campground, located on the Heart Lake property, offers thirty-four campsites, sixteen Adirondack-style lean-tos, and three tent cabins.

Johns Brook Lodge (JBL), located near Keene Valley, is a seasonal backcountry facility located in prime hiking country. It is 3.5 mi from the nearest road and is accessible only on foot. Facilities include coed bunkrooms or small family rooms. Cabins near JBL are available year-round.

Both lodges offer home-cooked meals and trail lunches.

JOIN US
We are a nonprofit membership organization that brings together people with interests in recreation, conservation, and environmental education in the wild lands and waters of New York State, with an emphasis on the Adirondack and Catskill parks.

ADK offers many opportunities to participate in club activities at all levels—from beginner hikes to Adirondack backpacks and international treks. Learn gradually through chapter outings or attend one of our schools, workshops, or other programs. A sampling includes:

- Alpine Flora
- Ice Climbing
- Rock Climbing
- Basic Canoeing/Kayaking
- Cross-country Skiing and Snowshoeing
- Bicycle Touring
- Mountain Photography
- Winter Mountaineering
- Birds of the Adirondacks
- Geology of the High Peaks

Membership Benefits
- Discovery:
  ADK can broaden your horizons by introducing you to new places, people, recreational activities, and interests.
- *Adirondac* Magazine
- Member Discounts:
  20% off on guidebooks, maps, and other ADK publications; discount on lodge stays; discount on educational programs
- Satisfaction:
  Know that you're doing your part so future generations can enjoy the wilderness as you do.
- Chapter Participation:
  Experience the fun of outings and other social activities and the reward of working on trails, conservation, and education projects at the local level. You can also join as a member at large.
- Volunteer Opportunities:
  Give something back. There are many rewarding options in trail work, conservation and advocacy, and educational projects.

For more information:

ADK Member Services Center
(Exit 21 off the Northway, I-87)
814 Goggins Road
Lake George, NY 12845-4117

ADK Heart Lake Program Center
P.O. Box 867
Lake Placid, NY 12946-0867

ADK Public Affairs Office
301 Hamilton Street
Albany, NY 12210-1738

Information: 518-668-4447
Membership: 800-395-8080 or
  membership@adk.org
Publications and merchandise:
  800-395-8080
Education: 518-523-3441
Facilities' reservations: 518-523-3441
Public affairs: 518-449-3870
E-mail: adkinfo@adk.org
Website: www.adk.org

Our Mission
The Adirondack Mountain Club (ADK) is dedicated to the protection and responsible recreational use of the New York State Forest Preserve, and other parks, wild lands, and waters vital to our members and chapters. The Club, founded in 1922, is a member-directed organization committed to public service and stewardship. ADK employs a balanced approach to outdoor recreation, advocacy, environmental education, and natural resource conservation.

ADK encourages the involvement of all people in its mission and activities; its goal is to be a community that is comfortable, inviting, and accessible.

LIST OF ADK PUBLICATIONS

Books *Price list available upon request*

Forest Preserve Series
    Adirondack Trails: High Peaks Region (Vol. 1)
    Adirondack Trails: Northern Region (Vol. 2)
    Adirondack Trails: Central Region (Vol. 3)
    Adirondack Trails: Northville–Placid Trail (Vol. 4)
    Adirondack Trails: West-Central Region (Vol. 5)
    Adirondack Trails: Eastern Region (Vol. 6)
    Adirondack Trails: Southern Region (Vol. 7)
    Catskill Trails (Vol. 8)
Adirondack Alpine Summits: An Ecological Field Guide
Adirondack Canoe Waters: North Flow
Adirondack Mountain Club Canoe and Kayak Guide: East-Central New York State
Adirondack Mountain Club Canoe Guide to Western & Central New York State
Adirondack Reader
An Adirondack Passage: The Cruise of the Canoe Sairy Gamp
An Adirondack Sampler: Day Hikes for All Seasons
Catskill Day Hikes for All Seasons
Catskill 67: The Catskill 100 Highest Peaks under 3500'
Climbing in the Adirondacks: A Guide to Rock and Ice Routes
Forests & Trees of the Adirondack High Peaks Region
Kids on the Trail! Hiking with Children in the Adirondacks
No Place I'd Rather Be: Wit and Wisdom from Adirondack Lean-to Journals
Ski and Snowshoe Trails in the Adirondacks
Views from on High: Fire Tower Trails in the Adirondacks and Catskills
Winterwise: A Backpacker's Guide

Maps

Trails of the Adirondack High Peaks Region
Trails of the Adirondack Northern Region
Trails of the Adirondack Central Region
Northville–Placid Trail
Trails of the Adirondack West-Central Region
Trails of the Adirondack Southern Region

National Geographic Trails Illustrated Maps in partnership with ADK:

Lake Placid/High Peaks (#742)
Lake George/Great Sacandaga (#743)
Northville/Raquette Lake (#744)
Old Forge/Oswegatchie (#745)
Saranac/Paul Smiths (#746)
Catskill Park (#755)

Adirondack Mountain Club Calendar

Adirondack Mountain Club, Inc., 814 Goggins Rd., Lake George, NY 12845-4117
518-668-4447 • Orders only: 800-395-8080 (Mon.–Sat., 8:30–5:00)

Membership

To Join

Call 800-395-8080 (Mon.–Sat., 8:30 AM–5:00 PM),
visit www.adk.org, or send this form with payment to:

Adirondack Mountain Club
Membership Department
814 Goggins Road
Lake George, NY 12845-4117

Check Membership Level:

- ☐ Individual — $50
- ☐ Family — $60*
- ☐ Student (full time, 18 and over) — $40
- ☐ Senior (65 or over) — $40
- ☐ Senior Family — $50*
- ☐ Individual Life — $1300
- ☐ Family Life — $1950*
- ☐ School

*Includes associate/family members
Fees subject to change.

Name _____
Address _____
City _____ State _____ Zip _____
Home Telephone ( ) _____
E-mail _____

- ☐ I want to join as a Chapter member*
- ☐ I want to join as a member at large

List spouse and children under 18 with birth dates:

Spouse _____
Child _____ Birth date _____
Child _____ Birth date _____

Bill my: ☐ MASTERCARD ☐ AMERICAN EXPRESS
         ☐ VISA   Exp. Date _____

Signature (required for charge) _____

☐ Check enclosed

* For details, call 800-395-8080 (Mon.–Sat., 8:30 AM–5:00 PM)

ADK is a nonprofit, tax-exempt organization. Membership fees, excluding $10 for membership benefits, are tax deductible, to the extent allowed by law.

Index

A

Acra Point, 21, 80 (map), 81, 87, 88 (photo), 89–90, 158
   combined with Burnt Knob, 88, 90, 159
Adirondack Mountain Club (ADK), 13, 165, 175, 176–179
Adirondack Mountain Club Fire Tower Challenge, 63
Alder Lake, 27, 39
   and Mill Brook Ridge Trail, access to Cradle Rock Ridge, 39, 40
   and Mill Brook Ridge Trail, access to Woodpecker Ridge, 30
   to Balsam Lake Mt. and Mill Brook Ridge, 28–29
all-terrain vehicles (see ATVs)
Andrew Gray Road, access to East Gray Hill and Old Clump, 139, 141
Appalachian Mountain Club, 165
Arbor Road, access to Pine Island Mt., 101
Arena quad, 20, 21, 28, 38, 40
Artists Rock, 84
Ashland Pinnacle State Forest, 95
Ashland quad, 20, 21, 94, 98, 104
Ashokan High Point (High Point or Shokan High Point), 21, 64 (map), 65, 66–68, 158
Ashokan Reservoir, 64 (map), 65, 71
ATVs (all-terrain vehicles), illegal trails, 32, 83, 134, 136, 160

B

B. G. Partridge Road, access to Huntersfield Mt., 95
Badman Cave, 84
Balsam Lake Mt. trailhead, Beaverkill Rd., access to High Falls Ridge, Neversink-Hardenburgh Trail, and Woodpecker Ridge, 31, 36
   to Balsam Lake Mt. and Mill Brook Ridge, 28, 31
bark road, 72, 160, 166
Barkaboom Mt., 21, 26 (map), 27, 40–42, 158
Barkaboom Road, parking area for Barkaboom Mt., 41
Batavia Kill Creek, 81, 87, 93
Batavia Kill lean-to, 89
Batavia Kill Trail, 89
Baum, Werner, 175
bear holes, 55
Bearpen State Forest, 108
Bearsville quad, 20, 21, 72, 78
Beaver Kill Creek, 27, 33, 34
Beaver Kill Range, 20, 26 (map), 27, 31–33, 158
   combined with High Falls Ridge, 36
   combined with Sand Pond Mt., 43, 159
   combined with Willowemoc, 35, 159
Beaver Kill Ridge. See Sand Pond and Willowemoc Mts.
Beaverkill Road, 27
   parking area for Balsam Lake Mt., High Falls Ridge, Woodpecker Ridge, and Neversink-Hardenburgh Trail, 31, 36
   parking area for Beaver Kill Range and Willowemoc, 33, 34, 43
   parking area for Cradle Rock Ridge, 40
Beech Mt., 37
Beech Mountain Nature Preserve, 27, 36, 38
Beech Mountain Road, 36, 37
Beech Ridge Road, 107
   parking for Sleeping Lion Mt., 115
Belleayre Mt., 20, 106 (map), 107, 109–110, 158
Belle Ayr (see Belleayre)
bicycling, 7, 27, 47, 65, 71, 81, 93, 107, 109, 118, 123, 145, 149
   See also Catskill Scenic Trail, Overlook Turnpike, and Plattekill Turnpike

Big Hollow Road (CR56), 81
  parking area for Burnt Knob and Acra Point, 87, 89
Big Pond, 27
Big Rosy Bone Knob, 69
Birch Creek, 119
Birch Creek Road, recreation area, 119, 120
birding, 7, 94, 118, 123, 150
Biscuit Brook Trail (Pine Hills–West Branch Trail), 48
Black Bear Road, 27
  parking area for Beaver Kill Range and High Falls Ridge, 31, 35
"Black Forest" (on West Wildcat), 58, 59
Blackhead Range, 81 (photo), 166
  combined with Burnt Knob, 88
Blue Line, 8
Bluebird Road (CR32C), access to Richmond Mt., 98
Bobcat Ski Center (Mt. Pisgah), 145, 147
bogs, 146, 161
Bookah, 13, 51, 72, 175 (photo)
Bookah's Bump, 89, 90
Bouton, Jim, 12, 59, 165, 167
Buck Ridge, 96
Burnt Knob, 18, 21, 80 (map), 81, 86–88, 158
  combined with Acra Point, 88, 90, 159
  combined with Blackhead Range or Windham High Peak, 87–88
  Burroughs, John, 138
  grave site and Woodchuck Lodge, 138
  monuments, 118, 119, 139
Bush Kill Creek, 65
bushwhacking, 7, 23, 153
  equipment, 156–157
  preparation, 153–155
  terminology and tips. *See glossary for catching feature, course of least resistance, drainage avoidance, handrails, waypoints*
butterflies, 94
Butternut Mt. *See* Red Kill Ridge

C

cairns, 17, 62
camping, 8, 27, 66, 84
canisters, 17
Cantwell, Mike, 12
Carl Mt. (Catskill 200), 79
Catasus-Chapman, Eileen, 13
  illustration, 9
caterpillars, damage to forests, 107, 163, 164
Catskill 67, 7–9, 15, 17, 20–21
Catskill 100 Highest, 8, 9, 19–21
  patch, 12
Catskill 3500, 7
Catskill 3500 Club, 8, 165, 166
Catskill Center for Conservation and Development, 76
Catskill Forest Preserve, 8
Catskill Mountain Club, 165
Catskill Park State Land Master Plan, 168
Catskill Scenic Trail, 107, 123, 145, 162
Cave Mt., 21, 92 (map), 93, 101–103, 158
  combined with West Cave Mt., 102, 104, 159
cemeteries, 130, 140, 141 (photo), 152
Chizzolin, Carlo, 175
Chriswell, Bill, 12, 13, 68
  photographs, 27, 42, 45, 69, 73
Churchill Mt., 21, 122 (map), 123, 134, 158, 159
Claryville quad, 20, 21, 31, 35, 60, 63
Codfish Point, 77, 78 (photo)
Colgate Lake, 71, 81, 85
Colgate Lake–Dutcher Notch Trail, 168–169
Colgate Road (CR78)
  parking for Stoppel Point, 85, 90
  parking for West Stoppel Point, 85, 90, 91
compass and map skills, 23, 153–154
Condon Hollow Road, parking for Sleeping Hollow and South Vly Mts., 113, 115
contour lines, 8, 152, 170

copperheads, 23
county high points, 19
  Greene (Hunter Mt.), 19
  Schoharie (Huntersfield Mt.), 20, 94
  Sullivan (Beech Mt.), 37
  Ulster (Slide Mt.), 19
Cowan Mt., 21, 122 (map), 123, 133–134, 158
Coykendall Mansion, 39
CR (county route), 25
CR6. *See* Spruceton Road
CR16. *See* Platte Clove Road
CR32C. *See* Bluebird Road
CR42. *See* Peekamoose Road
CR47. *See* Slide Mountain Road
CR56. *See* Big Hollow Road
CR78. *See* Colgate Road
Cradle Rock Ridge, 21, 26 (map), 27, 38–40, 158, 159
  combined with Mill Brook Ridge, 40
crampons, 105, 110, 157, 167
Cross Mountain Road, 27, 39
  Alder Lake Trailhead, access to Cradle Rock Ridge and Mill Brook Ridge, 28–29, 39
  parking area for Barkaboom Mt., 41
cross-country skiing, 29, 94, 118, 120. *See also* Catskill Scenic Trail, Plattekill Turnpike
Cruz, Liz, 11, 26, 46, 64, 70, 80, 92, 106, 122, 144
Cruz, Mike, 13
  photographs, 17, 77, 119
Curtis-Ormsbee Trail, route to East Wildcat, 49–50

D

DEC (New York State Department of Environmental Conservation), 23, 162
Deep Notch, parking area (on NY42) for Halcott and Sleeping Lion, 112, 113
Delaware River, 107, 123, 145
Denman Mt., 21, 46 (map), 47, 60–62, 158
  combined with Red Hill, 61, 159
Denning Road, trailhead East Wildcat, Lone, and Rocky Mts., 50
DEP (New York City Department of Environmental Protection), 24, 133, 162
  permits, 24, 65, 71, 107, 145, 162
Devil's Kitchen lean-to, 77
Devil's Path, 9 (illustration), 166
Diamond Notch Falls, 96
Diamond Notch Road (primitive bike corridor), 168
Dinch Road, trailhead for Red Hill, 63
Donahue, Reverend Ray L., 8
Dry Brook Ridge, 18, 20, 144 (map), 145, 146–147, 158
Dry Brook Ridge Trail, 146
Dudar, George, 12
Durham Road, access to Richmond Mt., 99
Dutcher Notch, 85
Dutcher Notch Trail, for access to West Stoppel Point, 91

E

East Gray Hill, 8, 21, 122 (map), 123, 140–142, 158
  combined with Narrow Notch Mt., 131, 159
East Highland Road, access to Narrow Notch Mt., 131
East Jewett Range, 21, 80 (map), 81, 88–89
East Kill Creek, 81, 93
East Kill Mt. *See* Onteora Mt.
East Rusk Mt., 100
East Wildcat, 20, 46 (map), 47, 49–51, 158
  combined with West Wildcat, 51, 59, 159
Echo Lake, 71
  combined with Plattekill Mt., 78
Echo Lake Trail, 78
Edgewood Mt. *See* Silver Hollow Mt.

Elk Creek Road, 107
equipment lists, 156–157
Escarpment Trail, 84–85, 87, 89
Esopus Creek, 47, 65, 71, 119
Evergreen Mt., 100
  combined with Pine Island Mt., 100
eye safety, 153, 160

F

Fall Brook lean-to, 32, 33, 35
ferns, 7, 33 (photo), 150 (photo), 163
  exceptional glades, 28, 31, 38, 43, 51, 58, 82, 150
  fiddleheads, 37 (photo)
Fir Mt., 20
  combined with Spruce Mt., 48
fire towers
  Overlook Mt., 75
  Red Hill, 63
  Utsayantha Mt., 131
first-growth forest, 29, 37, 40, 51, 58, 59, 163
fishing, 7, 8, 27, 47, 60, 65, 71, 81, 93, 107, 119, 123, 145
Fleischmanns quad, 20, 21, 109, 117
Flugertown Road, parking area for Sand Pond and Willowemoc Mts., 34, 43
Flynn Trail, access to Mongaup Mt., 37
forest fire, 103
Freehold quad, 19, 21, 86, 89
Frick Pond, parking area for Frick Pond, Hodge Pond, and Mongaup Mts., 36, 44
Frost Valley YMCA, 49, 60

G

Giant Ledge, 18, 21, 24 (photo), 46 (map), 47, 55–58, 158
Gillespie Road, parking for Roundtop (Kaaterskill quad), 82
Glade Hill Road Moore Hill Road parking area, access to Denman Mt., 61
Global Positioning System (GPS), 7, 23, 154, 156, 157, 164, 170
Guide to the Catskills, 8, 171
Gulf Mt. *See* Little Rocky

H

Hack Flats. *See* White Man Mt.
Halcott Mt., 20
  combined with Sleeping Lion, 112
Hallenbeck, George, 175
hang-gliding, 132
Harold Roberts Road
  and Plattekill Turnpike, 126, 127, 167
  parking area for North and South Plattekill Mts., 126, 127
Hemlock Mt., 48, 49
Henry, Dick, 12
Hensonville quad, 19, 20, 21, 101
herd paths, 17
High Falls Ridge, 21, 26 (map), 27, 35–36, 158
  combined with Beaver Kill Range, 36, 159
High Point. *See* Ashokan High Point
Highlanders View B&B, 137, 138
Hihn, Joanne, 13
  photographs, 33, 37, 91, 97, 111, 112, 114, 146, 147, 148, 175
hiking clubs. *See individual club names*
Hill Road, parking area for Huckleberry Loop, 147
Hobart quad, 20, 21, 124, 127, 133, 134, 137, 142
Hodge Pond Mt., 8, 21, 26 (map), 27, 43–45, 158, 159
Hoop Pole Mt., 67
Hoyt Hollow Mt. (Catskill 200), 79
Hubbell Hill, 21, 144 (map), 145, 151–152
Huckleberry Loop Trail, 146, 147
Hunter Mt., 19, 71
Hunter quad, 19, 20, 21, 86, 88
Hunter–West Kill Wilderness, 168
Huntersfield Mt., 20, 92 (map), 93, 94–96, 158
  combined with Richmond Mt., 95, 98, 159
Huntersfield Mt. lean-to, 93 (photo), 94, 95

Huntersfield State Forest, 94, 95
hunting
    on Frost Valley YMCA property, 60
    seasons, 16, 23, 158, 163

I

ice storms, 49, 53, 86, 95, 99, 161, 166
invasive species, 160, 163, 165
Irish Mt., 21, 106 (map), 107, 120–121, 159
Iron Wheel Junction, 44

J

Jim Cleveland Road, access to Huntersfield Mt., 94, 95

K

Kaaterskill. *See* Plattekill Mt.
Kaaterskill High Peak, 19
    combined with Roundtop (Kaaterskill quad), 82, 83–84
Kaaterskill quad, 19, 20, 21, 82, 84, 90
Kaaterskill Wild Forest, 82
Kanape Brook, 65
Kanape Brook Trail and trailhead (CR42), 66, 68, 69
kayaking. *See* paddling
Kelly Hollow, to Mill Brook Ridge, 29
Kenneth Wilson State Park, 65, 71
Kenyon Mt. *See* Meeker Hollow Mt.
King Post bridge, 77
Kudish, Michael, 11, 103, 146, 161, 163, 168, 169, 171, 174

L

Lake Capra, 85
lean-tos,
    Batavia Kill, 89
    Belleayre Mt., 109
    Devil's Kitchen, 77
    Fall Brook, 32, 33, 35
    Huntersfield Mt., 93 (photo), 94, 95
    Mill Brook Ridge and Kelly Hollow, 29
    Spruce Mt., 48

Leavitt, William H. and Elinore, 166
Leavitt Peak (SW Hunter), 8, 19, 166
LeBrun, Fred, 11
legend, to regional maps, 25
Lew Beach, 27, 37, 44
Lexington Mt. *See* Packsaddle Mt.
Lexington quad, 19, 20, 21, 96, 99, 103
Little Ashokan, 66
Little Pisgah, 21, 144 (map), 145, 149–151, 159
Little Pond, 27
Little Rocky (Gulf Mt.), 21, 64 (map), 65, 68–69, 158
Little West Kill. *See* Roundtop (Prattsville quad)
Little West Kill Creek, 93
Lone Mt., 19, 50
Long Path,
    and East Wildcat, 50
    and Stoppel Point, 84
    on Richmond Mt., 99
Long Pond–Beaver Kill Ridge Trail, to Sand Pond Mt., 43
Lookout Rock, 84, 85
Lower Meeker Hollow Road, 145
    access to North Plattekill Mt., 124
    access to South Plattekill Mt., 129

M

map skills, 23, 153–154
mapping software, 154
maps (this book), 8
    east peaks, 70
    legend, 25
    north peaks, 92
    north-central peaks, 106
    northeast peaks, 80
    northwest peaks, 122
    south-central peaks, 46
    southeast peaks, 64
    southwest peaks, 26
    west peaks, 144
Margaretville quad, 20, 21, 147, 149, 151
Marv Rion Road, access to Huntersfield Mt., 94, 95

Mary's Glen Trail, 84
Matyas Road, 119
   trailhead for Rochester Hollow and Rose Mt., 119
Meade, Walter, 121
Meads Mountain Road, parking area for Overlook and Plattekill Mts., 75, 78
Meeker Hollow Mt. (Kenyon Mt.), 8, 21, 122 (map), 123, 142–143
   combined with North Plattekill Mt., 124–126, 159
Michael Kudish Natural History Preserve, 174
MICROspikes, 105, 110, 157, 167
Mill Brook, 27
Mill Brook Ridge, 20, 26 (map), 27, 28–30, 158, 159, 167
   combined with Balsam Lake Mt., 28
   combined with Cradle Rock Ridge, 40
Mill Brook Ridge Trail
   access to Woodpecker Ridge, 30
   as part of route to Cradle Rock Ridge, 39, 40
   to Mill Brook Ridge via Balsam Lake Mt., 28
Mill Brook Road, access to Mill Brook Ridge, 29–30
Miller, Cheryl, photograph, 75
Milt's Lookout, 85
Mink Hollow Road
   parking for Olderbark Mt., 72
   primitive bike corridor, 168
Mink Hollow Trail (Map 4), 72
Mink Hollow trailhead (Map 6)
   access to Pine Island Mt. and St. Anne's Peak, 97, 101
   trailhead for West Kill Mt., 96
Mombaccus Mt., combined with Little Rocky, 68
Mongaup Mt., 21, 26 (map), 27, 36–38, 159
   combined with Sand Pond Mt., 43
   combined with Willowemoc, 35
Mongaup Pond, 27

Montgomery Hollow (Walt's Knob), 21, 106 (map), 107, 121, 158, 159
Montgomery Hollow Road (North and South), 107
Moore Hill Road–Glade Hill Road parking area, access to Denman Mt., 61
Moresville Range NW Peak, 20, 122 (map), 123, 129–130, 159
Moresville Range SW Peak, 21, 122 (map), 123, 136–137, 159
Morrissey, Spencer, 12, 172
Morse Road (Relay Road), parking areas for East Gray Hill, Narrow Notch Mt., and Old Clump, 130, 139, 140
Mt. Pisgah, 20, 144 (map), 145, 147–148, 158, 159
Mt. Pisgah Road, parking areas for Richmond Mt., 99
Mt. Pisgah State Forest, 99
Mountain Brook Road
   and Plattekill Turnpike, 167
   parking for North Plattekill Mt. and Round Top (Hobart quad), 126, 135

N

Narrow Notch Mt., 20, 122 (map), 123, 130–131, 159
   combined with East Gray, 131, 159
NE Halcott. *See* Sleeping Lion Mt.
Nesbitt Cemetery, 140, 141 (photo)
Neversink River, 27, 47, 49
Neversink-Hardenburgh Trail, 36
New Kingston Road, 145
New Kingston Mountain Road, access to South Plattekill Mt., 127
New York City Department of Environmental Protection (DEP), 24, 133, 162
   DEP permits, 24, 65, 71, 107, 145, 162
New York State Department of Environmental Conservation (DEC), 23, 162
New York–New Jersey Trail Conference maps, 15, 18, 173

Newman's Ledge, 84
North Lake, 84
North Plattekill Mt., 20, 122 (map), 123, 124–126, 158
   and Plattekill Turnpike, 126, 167
   combined with Meeker Hollow Mt., 124, 142, 159
   combined with Round Top (Hobart quad), 126, 136, 159
   combined with South Plattekill Mt., 126, 129, 159
North Point, 10 (photo), 84
North-South Lake, 71, 81
North-South Lake State Campground, 84
NW Moresville Range. *See* Moresville Range NW Peak
Notch Inn Road, for access to Olderbark, Plateau, and Silver Hollow Mts., 74, 79
NY23A, access to Roundtop (Kaaterskill quad), 82
NY42
   access to Packsaddle Mt., 104
   parking area for Halcott and Sleeping Lion Mts., 112

O

O. S. Baptist Church (Old Yellow Church), 124
Oelberg. *See* Olderbark Mt.
Old Clump, 21, 122 (map), 123, 138–140, 158, 159
Olderbark Mt., 20, 70 (map), 71, 72–74, 158
   combined with Plateau Mt., 73
Onteora Lake, 65, 71
Onteora Mt. (East Kill Mt.), 20, 80 (map), 81, 86
Ontiora Mt. *See* Roundtop (Prattsville quad)
Overlook Mt., 21, 70 (map), 71, 75–76, 158
   combined with Plattekill Mt., 76, 78, 159
Overlook Mountain House ruins, 75
Overlook Turnpike, primitive bike corridor, 168

P

Packsaddle Mt. (Lexington Mt.), 21, 92 (map), 93, 103–104, 158
   combined with Pine Island Mt., 100, 159
paddling, 7, 27, 47, 65, 71, 81, 93, 107, 123, 145
Pakatakan Mt., combined with Dry Brook Ridge, 146
Panther Mt., 19
   combined with Giant Ledge, 58
Panther Mt. trailhead (CR47), 53
peak ratings, 24
Peekamoose Mt. quad, 19, 20, 21, 49, 53, 58, 62
Peekamoose Road (CR42)
   access to Van Wyck Mt., 54
   Kanape Brook trailhead, 66
Pepacton Reservoir, 145
Phoenicia quad, 19
Phoenicia–East Branch Trail
   and East Wildcat, 50
   and Giant Ledge, 55
Pine Hills–West Branch Trail (Biscuit Brook Trail), 48
Pine Island Mt., 21, 92 (map), 93, 99–101, 158
   combined with Evergreen Mt., 101
   combined with Packsaddle, 100, 103, 159
plane wreck, 55, 67, 85
Plateau Mt., 19, 166
   combined with Olderbark Mt., 73
Platte Clove Preserve, 76
Platte Clove Road (CR16), 71, 77 (photo), 81
   trailhead to Kaaterskill High Peak, Overlook, Plattekill, and Roundtop Mts., 76, 82
Plattekill Falls, 22 (photo)
Plattekill Mt. (Kaaterskill), 21, 70 (map), 71, 76–78, 158
   combined with Echo Lake, 78
   combined with Overlook Mt., 76, 78, 159

Plattekill State Forest, 124, 127, 136, 167
Plattekill Turnpike, 123, 126, 127, 135, 136, 145, 167
Ploutz Road, access to Dry Brook Ridge, 147
Pople Hill parking area, access to Little Rocky, 69
Porcupine Road, access to Van Wyck and Woodhull Mts., 54, 62
Prattsville quad, 20, 108
private property, 15, 24, 168
public property, 23. *See also* DEC, DEP

Q

quad. *See topographic maps and individual quad names*
Quaker Cove, 33
Quick Lake Trail, 44

R

Rankin, Laurie, 12, 28, 34
Rankin, Tom, 12, 34
rating system (explained), 24
rattlesnakes, 23, 75 (photo), 76
Red Hill, 8, 21, 46 (map), 47, 63, 158
 combined with Denman, 61, 159
 combined with Woodhull, 62
Red Kill Ridge (Butternut Mt.), 21, 106 (map), 107, 117–118
Red Kill Road, access to Red Kill Ridge, 118
Relay Cemetery, 130, 140
Relay Road (Morse Road), parking area for East Gray Hill, Narrow Notch Mt., and Old Clump, 130, 139, 140
Relay State Forest, 130, 131
Richmond Mt., 20, 92 (map), 93, 98–99
 combined with Huntersfield, 95, 98, 159
Rip Van Winkle Hiking Club, 165
Rochester Hollow, 118, 119
Rock Shelter Trail, 84
Rocky Mt., 20, 50
Rondout Creek, 47, 65

Rose Mt., 21, 106 (map), 107, 118–120
Roses Brook Road, 143, 145
Round Top Mt. (Hobart quad), 21, 122 (map), 123, 134–136, 158
 and Plattekill Turnpike, 167
 combined with North and South Plattekill, 126, 136, 159
Roundtop Mt. (Kaaterskill quad), 20, 80 (map), 81, 82–84, 158
 combined with Kaaterskill High Peak, 82, 83–84
Roundtop Mt. (Ontiora or Little West Kill; Prattsville quad), 20, 106 (map), 107, 108, 159
Roxbury Mountain Road, 145
 access to Meeker Hollow Mt., 143
Roxbury quad, 20, 21, 116, 117, 120, 121, 129, 130, 136, 138, 140
Rusk Mt., 19, 100
Ryndak, Ralph, 165, 167

S

Sand Pond Mt. (Beaver Kill Ridge), 18, 21, 26 (map), 27, 42–43, 158
 combined with Beaver Kill Range and Willowemoc, 43, 159
 combined with Mongaup, 43
 combined with Willowemoc, 34, 43, 159
Sand Pond Ridge. *See* Sand Pond Mt.
Schaefer, Mark, 8, 12, 13, 82, 138
 photographs, 14, 22, 24, 47, 67, 71, 78, 81, 85, 93, 102, 107, 108, 125, 128
Schepart, Moonray, 12, 13
 photographs, 29, 52, 60, 100
Schoharie Creek, 71, 81, 93, 107
Schoharie Reservoir, 107
Schultice Mt. *See* Shultice Mt.
Schutt Road, parking area for Stoppel Point, 84
SE Warren. *See* Southeast Warren
Seager quad, 19, 20, 30, 146
seep, 40, 41, 169
Shandaken quad, 19, 20, 21, 48, 51, 55

Shandaken Wild Forest, 120
  recreation area, 120
Shin Creek, 45
Shin Creek Road, 27, 36
  access to Hodge Pond and Mongaup Mts., 37, 38, 44, 45
Shokan High Point. *See* Ashokan High Point
Shultice Mt. (Schultice Mt.), 20, 106 (map), 107, 116–117
  combined with Irish Mt., 159
Silver Hollow Mt. (Edgewood Mt.), 21, 70 (map), 71, 74, 78–79, 158
  combined with Carl, Hoyt Hollow, Tremper, and West Silver Hollow Mts., 79
Silver Hollow Notch, 74
Ski Plattekill, 124, 137
Ski Run Road, parking area for Rountop Mt. (Prattsville quad), 108
Ski Windham, 101, 102, 104
Sleeping Lion Mt. (NE Halcott), 20, 106 (map), 107, 112–115, 158
  combined with Halcott Mt., 112
  combined with South Vly, 116, 159
Slide Mountain Road (CR47)
  access to East Wildcat, 51
  access to Giant Ledge, 56
  access to Spruce Mt., 49
  parking area for East Wildcat, Slide, Spruce, and Winnisook Lake Mts., 48, 49, 52
  parking area for Giant Ledge, Panther, and Winnisook Mts., 53, 55
  parking area for Pine Hills–West Branch Trail (to Fir and Spruce Mts.), 48
  parking area for West Wildcat, 58
Slide Mountain trailhead (CR47), 49
snowshoeing, 52, 66, 79, 90, 102, 110, 114 (photo), 118, 120, 126, 127
solo hiking, 153
South Bearpen, 20, 106 (map), 107, 111–112, 158

South Mountain Road, access to Huntersfield Mt., 95
South Plattekill Mt., 20, 122 (map), 123, 127–129
  and Plattekill Turnpike, 126, 167
  combined with North Plattekill Mt., 126, 129, 159
  combined with North Plattekill and Round Top (Hobart quad), 126, 136, 159
South Vly, 20, 106 (map), 107, 115–116
  combined with Sleeping Lion, 116, 159
Southeast Warren, 21, 122 (map), 123, 137–138, 158
Southside Road, parking for Dry Brook Ridge Trail, 146
Spruce Mt., 20, 46 (map), 47, 48–49
  combined with Fir Mt., 48
  combined with Winnisook Lake Mt., 51, 159
Spruceton Road (CR6), 93
  access to Pine Island and Packsaddle Mts., 100, 103
  Mink Hollow trailheads, 96, 97, 101
  trailhead for St. Anne's Peak, 97
  trailhead for West Kill Mt., 96
St. Anne's Peak (West West Kill), 18, 20, 92 (map), 93, 96–97, 158
  combined with West Kill Mt., 96–97
Stamford quad, 20, 21, 131, 134
Stone Hollow Road, access to South Bearpen Mt., 111
Stone Tavern Farm (B&B), 124, 142, 143
Stoppel Point, 10 (photo), 18, 20, 80 (map), 81, 84–86, 158
  combined with West Stoppel, 91, 159
Stork's Nest Road, trailhead to Stoppel Point, 86
Sundown Wild Forest, 63
Sunset Rock, 84, 85
SW Hunter (Leavitt Peak), 8, 19, 166
SW Moresville Range. *See* Moresville Range SW Peak
swimming, 27, 47, 65, 81

T

Table Mt., 19
  combined with Van Wyck Mt., 55
Taconic Hiking Club, 165
Thompson Hollow Road, access to Hubbell Hill, 151
timber rattlesnake, 23, 75 (photo), 76
topographic maps, 153–154, 170.
  See also individual quad names
tracklogs, 154
Trail's End Road, for access to Little Rocky, 69
trailless hiking. *See* bushwhacking
Tremper Mt. (Catskill 200), 79
Tunis Pond, 36
Turnwood, 27, 37, 44

U

Ulster and Delaware Railroad, 162
United States Geological Survey (USGS) Board of Names, 166
United States Geological Survey (USGS) maps, 8, 18, 154, 167, 170.
  See also individual quad names
Upper Meeker Hollow Road, 145
  access to Meeker Hollow Mt., 142
  access to North Plattekill Mt., 124
  access to South Plattekill Mt., 129
Utsayantha Mt., 20, 122 (map), 123, 131–133, 158, 159

V

Van Wyck Mt., 21, 46 (map), 47, 53–55, 158
  combined with Table Mt., 55
  combined with Woodhull Mt., 53, 62, 159
Vega Mountain Road, 107
Venture Out maps, 15, 18, 173
Versandi, Tony, 12, 13
  photographs, 10, 18, 54, 56, 79, 88, 110, 132
Via, Barbara, 11, 13
  illustrations, 7, 48, 63, 65, 126

Vly Creek, 118

W

Wallkill Valley Rail Trail, 65
Walt's Knob. *See* Montgomery Hollow
Warner's Creek, 74, 79
waterfalls, 22 (photo), 89, 96, 97 (photo), 119
Weaver Hollow Road, 145
  parking for Mt. Pisgah, 148
West Cave Mt., 21, 92 (map), 93, 104–105, 158
  combined with Cave Mt., 102, 104, 159
West Kill Creek, 93, 97 (photo), 107
West Kill Mt., 19
  combined with St. Anne's, 96–97
West Kill quad, 20, 21, 111, 112, 115, 118
West Shokan quad, 19, 20, 21, 66, 68
West Silver Hollow Mt. (Catskill 200), 79
West Stoppel Point, 21, 80 (map), 81, 90–91
  combined with Stoppel Point, 91, 159
West West Kill. *See* St. Anne's Peak
West Wildcat Mt., 21, 46 (map), 47, 58–60, 158
  combined with East Wildcat, 51, 59, 159
White Man Mt. (Hack Flats), 21, 106 (map), 107, 117, 159
Wild Meadow Road. *See* Black Bear Road
Wildcat Range, 50, 51, 58, 59
Wildcats. *See* East Wildcat, West Wildcat
wildflowers, 7
wildlife, 7
Willowemoc Creek, 27, 47
Willowemoc quad, 20, 21, 34, 36, 42, 43
Willowemoc Mt. (Beaver Kill Ridge), 18, 20, 26 (map), 27, 34–35, 158, 159
  combined with Beaver Kill Range or Mongaup Mt., 35, 159
  combined with Sand Pond Mt., 34, 43, 159

wind farm (proposed), 130, 137
Windham High Peak, 20
  combined with Burnt Knob, 87
Winnisook Lake, 52
Winnisook Lake Club, access to Giant
  Ledge via DEC right-of-way, 56
Winnisook Lake Mt., 20, 46 (map), 47,
  51–53, 158
  combined with Spruce, 51, 159
  combined with Spruce, Fir, and
    Hemlock, 53
winter hiking, preparation, 157
Woodchuck Lodge, 138.
  See also Burroughs, John
Woodhull Mt., 21, 46 (map), 47, 62–63
  combined with Van Wyck, 53, 62,
    159
Woodland Valley, to Giant Ledge, 57
Woodpecker Ridge, 20, 26 (map), 27,
  30–31, 158, 159
Woodstock quad, 20, 21, 75, 76
Woodworth, Neil, 13

Y
Brian Yourdon, 12

Notes: